TERRESTRIALS

Terrestrials

A Modern Approach to Fishing and Tying
with Synthetic and Natural Materials

Harrison R. Steeves III
Ed Koch

STACKPOLE
BOOKS

Published by
STACKPOLE BOOKS
5067 Ritter Road
Mechanicsburg, PA 17055

Printed in the United States of America

10 9 8 7 6 5 4 3 2 1

First edition

Library of Congress Cataloging-in-Publication Data

Koch, Ed.
    Terrestrials : a modern approach to fishing and tying with synthetic and natural materials / Ed Koch, Harrison R. Steeves III.
        p.   cm.
    ISBN 0-8117-0629-X
    1. Fly tying.   2. Flies, Artificial.   3. Fly Fishing.
I. Steeves, Harrison R.   II. Title.
SH451.K596   1994
799.1'755—dc20   93-50195
                                                                CIP

DEDICATION

For my wife, Elissa, a loving and beautiful lady who has always understood and even encouraged my eccentricities, the greatest of which has been my passion for trout. For my son Charles, a novitiate at present, but in whom a fifth generation of trout fishermen resides. Without the two of you this would never have been accomplished.

For my mother, whose love for her son has been a source of strength over the years. And for my father, who taught me the sport, and with whom I wish I could fish for trout once more.

—H. R. S.

To Betty Ann, for her love.

—E. K.

CONTENTS

SPECIAL THANKS

The art in this book is the work of four talented artists. David P. Krupa sketched the chapter-opening scenes. Dave Hall made the terrestrial insect drawings. Creed Taylor illustrated the tying sequences. Norm Shires took the color photographs.

ACKNOWLEDGMENTS

Thanks to both Creed Taylor and Dave Hall for lending their considerable talents toward the illustration of this book.

Thanks to Stephen Hiner, Pete Bromley, Cliff Rexrode, Stewart Asahina, Gary Griffin, Scholey Pitcher, Miller Williams, John Rucker, and all the others with whom I have shared adventures, streamside philosophy, traveling time, and fast food.

Thanks to Gus Blagden, a true sportsman who, had he lived, would surely have ranked among the greats. He died as a young man, but he taught me the ethics of the sport, although he never knew it.

—H. R. S.

To Harry Steeves, a good friend, angling companion, and master fly tier, for his invitation to participate in this work.

To Norm Shires, a friend and angling companion for some thirty years, for his photographic excellence.

To Dave Krupa, a wildlife artist whose pencil sketches throughout the book are reminiscent of a bygone era in angling literature.

—E. K.

EDITOR'S NOTE

If you look carefully at the acknowledgments and the credits in this book, you'll see that a good number of contributors participated in the making of *Terrestrials*. Every book is a collaborative effort, but this book happens to be especially so.

First of all, the book has two authors. The idea for the book was Harrison Steeves's. He put together a healthy manuscript and began talking about it with his fly-fishing friend Ed Koch. Together they decided to collaborate. This is Harrison's first book and the manuscript seemed to spill easily and gracefully out of him. This is book number four for Ed and Stackpole. Ed continues to bring an enthusiasm to each new book, and that spirit infuses the project.

Harrison found Creed Taylor to do the terrific step-by-step pen and ink drawings of the flies and Ed enlisted David Krupa to do the chapter openers; both are artful touches. Dave Hall drew the bugs, true and otherwise, and Norm Shires worked his usual magic with the color photographs. When the manuscript was nearly ready, my trusted team of readers, the three Davids, gave their valuable suggestions.

Thank you all, those I've named and others, the in-house staff and our unsung freelancers. You were great to work with. This kind of team making this kind of book is why *Terrestrials* is an editor's dream.

—J. M. S.

INTRODUCTION

. . . the eagle-eyed watcher watched until his eyes narrowed and became pin-points, and he ceased to be a man and became an optic.

"Wait," he breathed, "wait until I screw into one other inch of sight."

And they waited, looking no longer on that scarcely perceptible speck in the distance, but straining upon the eye of the watcher as though they would penetrate it and look through it.

— James Stephens, *Irish Fairy Tale*

THERE WAS A TIME, not so terribly long ago, when the average fly fisherman hung up his gear as the major hatches of the spring and early summer dwindled away. The members of the fraternity of the damned slowly began to put their gear and their lives back into some semblance of order. Reels were cleaned, rods were caressed and put away for the season, flies were again neatly arranged in their little "fly hotels" (as the wife of a friend calls her husband's fly boxes). Each tenant was given its own space or roomed with other members of its genus. It was particularly satisfying to rearrange and compartmentalize one's collection if the tenants were housed in a beautiful Wheatley Ritz-Carlton. It was a time of restoration; a time to savor the memories of the season, to sort and edit slides, to reacquaint ourselves with our families and our jobs, and to clean all the crap off the fly-tying tables.

1

For more and more of us, however, the ending of the major hatches heralds not the death of a season but the birth of the most exciting time of the year. There are a few hatches still going on; there are the maddening Tricos, midges, craneflies, and always stoneflies of one sort or another. Caddis are usually around, and now that they have reached prominence and been given their rightful place in the pages of American angling literature, more and more people are taking advantage of these prolific hatches. There are still some excellent mayfly hatches. The ubiquitous *Baetis* and all the other tinies have begun to come off, so if the angler wants to fish small flies, these are sometimes available. There are other less well-known but plentiful hatches in isolated areas. The White Fly, for example, creates a late-summer madness along Pennsylvania's Yellow Breeches. But unless one lives fairly close to one of these areas, these hatches are experienced only from the pages of magazines. In short, there are enough hatches to carry the diehard into the fall, and even into the time of year when one stands frozen in the pool, waiting for the sun to come over the trees and melt the ice in the guides of the rod.

This, however, is a time of the year that for many of us is even more exciting than the blizzard hatches of the early season or the fine and delicate fishing when the leaves begin to turn. It might be termed the "middle season" of the year, which to most of us simply means summer. It's a time of lazy fishing and unhurried mornings. There is none of the rush to get to the stream in time for the hatch—the hatch is going to last all day. It's a time when the angler can leave the stream in the early afternoon without fear of missing the spinner fall or the late-hatching caddis. It's a time of bank sitting, contemplation, and conversation with one's angling partner. It's a time of many fish and big fish, of broken tippets, of strikes that are too early or too late. It's a time of agony and ecstacy; a time of morning mists and evening fireflies; a time to listen to the purring of the crows in the midday heat; a time to explore those places where the air smells of molding leaves, of mosses, and of snakes; a time of rebirth for many of us. For those of you who pursue trout during this time of the year, it may just prove to be that time when you learn more about trout and trout habits than you have ever learned before.

During this time of the year the angler becomes more of a hunter than a fisher. The powers of observation are honed and polished. The ability to stalk a fish becomes more important than the ability to classify the food object (indeed, angling entomology flies right out the window, which is a real blessing for many). One develops a type of tunnel vision, in which only the quarry is seen and all other visual information is excluded as useless and irrelevant to the immediate situation. A dimple under a bush on the far bank will, for example, become an immediate point of focus, and the angler becomes an eye, a single lens, intent only on that point until the point is resolved. The angler becomes a heron, an osprey, a predator of the highest order, riveted to that point and deaf and blind to all other sensory input, which is simply filtered out and discarded as trivial.

Those who fish during this season will most assuredly become watchers. They will remain riveted, concentrated, and immobile—fixed on that ethereal shape, that suspected disturbance, that shadowy outline that wavers below the surface. A slight bulging of the interface, unnoticed by others who have passed before, will assume Brobdingnagian proportions, as well might be the fish that caused it.

The practice of this art of recognition comes only with time and experience. You will learn to look into and past the surface, to strip away each layer of the stream's dimension, and to examine each region of the aqueous layer cake. There are no books, no videos, and no shortcuts. But somehow, with practice, you will develop an almost mystical ability to determine the presence of your quarry. Given time, you will learn to look for what should not be there rather than what is there.

It is a time for patience; a time not only for intensity of observation, but also for the utmost stealth. The angler who charges forth into the water is doomed to certain failure. The crunch of gravel underfoot, the careless waving of the rod overhead, and the gentle (or not so gentle) waves of the hurried angler serve only as warning signals to the prey. It is a time to mimic the stoic heron rather than the frenzied behavior of the chattering kingfisher. There is no frenetic hatch feeding to distract the quarry. Trout are probably more aware of the angler now than at any other time of the year, and any disturbance, no matter how slight we may perceive it to be, will serve as a distinct warning. There are times when it seems that the very act of breathing will cause the object of our stalk to slowly but defiantly retreat into the watery shadows of its domain and our memory.

This is the season of the watcher and the hunter. This is the season of the terrestrial.

—H. R. S.

FOR FIFTY PLUS YEARS now I have fished. As a young lad, I chased minnows in pools and holes of a small mountain brook with a stick, a piece of string, and a safety pin. Worms were our staple bait when they could be found, or bacon pieces when they were available. Numerous minnows and chubs fell prey to our clumsy tactics of splashing the baited pin on the water, as they dashed from all parts of the pool to feed greedily. Everything we caught was quickly returned to the brook, ensuring us something to fish for the next day. Nobody told us to throw them back; somehow we just knew that if we killed every fish we caught, the next day we would have no quarry to defeat.

The beautiful, brightly colored brook trout that shared the many holes and pools with the minnows were a different story altogether. Instead of dashing and darting madly about when our loaded pins splattered the pool, the brookies darted for the cover of the streambottom, rocks, or undercut banks. The brookies managed to elude us for many summers.

When we finally reached our threshold of frustration, we would wander the banks searching for ants, inchworms, crickets, hoppers, spiders, or whatever, and throw them into the pools we knew held brookies. We would stay well back from the stream's edge, hiding behind trees or brush so as not to scare the hyper natives. Inevitably the streamwise brookies would devour almost every live insect we fed them. Somehow it never crossed our young minds to impale the live insects on our safety pins.

It was almost twenty years before I was again to encounter those land-bred insects in my fishing experiences. The interval had been filled with fly-fishing memories, a partial mastering of wet flies, nymphs, streamers, and dry flies, plus the art of tying my own imitations.

The year was 1957, and I had settled in Carlisle, Pennsylvania, after discharge from the Marine Corps. It was that year that Joe Brooks introduced the fly-fishing fraternity to terrestrial fishing with his article "On the Jassid" in *Outdoor Life*. Two relatively unknown anglers at that time, Charlie Fox and Vince Marinaro, had spent the better part of a decade on Carlisle's Letort Spring Run in search of a solution to the selective-feeding, free-rising browns. The Jassid, a leafhopper imitation, was the first of the new terrestrials to be proven successful. Other patterns followed— a floating ant pattern in black and brown, a Japanese beetle, a cricket, and a grasshopper. Others were developed in the ensuing seasons, some by other Letort regulars. Mike Schell, one of the youngest Letorters, created a grass beetle. It is a little larger than the Jassid but smaller than a beetle, and it has been a favorite of mine for many years.

Thirty-plus years have passed since the introduction of the original terrestrial patterns. Not since the revolution in New York of dry flies, fly patterns, and techniques some sixty years earlier has such an impact been made on American angling.

Strangely little literature has been forthcoming, however, since the inception and acceptance of the original terrestrial development. A work by Gerald Almy was published by Stackpole Books in 1978, and in 1989, Stackpole published my *Terrestrial Fishing,* a history of the development of the terrestrials along with stories and anecdotes about what took place during that time period in the Cumberland Valley of Pennsylvania.

History has repeatedly confirmed that change is inevitable. Fly fishing and fly tying have not been exempted—thank goodness. Things keep getting better and better.

For a century or more, fly-tying materials had remained fairly constant; not so over the past forty years, however. They have entered the space age. Today, 50 to 70 percent of fishing tackle and fly-tying materials are synthetic. The purpose of this work is to inform, to a limited extent, about the uses and advantages of synthetics in tying and fishing terrestrials. We've come a long way.

Some years ago I received a letter from a fellow angler and fly tier by the name of Harrison (Harry) Steeves, a biologist at Virginia Polytechnic Institute. Harry has been tying for some forty years. Enclosed in his letter were some unique terrestrial patterns, tying instructions, and tying materials for the patterns. The materials were all the new synthetics. It was the beginning of a friendship that I hope will continue for many years. I have met a lot of fly fishermen and tiers over the years, but not more than several dozen or so are the dedicated kind of person who contributes more to the sport of fly fishing than he takes. With certainty, Harry is one of that elite group! I met him shortly after the letter, at a fly fishing and tying symposium in Pennsylvania. We have since spent countless hours fishing, tying, and testing. It was Harry who first raised the possibility of this book on the porch of the Carriage House at Allenberry on the Yellow Breeches in Pennsylvania after a remarkable day on the river testing the new synthetic terrestrial patterns. It's taken almost five years to complete. I hope everyone who reads this book will gain as much from it as Harry and I have from writing it.

—E. K.

1

The History of Terrestrial Fishing

FLY FISHING IS not new, and angling literature hundreds of years old, if researched, would divulge terrestrial patterns used. Used rarely, perhaps, as compared with more popular patterns of the day, but nevertheless included for specific occasions.

This work deals with the more recent developments of terrestrials in America over the past forty years and the changes that have taken place. In order to begin to fathom exactly what has taken place, it is necessary to consider the number of terrestrial patterns developed in the mid-1950s and the total number of patterns described in this book.

During the 1950s, a group of dedicated fly fishers in Carlisle, Pennsylvania, were faced with a perplexing dilemma. The Letort Spring Run, one of the Cumberland Valley's premiere limestone streams, had a wonderful head of stream-bred brown trout as well as a fair population of brook trout. Both species appeared to coexist without the danger of either taking over the stream. Early-season fly fishing was great, and a fair number of hatches lasted through June. The Letort trout were well known in the local area for their free-rising antics day after day. By the end of June, a dramatic change took place and the mayflies disappeared. But the trout continued their voracious feeding through July, August, September, and often into October. A day on the river would often present the angler as many as three dozen free risers working as greedily as they had through the spring and summer. The problem: They were not feeding on mayflies, and few if any of the regulars along the Letort's banks ever caught even a pair of the free risers on top. Cress bugs, shrimp, or an occasional streamer pattern produced trout fished deep. It was frustrating, to say the least.

Charlie Fox and Vince Marinaro had been fishing the Letort for some twenty years and intimately knew easily 90 percent of the browns in the river—where they lived, where they fed, and where they spawned. To Charlie and Vince, each brown was like a part of the family. They could walk visitors along the banks and point out dozens of browns. They even named them: the rose bush feeder, the S bend brown, the hanging willow feeder, the monster under the buttonwood roots, and on and on. Their intimacy with the river and its browns amazed visitors for years.

Finally, after years of frustration, Charlie and Vince uncovered the Letort's guarded secret of the surface-feeding browns of summer. Tiny insects were everywhere. Not the aquatic insects that they were expecting to find, but rather terrestrials, land-bred critters and small compared with typical patterns of spring. They were elated with their discovery, but not for long. Frustration began to set in again as they thought about the challenge of trying to imitate what they had found.

—E. K.

In the early 1980s, the inevitable happened, not only to terrestrial patterns, but to all fly patterns and the entire fly-tying material industry. Synthetics—artificial fly-tying materials—were introduced. The entire fly-tying fraternity went crazy. The new materials were more durable and easier to work with than the naturals used for centuries, and they often were less expensive. Anglers for trout, bass, and other warm-water species, as well as saltwater fishermen quickly picked up on the advantages of the new synthetics. As much as half of all fly-tying materials offered in suppliers' catalogs today are the new synthetics, from threads to imitation fur, wing and body materials, hair, and even jungle cock eyes, and often they float or sink better. They are undoubtedly more durable. Color ranges are wider, and the bleaching, dyeing, and tying processes that added drastically to the cost are unnecessary. This new generation of synthetic materials was not only welcomed by fly tiers, but accepted like nothing I had ever seen in fifty years of fly tying. These new synthetics, as well as the role synthetics played in the development of new patterns for terrestrial fly fishing, are our major reasons for doing this book.

2

The Terrestrial Menu

PICTURE IF YOU will your favorite stream in midsummer. If it happens to be a meadow stream, the banks may be lined with rushes, high grass, shrubs, and assorted low-growing vegetation. On the other hand, the predominant vegetation may be mature sycamores, oaks, and maples if you live in the East, or cottonwoods and willows in the West. In any case, there will be a lush understory of varied plant growth ranging from shrubs and bushes to vines, grasses, and other flora. All of this vegetation is in full summer foliage and represents a grand hotel and dining area for the assorted terrestrials that inhabit its confines.

Ants trek endlessly along established paths, following a trail of pheromones to the beginning or end of some specific task. Cicadas and katydids drone in the higher foliage. Moths and butterflies flit through the leaves like bright spots of paint on an artist's green canvas, and their corpulent larvae chew endlessly on their favorite food. Fat little beetles rove through the undergrowth doing whatever fat little beetles do, while their cousins the ground beetles prowl like iridescent tigers through the detritus searching for prey. The true bugs are also busy, chewing, sucking, copulating, laying eggs, and carrying out other buggy chores.

You could devote your entire life to studying the terrestrial insect population that inhabits a single mile of stream and only scratch the surface of this incredibly intricate and complex ecosystem. It is a task few would choose to undertake, but a simple understanding of the incredible diversity of life that exists within this ecosystem might just make you a better trout fisherman. That reason alone should be sufficient motive for those interested in fly fishing to undertake a more in-depth study of the truly terrestrial organisms that make up a significant portion of the trout's diet.

Most anglers are probably already aware of the tremendous numbers of insects that are potentially available to trout. But one question that is rarely asked is why there is such a staggering number present. Why have the insects been so successful from the evolutionary point of view? The answer is simpler than it may appear to be, but we have to go back in time in order to explain it. Let's go back and take a quick look at what happened.

GENESIS AND EXODUS

The insects have been around for a long time, much longer than the mammals, the group of organisms to which fly fishers belong. While fossilized forms of insects are not often picked up by the roadside, there are plenty of them to be found by knowledgeable persons. Through the magic of modern dating techniques, we know that the ancestors of today's insects appeared about 600 million years ago and lived in the water. After approximately 160 million years, some of these ancestral forms made it out onto the dry land, and it is from them that our modern insects evolved.

The whole group to which the insects belong is then a very ancient group, but even more important than that, they were the first forms of animal life to crawl out onto the dry land and manage to make a living. This wasn't easy and it didn't just happen overnight. It required a lot of changes in the way these organisms lived. Life in the water is easy, but life on land is very difficult. You have to deal with the problems of drying out, developing complicated organ systems, fighting the force of gravity, getting rid of waste products, and a host of other problems as well. But the ancestral terrestrial insects managed to do all of these things, and to do them reasonably well. They developed an external skeleton for support, protection (both from drying out and from predators), and muscle attachment; fairly good respiratory systems; decent "kidneys"; and a bunch of other things.

In short, they managed to make it, but more important, *they were the first of all the animals to do so.* Why was this so terribly important, and what does it have to do with the tremendous numbers of terrestrial insects that we see today? Simply this: As the first group out, they had the opportunity to invade every nook and cranny. There was no competition for anything (except from other insects). They had first crack at whatever food supply (vegetation) was present, and aside from other insects there were no predators. As a result, they literally took over the ancient world. As a matter of fact, from the numbers point of view, they still own the world. Nothing has ever been able to displace them from this position. If mankind were wiped off the face of the earth, it would have no effect on the insects (other than a possibly beneficial one). They would continue

to reproduce, grow, feed on plants or each other, be parasites and predators, and serve as one of the most important food sources for trout.

Another factor that was a major contributor to the huge numbers of terrestrial insects was the appearance of the flowering land plants. Strange, isn't it? Not really, when you think about it. Look at all the flowering plants present today. They are the dominant form of terrestrial plant life, and how many of them depend on insects for reproduction? Virtually all of them require some sort of insect mechanism for pollination purposes. Cone-bearing plants like pine and spruce trees don't need insects—wind does the job for them—but most flowering plants absolutely require the insects for sexual reproduction, and they have evolved hand in hand with each other. When the first flowering plants appeared about 225 million years ago, the insects must have had a field day. A whole new source of food and housing was opened up to them, and they certainly took advantage of it. When the flowering plants reached dominance on the land some 100 million years ago, the terrestrial insects were right there with them, and they have remained there ever since. One might even make the statement that "as the flowering plants go, so go most of the terrestrial insects."

Scientifically speaking, the terrestrial insects have had more than 400 million years to evolve and undergo species formation. They have adapted to just about every available ecological situation imaginable, and during a great deal of their evolutionary history they had no competition for food, space, or any other necessary resource. Could any organism ask for more?

The entire course of insect evolution is a process termed *adaptive radiation*. In essence, this is the process during which a single species undergoes *divergent evolution* and gives rise to new and different species of organisms. It is a common evolutionary pattern when new environmental resources become available to a species and is a valuable method of reducing competition between organisms. Charles Darwin was the first scientist to describe this phenomenon, but since his original publication in 1859, many other examples have been cited. For approximately 400 million years, the insects had virtually the entire terrestrial environment to themselves, and during this time they certainly took advantage of it! They flew, crawled, hopped, jumped, and shuffled into every available ecological niche, and there they remain to this day.

This hasn't been without its problems, however. For example, the exoskeleton (that hard covering on the outside of the beetle) places some severe limitations on the terrestrial insects. They don't get very big because the exoskeleton can support only so much weight. This is why you don't see 2-foot beetles crawling around in the bushes. The beetle's cousin the lobster, however, can grow to well over 50 pounds in weight. Why? Simply because it lives in the water and its body is buoyed up by a force equivalent to the weight of the amount of water its body displaces.

There used to be some really large winged insects about 350 million years ago, but most of these primitive orders of insects are extinct. Some primitive insects did manage to survive up to the present time, and it is rather interesting to note that the only ones that did are the mayflies (Ephemeroptera) and the dragonflies and damselflies (Odonata).

NUMBER CRUNCHING

"There are a lot of arthropods. You can get the idea by imagining Noah trying to load his ark with animals. If, by chasing, swatting, and kicking, he could have gotten one pair aboard per minute, he would have spent eighteen months, night and day,

simply loading his quota of crickets, crabs, lice, flies, centipedes, aphids, wasps, weevils, dragonflies, lobsters, ticks, and the like into the vessel."
—*Wallace, King, and Sanders,* Biology, The Science of Life

A primary consideration for a study of this sort is to try to visualize the immensity of the problem at hand. While the number of insects potentially available to a trout is staggering, there are some things we can do to make things just a bit simpler. Since this work is involved with only the truly terrestrial insects, we can eliminate all those insects in a trout's diet that spend the majority of their life cycle in the water. We thus discard all of the mayflies, stoneflies, caddisflies, craneflies, midges, dragonflies, dobsonflies, and so forth. In all of these insects, the sexually mature aerial (or terrestrial) stage in the life cycle occupies a relatively short portion of the entire cycle. Indeed, if one examines the life cycle of these insects, it might appear that the adult phase is nothing more than the nymph's method of producing more nymphs! The nymph certainly occupies a much greater portion of time in the life cycle, and the nymphs are entirely aquatic.

So if we eliminate all of the above, and thus eliminate the great majority of flies so dear to the hatch fisherman's heart, what do we have left in the way of terrestrials? A great deal. We have all of the daddy longlegs, the spiders, the ticks, the mites, and the scorpions. We have a few crustaceans, the pillbugs or sowbugs, that are truly terrestrial. And we have the millipedes and the centipedes. Last, but by no means least, we have a huge mass of insects.

From the above list of leftovers we can easily eliminate the ticks, mites, scorpions, and pillbugs as important food sources for trout. Of minor importance would be the centipedes, millipedes, and daddy longlegs. The spiders may be quite important. There are a great many species around, many of them unquestionably fall into the water, either as adults or juvenile spiderlings being blown along by the wind, and trout undoubtedly eat them.

This then leaves us to deal with the insects. In considering the truly terrestrial insects as a food source for trout, we have a veritable smorgasbord from which to choose. The numbers are truly staggering and can be appreciated only if we break this group, the class Insecta, into its different orders with an indication of the number of different species within each order (and these are only the species that have been described). On a worldwide basis, the breakdown of the major orders would be more or less like the following (keep in mind that the figures will vary somewhat according to the author!):

• Coleoptera: the beetles, 300,000 species
• Lepidoptera: moths and butterflies, 140,000 species
• Hymenoptera: bees, wasps, and ants, 90,000 species
• Diptera: flies and mosquitoes, 80,000 species
• Hemiptera: true bugs, 40,000 species
• Homoptera: aphids, scale insects, leafhoppers, cicadas, and plant lice, 32,000 species
• Orthoptera: grasshoppers, crickets, 12,500 species
• Blattaria: cockroaches, 4000 species
• Neuroptera: ant lions, dobsonflies, and lacewings, 4,000 species

The less important orders (such as the Zoraptera, Protura, Collembola, and Isoptera) are not included in the above list. The Diptera remain, however, since many of the flies are terrestrial. And finally, let's eliminate all those species of the orders listed above that occur outside the United States. The list of available terrestrials within the United States is still overwhelming. For example, on the North American continent, north of the Mexican border, there are 23,701 species of beetles and approximately 10,000 species of Hemiptera and Homoptera (the two groups that most laypersons simply call "bugs"). Within these three groups alone we are then dealing with well over 30,000 species of terrestrial insects! Add to this the 17,000 species of Hymenoptera, the 11,000 species of Lepidoptera, and a few extra thousand species of assorted orders such as the Orthoptera, and we are looking at a potential trout menu of about 65,000 species. Wait a minute! Don't forget the approximately 9,000 species of Diptera that are terrestrial, so the total figure now comes to about 74,000 species of potentially available food items.

These are pretty impressive figures, particularly when you consider that there are only about 600 species of mayflies (Ephemeroptera), 1,200 species of caddisflies (Trichoptera), and some 9,000 species of "flies" (Diptera) that would be considered aquatic. The ratio then of terrestrial to aquatic insect species is 74,000:11,000, or about 7:1. Watch out, though, because this is just a species ratio and not a total numbers ratio. It really gives no idea at all as to how many more terrestrial insects there are than aquatic insects, but we can assure you that the ratio of total numbers of terrestrial to aquatic insects is phenomenal.

But when you start throwing figures like this around, you have to take into consideration a lot of variables. For example, how many species of mayflies, caddisflies, and dipterans are of real importance to the trout's diet? How many are residents of streams, lakes, ponds, and rivers that are exclusively warm water and in which there are no trout? The same holds true for the terrestrials. How many species occur in areas of the country where there are no trout? How many species are geographically or environmentally isolated and unavailable as food items? It is impossible to answer questions like this simply because no one has ever bothered to put this kind of data together, and probably never will! The point remains, however, that even when we eliminate a huge number of terrestrial insects as unimportant or unavailable, the population that remains important and available is still tremendous.

AQUATIC VERSUS TERRESTRIAL

The *aquatic* "flies" that are important to a trout's diet are important for a number of reasons. First of all, they are normal inhabitants of the aquatic

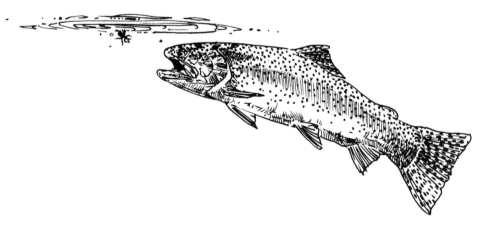

ecosystems where we find trout. They carry out their life cycle in cold-water environments in which trout are present, and both the larval and adult stages of the life cycle are consumed by trout. Second, they occur in sufficient quantity to make it worthwhile for the trout to gather them in as food items. And finally, *the nymphal or larval stages are always present and available as food for the trout.* In other words, they are key items in the aquatic food web, in which the trout might be considered one of the top predators.

On the other hand, the *terrestrials* that are taken as prey by a trout are taken as *chance offerings.* They really don't want to get in the water—it's the last thing on their buggy little minds—but it frequently happens. Whether they are blown in, chased in, fall in, jump in, fly in, or are thrown in by some angler trying to locate a fish, the fact remains that they did not do it on purpose. But it happens all the time, and many of us are thankful that it does. So are the trout, for the happenstance terrestrial plays a central role in the nutrition of the fish when the major aquatic hatches are long gone.

What the above points out is simply that while the aquatic insects are always present for the trout, the terrestrials that become available are random chance events. But the sheer numbers of the terrestrials that inhabit streambanks ensure that enough of these chance events will occur so that the trout is constantly supplied with a random sampling of choice morsels from which to choose. Every angler should at some point simply lie down with his nose a foot from the surface of the water and observe what passes. There is a constant stream of terrestrials. If you are not inclined to do this, then at least sample the surface using a fine-meshed seine to get an idea of what is going by.

MAKING A CHOICE

At this point a problem becomes apparent. If all these terrestrials are constantly on the surface during the "middle" or "terrestrial" season of the year, how does one ever determine which terrestrial the fish are feeding on or which one a fish might prefer? Sometimes it is very obvious. There are occasional times when the water is covered with one particular type of terrestrial, such as flying ants. In this situation there really is no problem, unless you don't have the proper fly to mimic the natural. Sometimes, however, it is not so evident, since many terrestrials are quite small. Seeing a size 22 black ant on the surface isn't that easy, particularly if you wear bifocals. If, during the terrestrial season, you are surrounded by riseforms and see nothing hatching, put your nose to the water. If there happen to be tiny ants on the surface and if you happen to have a tiny ant of the right color, you might experience one of the finest moments of your career. But this is a very obvious situation with a relatively simple solution. Sometimes the situation is not so obvious nor the solution so simple.

Pete Bromley, Steve Hiner, and I stood on the old steel bridge on the upper Beaverkill. Just below the bridge there were half a dozen nice fish, all of which were periodically rising.

Pete posed the natural question: "What's coming off?"

"I don't see anything," said Steve.

I didn't see anything either, but the fish continued to rise and we continued to watch. There was one fish in particular, right below us, that would periodically feed madly, darting left and right, obviously taking something from the surface.

"What in the hell is he taking?" exclaimed Pete. We had been watching for five minutes, and during that time the fish had gone through three or four of these rapid periods of rising, punctuated by periods of relative calm. During these calm periods it would return to its holding station in midstream, about 8 to 10 inches below the surface.

I went back to the car and got the binoculars from the glove compartment. When I returned, Pete said excitedly, "He's feeding on something small and white, but it's not a mayfly."

A few minutes later the fish went into one of its rapid-feeding periods. Using the binoculars, Pete carefully searched the water for the small, white objects that were attracting so much attention.

"I've got 'em," he said. "They're spruce budworms. Look upstream. There's a big spruce tree, and every time the wind blows it knocks a bunch of budworms in the water. That's why these guys are feeding only periodically."

"You're right," said Steve. "Want to see something else interesting? Watch those fish about thirty feet away and to the right. They aren't feeding at all.

They're not in the right place. The only fish that are feeding are the lucky guys that happen to be in the chum line."

What did we do about it? Nothing. The bridge happened to mark the upper property boundary of the Fly Fishers of Brooklyn. The property was heavily posted, and we have always respected other people's property. What could we have done about it? Maybe a lot. I just happened to have some unweighted cream-colored caddis larvae of about the right size. We also had a good collection of other stuff, notably some #14 White Flies for the Yellow Breeches. With a careful trimming of the wings, hackle, and tail, these probably would have worked just fine. But we'll never know.

—H. R. S.

Assuming that you approach an unfamiliar stream during terrestrial season, how do you ever pick a pattern to start with? There are always beetles and crickets about. The air is filled with honeybees, wasps, terrestrial flies, and such. The grass, shrubs, trees, and bushes are crawling with caterpillars, leafhoppers, ants, and spiders. All of these are happily munching away on plants (or each other), copulating, laying eggs, pupating, molting, or engaging in some other necessary activity. Unlike mayflies, however, they aren't doing this right in front of your face or on the surface of the water. Most of these insects are shy and you really have to look for them. The one exception might be the grasshoppers, which take off in front of you like so many lumbering jets. If a great many (or even a few) grasshoppers do take off in front of you, then by all means grab some and see if you have anything comparable in your fly box. Many times the problem can be solved right there. But suppose there are no hoppers around, what then? The scientific solution would be to have with you a large insect-collecting net with which to sweep the streamside foliage. How many times have you ever seen anyone doing this? And yet, if you really wanted to determine the predominant insect life-forms along that stream, that is exactly what you should do. But most of us just aren't going to do this.

The next best thing is to wander along the bank looking at all the foliage and trying to determine if a particular type of terrestrial seems to be relatively abundant. Are there Japanese beetles on the multiflora rose and grapevines that overhang the stream? Are there a lot of crickets down among the grass? Is there some sort of caterpillar in abundance? Careful observation of the streamside flora will often reveal the most abundant fauna. It is not uncommon, for example, to find hordes of ants (particularly carpenter ants) in the streamside foliage. If there just happens to be an actively feeding trout below a bush or tree that's loaded with carpenter ants, it's a safe bet he's feeding on them. Remember, all ants are not tightrope artists. Some will drop, and when they do . . .

This brings us to another method. Suppose while you're sneaking along the bank you spot a rising fish. You of course have no idea what it's feeding on, but there's something that may help you figure it out. Get well below the fish, and if you don't have an insect net, put your nose to the water. Don't just give it a casual glance—really look at the water. You may at first see nothing, but give it time. Whatever it is might be so small that you will have to really scan the surface, even if there are quite a few of them. On the other hand, if it is a fairly large item like a Japanese beetle, the fish may be getting most of them, but sooner or later one will get by. When it does, you might just have the problem solved.

And finally, there is the method that many of us use, which is based on experience. Even in unfamiliar waters, we have tested and proved designs with us. They have caught many fish under varied and difficult conditions and occupy a particularly prominent place in our boxes. It might be a cricket pattern, a beetle, or an ant, but whatever it is *we know it works,* even when fish are not actively feeding. We simply knot the pattern to the tippet and step gently into the water, fishing blind, but confident in the knowledge that it has worked on many previous occasions and it will surely work again. That's how many of us pick a pattern. There really isn't any mystery to it, which is sort of sad when one considers the multiple convolutions and considerations of the average angler when presented with a mayfly hatch.

3

Terrestrial Design

WHEN MARINARO PERFECTED his design for the Japanese beetle, fly fishing took a quantum leap forward. The further development of the jassid and the Letort cricket and hopper put the terrestrial movement into high gear, and it has been churning forward at a steady rate ever since. But many of the authoritative pronouncements over the course of the years are erroneous. There have been certain contradictory statements, even by the same author in the same publication. Many statements that have been made have never been questioned, simply because they were uttered with such a sense of authority that to contradict the author would have appeared blasphemous (particularly if that author happened to be one of the grand gurus of the art). If this happened to be the case, his sage pronouncements were usually greeted by a collective affirmative nodding of the audience, and the theorem was graven into the bronze tablets of fly-fishing lore.

We are not saying that these authors ever purposely misled anyone; they certainly did not! It was (and still is to a certain extent) simply a matter of fly fishermen taking something at face value because no other information on the subject happened to be available. Even today, with so many well-educated and erudite individuals writing about fly fishing, there are still many misleading statements. A current author, for example, indicates trout preferences for certain flies by giving percent takes versus percent refusals. The same author also compares a couple of flies' effectiveness by giving categories such as "possible," "probable," and "acceptable." In this instance, "possible" indicated that a trout might take the fly, since it floated through the fish's window of vision; "probable" indicated that a fish rose to the fly but apparently refused it; and "acceptable" indicated that the trout actually completed the rise and took the fly. From the figures recorded for the two flies tested, the author concludes that one was more effective than the other. The average fly fisherman would probably read this and take it at face value. But there is a great deal wrong with this study. In the first place, there is no way that one can dismiss all the variables present, which are too numerous to mention. In the second place, even if one could eliminate the multiple variables, hundreds or even thousands of trials would have to be done in order to establish any significant difference between the two designs. The fact that one acceptable for twelve possibles was operative for one fly and two acceptables for eight possibles for the other just won't do it! This is nothing but so much data dust.

When reviewing much that has been written on the subject of terrestrial design, it is apparent that some of the dictums proposed over the years are seriously in error. Terrestrial patterns are designed with certain things in mind, and it is imperative that you have a real understanding of such things as why terrestrials float, how they float, and what their key attractants are. In other words, what is it about a particular terrestrial pattern that makes it so successful? There is a great deal known about these subjects, but there is a tremendous amount yet to be learned. With all the new materials available today, it should be possible to produce terrestrial designs that are more effective than ever.

TERRESTRIAL PROPERTIES OF FLOTATION

Before we get into the actual materials used to tie the floating terrestrials, two questions need to be answered: "Why do terrestrial insects float?" and "What do they look like when they float?" Answers to these questions have been proposed before, but some of these answers are not acceptable.

Caddisflies and mayfly duns float on the surface of a stream for the simple reason that they are supported by the surface tension of the water. Their feet do not break through the watery film, which has a certain degree of elasticity, or surface tension, and they remain high and dry. The same holds true for many of the smaller terrestrials. Tiny ants, very small bugs, leafhoppers, and the like probably owe their floatability in a large measure to surface tension. Even very small beetles will be supported by surface tension, but there is an additional factor at work that allows the terrestrials to float rather well.

If a human is in a swimming pool, the ability to float is easily controlled. You can try this if you want to. Simply inflate your lungs with air, and you will float quite nicely. If you exhale, however, you will begin to sink—rather slowly, but nevertheless you will begin to sink. The air in your lungs gives you the buoyancy necessary to float, and once it is expelled you lose that ability. Terrestrial insects operate in a similar manner, but one that is not so controllable.

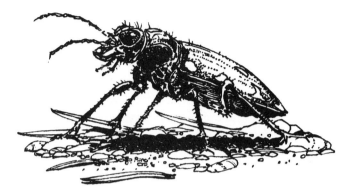

Terrestrials do not have lungs like humans, but they do have a respiratory system filled with air. It is quite unlike the respiratory system found in humans, and consists of a system of circular tubes, or trachea, that extend into and branch throughout the body of the insect. These tubes become ever smaller in diameter and terminate in very small tubes, the tracheoles, which have closed ends and may be filled with fluid. Both the trachea and tracheoles are lined with cuticle. The tracheoles are closely apposed to each cell of the body, and it is through these that actual gaseous exchange takes place. Oxygen diffuses out of the tracheoles to the cells, and carbon dioxide (a waste product of cellular metabolism) diffuses from the cells to the tracheoles. The trachea open to the surface of the body through spiracles, which are supplied with valves. The function of the spiracles is to either open or close the entire network. The truly terrestrial insects have what is termed an open tracheal system, with functional spiracles that may be opened or closed depending upon conditions. They thus operate not only for gaseous exchange, but also as an important means of retaining water and preventing the terrestrial from drying out.

From the above discussion it should be obvious why the larger terrestrials float. They represent large hunks of nutrition permeated with an incredibly extensive system of tubes that contain air. They are thus lighter than water, although not by much, which explains why the big boys float so low in the surface (more about this later). If it were possible to take a chunk of meat, thread an extensive system of soda straws through it, and then plug the outside openings of the soda straws, you could achieve the same effect.

Now there are those who might wish to argue with the above "theory of flotation," but there is a very easy way to prove that it is true. One simply has to remove all the air from the tracheal system of an insect and then drop it into a saucer of water. Easy to say, but not so easy to do unless one has access to the equipment necessary to accomplish the procedure. Fortunately, we do.

I was sitting in my laboratory one day when a movement on the floor caught my eye. Aha! A cricket—a juvenile cricket, but a cricket nevertheless. It was perfect; all I had to do was pop it into a little 70 percent alcohol and add it to my terrestrial collection to use as a model. By the way, crickets in my lab are nothing new—the guy upstairs orders them by the thousands to feed to his lizards. As I was getting ready to drop this little guy into the alcohol, another thought entered my mind. This would be the perfect time to try sinking a terrestrial by evacuating the air from the tracheal system.

There is an easy way to do this. I have a vacuum pump and a vacuum flask, perforated stainless steel capsules for processing tissue samples, and a door that locks so none of my colleagues can see me wasting time. OK, here's what you do. You put the cricket in the perforated stainless steel capsule and drop it into the vacuum flask, which has a couple of inches of water in it. You have to sink the cricket initially. If you don't, the tracheal system will just fill up with air once you release the vacuum and you've accomplished nothing. The flask is hooked up to the vacuum pump, the pump is turned on, and you pull a negative 20 pounds of pressure. A lot of bubbles come out of the cricket—air is obviously being pulled out of the trachea. By the way, you also have to perforate the abdomen (stick it with a pin) or else a big bubble of trapped air forms, which will float the cricket once the vacuum is released. Let the system sit for a couple of minutes, release the vacuum, and all of the space in the tracheal tubes then fills up with water. Take the cricket out of the capsule, drop it into a beaker of water, and it sinks like a rock. The waxy

cuticle remains intact, but it sure doesn't have the ability to float the cricket. Convinced?
—H. R. S.

This then, is why the larger terrestrials float. It has nothing whatsoever to do with the physical qualities of the cuticle (the chitinous major exoskeletal component). The waxy covering of the cuticle likewise has little to do with the floatability of the terrestrials. The major function of this waxy covering is to prevent water loss from the surface of the body, since the cuticle is permeable to water. While it may effectively prevent waterlogging of a terrestrial over very long periods of time, it really has very little (if anything) to do with the initial ability of the terrestrial to float.

In designing a terrestrial with the proper flotation qualities, one should therefore keep in mind the following: The smallest terrestrials float because of surface tension properties of the water as well as their natural buoyancy as a result of air within the tracheal system. They float relatively low in the water, however, so that their entire silhouette is visible to the trout. The larger terrestrials, such as beetles, hoppers, and crickets, will float much lower in the water. In many instances, the bulk of the organism may be below the surface of the water. The outline and/or silhouette of these terrestrials is therefore highly visible to the trout.

These observations on the flotation properties of terrestrials are certainly not recent revelations. Vince Marinaro was perhaps not the first to make these observations, but he was certainly the first to put them into print with the publication of *A Modern Dry Fly Code* in 1950. There was little that escaped his scrutiny. Like Rudyard Kipling's sailor, he can be described as a "man of infinite resource and sagacity." Marinaro observed that ants did not sink but floated quite well, not so surprising a revelation. His second observation, however, that they floated "partly submerged and flush with the surface," is of extreme importance. As a result of this observation, Marinaro trimmed his ant patterns so that they would ride "low and flush in the surface in the manner of the naturals." In performing this simple operation, Marinaro laid the groundwork for what should be one of the primary considerations of terrestrial design—that is, to design the terrestrial pattern to float low in the water. His observations extended to grasshoppers as well, as indicated by the following: "the large ants, black or red for example are partly sunken with wings awash. So too are the grasshoppers and Japanese beetles."

Other authors have also noticed and commented upon this phenomenon of terrestrial flotation. One of the more recent comments was made by Mike Lawson, who stated: "Large, high-floating flies usually don't work very well. Natural grasshoppers float in the surface film, not on it, sort of like an iceberg" (*American Angler and Fly Tyer,* Fall 1990). The iceberg analogy is most appropriate.

It is therefore imperative that most, if not all, terrestrial patterns be designed to imitate the partially submerged natural, rather than having them ride the current like a cork.

THE BODY

There is no doubt that the body comprises the bulk of terrestrial insects. It is therefore not surprising that it has attracted the greatest attention from tiers. In some instances the body has been considered so important in designing a specific terrestrial that it is just about the only component of the fly! Beetle imitations are a good example of this. Most of them are tied as nothing more than an opaque body with a few spindly legs attached, but they work. Vince Marinaro felt so strongly about the importance of the body in terrestial design that he made the statement that when designing grasshoppers and Japanese beetles "it is plain that in these cases it is imperative to construct and fish a body only." Toward the end of the same publication, *A Modern Dry Fly Code,* he states, "The bodies of terrestrials are of paramount importance." We agree with the latter statement but not the former. The wings and legs of most terrestrials are too important to disregard, and we consider them to be essential components for many successful imitations, particularly hoppers and beetles. But his latter statement rings true: Yes, the bodies of terrestrials are "of paramount importance." They are probably the first characteristic of a terrestrial that a trout notices when the hapless insect floats into the trout's window of vision. And since most terrestrials float low and partially submerged in the interface, they are indeed extremely noticeable.

Excluding certain ants, the bodies of terrestrials are opaque, so the tier is presented with only the problems of size, shape, and color. All of these characteristics are easy to duplicate due to the abundance of both synthetic and natural materials currently available. Since the bodies of imitation terrestrials must automatically be constructed with a certain amount of bulk, they will ride low in the water presenting a natural silhouette. So in designing bodies for terrestrial insects there are really no major problems to overcome. Judicious use of the available materials will allow the tier to produce elegant and effective bodies for any terrestrial he chooses.

Body Materials

Hollow (chambered) Hair. Deer and caribou are probably the most commonly used types of hollow hair. They have the advantages of being very cheap, available in an entire spectrum of colors, and very easy to tie with. Since they are essentially hollow, they have excellent flotation qualities, quite similar to a natural terrestrial (a beetle, for example). They lend themselves to a variety of techniques and have proved their worth for many years. You could probably tie nothing but hollow-haired terrestrials for the rest of your life and do just fine. The major problem with hair of this type is that it is quite fragile, and after only a few fish your fly will look terrible. It will still catch fish, however, but there is something about fishing a fly that looks like a haystack that's been through a tornado that is not aesthetically pleasing. This is particularly true for patterns like the Crowe Beetle and any bullet-headed terrestrial such as Mike Lawson's Henry's Fork Hopper. What keeps us tying these patterns is their proven effectiveness and the fact that they are so quick and easy to tie.

Closed Cell Foam. Closed cell foam, in one form or another, has been around for years. Forty years ago we fished rubber crickets for bluegills, and it was a deadly pattern. Do you remember that fly? The body had three parts, just like an insect, and it had long, dangly rubber legs that gave it an irresistible action. That same fly today is an excellent trout producer. The advantages of the new foams available are that they are relatively cheap, may be bought precut or in sheets for custom sizes, and are almost indestructible. One can also tie very quickly with this material without all the mess that is ever-present with hollow-core hair. Foam is available in sheets of different thicknesses and in round lengths as well. It is, in short, a very versatile and durable material. The major drawback is that it is not available in a tremendous variety of colors. Black, gray, olive, insect green, and yellow are readily available, but there are no good browns, tans, dark greens, or iridescent metallics (but there is a way to remedy this, as discussed later).

Macramé Cord. Macramé cord is a comparative newcomer on the scene and has a definite place in tying large-bodied terrestrials. Available in more colors than even deer hair, it is extremely versatile and lends itself well for tying the bodies on large hoppers, crickets, locusts, cicadas, and the like. Its only drawback is that it is not terribly useful for tying anything smaller than about size 10. Even then, one can use only macramé cord of 2.5 to 3 millimeters in diameter. When combined with one of the hollow hairs and greased, these flies have good flotation properties. They tend to settle down deep in the surface, just as one would expect a large terrestrial to do. Also, the material is extremely durable, and a fly tied with macramé cord will still have a body long after the rest of it has been torn apart.

Plastic Canvas Yarn. Plastic canvas yarn is a two-strand synthetic yarn that is a wonderful material for tying small-bodied hoppers, crickets, beetles, and the like. It is available in any color you might like, and is relatively inexpensive and virtually indestructible. The cord may be used as is and furled to form bodies on anything from size 10 to size 14 flies. The two strands are easily separated, and a single strand may be used to form furled bodies down to about size 18. When dressed with floatant, it floats well, since air is trapped within the interstices of the fibers. Flotation is even better if the fly is tied with a deer-hair bullet-head, a trimmed deer-hair head, or a heavily hackled head region.

Cork and Balsa Wood. Cork and balsa wood have been used for years in the manufacture of flies. The success and effectiveness of the MacMurray terrestrial patterns and Corkers speak eloquently for both. Their flotation qualities need no comment. The MacMurray patterns are very easy to tie, since you can buy the preformed bodies in all different sizes. They are, however, relatively fragile and have the tendency to explode after a few fish. But sacrificing a MacMurray ant for a 20-inch trout

is a small price to pay! Likewise, terrestrials with cork bodies are relatively easy to tie but are somewhat time-consuming. Corkers allow the tier the luxury of artistic expression; they may be shaped and painted according to your desires, which certainly contributes to their versatility.

WINGS

In fishing many of the terrestrials, the importance of the wings as attractors has often been overlooked. The wings play a prominent role in the design of many terrestrial patterns, but others have routinely been tied with little if any attempt to include wings. When a winged terrestrial insect (and most have wings at some stage in the life cycle) hits the water, its first reaction is to try to get the hell out. How does it accomplish this? It attempts to fly out. Even if the terrestrial is a beetle, many of which show little inclination to try to fly out of the surface film, there is often an attempt to free the wings.

As a result, many terrestrials spend their time flopping around on the surface, wings extended, vainly trying to fly out of their watery prison. Some of them produce some rather spectacular wave motion patterns. If you have the opportunity, spend a few minutes watching a bee trapped on the surface of a stream. The wings vibrate at an unbelievable frequency! (You can get the same effect by whacking a tuning fork and sticking it into a dish of water.) This activity is certainly going to attract a predatory fish. The relatively slow wing flapping exhibited by moths and butterflies is also a powerful attractant. Indeed, any kind of motion, even the futile waving of a beetle's stubby legs, can act as an attractant for a hungry fish. Even if the wings are not in motion, their outstretched reflective surface presents a highly visible optical cue.

When we have paid so much attention to the importance of the wings in designing mayfly and caddisfly imitations, how can we have been so blind to their importance in the design of certain terrestrials? The answer may lie partially in the fact that the wings of many terrestrials are not particularly noticeable unless they are in flight. The wings of beetles are, for example, hidden under the elytra. Others, such as ants, crickets, and hoppers, have wings only during a portion of the life cycle. The wings of a waterborne terrestrial, even when unfurled, are not as noticeable as those of either a mayfly or a caddisfly—at least not to the angler! As a result, many patterns have been devised in which wings have been either omitted or given only a minor role. With all the excellent wing material available, this seems a real oversight, particularly since the wings probably play a major role as attractors.

The omission of wings on many of the terrestrial patterns may also be due somewhat to the work of Vince Marinaro. Marinaro exhibited a certain ambivalence concerning the importance of wings, and this ambivalence may have either consciously or subconsciously inhibited others from including them as an important factor in terrestrial design. It is not clear what his feelings were. He describes floating ants as having "wings sodden and blending with the background so as to make them completely invisible to the angler." This does not, however, mean that the wings are completely invisible to the fish! As indicated previously, he has described ants as "partly sunken with wings awash" and indicates the same for hoppers and Japanese beetles. And yet he also describes the wings of hoppers as being "transparent and watery" and those of Japanese beetles as "folded and invisible" when they are in the water. Because of this he indicated that it was "imperative to construct and fish a body only" for both the hopper and the Japanese beetle. Regarding the Japanese beetle, he further states that "in almost every case the living beetle falls to the water with wings tightly folded and invisible beneath the coppery brown wing covers."

Other authors have reinforced Marinaro's statements regarding the unimportance of beetle wings. Almy, for example, states that "with few exceptions, the beetles do not spread either pair of wings prominently when they are on the water." This is just not so. Personal observations have shown that many terrestrials do open their wings in the water, even grasshoppers and beetles. They do so while they are alive, and the wings certainly are open after they die because of the relaxation of the controlling musculature. Trout streams are filled with beetles, both alive and dead, and if you examine them it immediately becomes apparent that many float in the surface with both the elytra and wings fully open.

Certain new terrestrial designs presented in this book were therefore conceived with the idea that the wings are extremely important components. The success of these patterns compared with designs in which wings are not included leads us to believe that they are indeed important—that wings represent major visual cues that elicit a feeding response from trout. This seems to be especially true for beetles, hoppers, and crickets.

Other terrestrial patterns have routinely been tied with prominent wings. This is not surprising, since it is difficult to ignore the naked and exposed wings of terrestrials such as the true land flies, wasps, moths, butterflies, and others. In some cases, however, even the exposed wings of certain of these terrestrials have been given short shrift. For example, Almy states that the wings of many true land flies are held over the back and thus "visibility to the trout is minimal." He also indicates that "other flies have smoky gray or mottled wings and these may be visible to fish where they extend over the body." This may very well be true when these flies are at rest in a terrestrial setting, but we are not particularly concerned with how they look on land. When they are suddenly dunked into the water, the picture changes dramatically! The wings splay out and vibrate frantically as the fly makes a determined but often futile attempt to extricate itself. In this situation, the wings become a primary attractant, and to ignore them as such is to make a regrettable error.

The attractant properties of wings in terrestrial design should therefore be of primary importance. There are many new and exciting materials available for tying wings, and these are listed. The modern designer should take full advantage of them.

Wing Materials

Krystal Flash. Krystal Flash is a real boon for tying hopper and other terrestrial wings. It is bright, flashy, stiff, and available in a variety of colors. This is a real attractor. It isn't cheap, but for the casual tier, an envelope of this goes a long way.

Kreinik Braided Metallics. Kreinik braided metallics are an absolutely superb material for tying wings on small hoppers, crickets, beetles, and just about everything else. It is soft and flexible and is available in an entire spectrum of colors and sizes, with as much sparkle as Krystal Flash. It's relatively inexpensive considering the quantity on a spool. We have found that the best all-around color for wings is the mallard, but many of the others are also highly effective.

Z-lon. At $4.95 a package, Z-lon has to be one of the most expensive materials on the market. It's a good winging material, but it lacks the flash so often seen in the wings of terrestrials. It's useful for the smallest of terrestrials but is prohibitively expensive for the larger sizes.

Macramé Cord and Plastic Canvas Yarn. Macramé cord and plastic canvas yarn are cheaper by far than Z-lon but they have almost the same qualities and are available in many different colors. They lack the desirable flash and sparkle of other materials, but they are still quite useful and you can use them in large quantities.

Nylon Organza. Nylon Organza is a great but overlooked winging material. You can purchase it through fabric stores, and a yard of material should last even the most dedicated tier a lifetime. Cut a piece about 1½ inches square, pull the fibers apart, and you have some of the nicest wings you could imagine.

LEGS

The legs of certain terrestrials are undoubtedly attractive to trout. Grasshoppers in particular seem to be more effective if tied with prominent legs. The same may or may not be true for crickets. As far as beetles are concerned, most patterns make some attempt to provide legs. Why legs on beetle imitations have historically been deemed so important but wings have usually been omitted is a real mystery. The legs of beetles are for the most part stubby and inconspicuous, whereas the wings are real

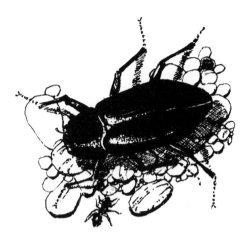

attractors. Nevertheless, most beetle patterns are tied with a few spindly legs, perhaps for the sake of tradition.

Even Marinaro seemed to pay more attention to the legs of beetles than to the wings. He makes the statement in his *Modern Dry Fly Code* that the wings of the Japanese beetle are not important but that it is acceptable to try to match the color of the legs with that of the natural. To his credit, however, he did not consider the hackle used to form the body of the beetle as representative of legs. In this instance he was simply reinforcing his belief that the body of the terrestrial was the most important design component, and that the hackle added to the overall opacity and outline of the body.

Gerald Almy has likewise indicated that "legs can sometimes be important features in beetle imitations. At other times legless patterns seem to score just as well."

We feel that legs are not terribly important on the smaller terrestrials. There, the general shape and color of the body and the wings are going to play a much more important role than the six stubby, little legs. On many of our most effective terrestrial patterns the legs are totally omitted or only hinted at through the judicious use of hackle. After all, if Vince Marinaro could glue a coffee bean to a hook, use it as a beetle imitation, and catch fish with it, how terribly important could legs be? If, however, he had somehow added wings to the coffee bean, he might have had a real winner!

Leg Materials

Trimmed and Knotted Hackle. Trimmed and knotted hackle makes excellent hopper legs and is a good way to get rid of all those large hackles you can't use any other way.

Knotted Turkey Quill and Knotted Pheasant Tail Fibers. Knotted turkey quill or pheasant tail fibers are also excellent for hopper legs and are relatively cheap.

Elk Hair. Elk hair makes an acceptable hopper leg if tied in long under a turkey quill wing and divided into equal portions along each side. It is cheap and easy to use, and it comes in many colors.

Moose and Elk Body Hair. Moose or elk body hair is good for beetle legs when tied in under the body and figure-eight wrapped on top of the hook shank.

Rubber. Rubber should be used more often for terrestrial legs. In the larger terrestrial imitations, it lends a lifelike appearance and endows the fly with an almost irresistible action. If they work so well for flies like the Madame X, then why not use them on some of the smaller terrestrials?

Hackle. Hackle is particularly useful for ant patterns, but it may also be used for the smaller terrestrials as a sort of joint wing-leg technique.

Cul-de-Canard. Why not? Right now cul-de-canard (CDC) is being used for everything from midge pupae to strike indicators. It has terrific action in the water, its flotation properties are good, and it's now available in quantity. It isn't cheap, but you can tie a lot of legs on small stuff with what you get in a package.

COLOR

No discussion of terrestrial design is complete without some mention of color. When contemplating the great diversity of terrestrial insects, color must certainly be considered an important component. Many terrestrials are relatively dull, while others exhibit a veritable rainbow of colors that is impossible to duplicate. Though black, browns, and grays may predominate, there are also brilliant yellows and greens, iridescent purples and peacock colors, lovely pastels, and vibrant combinations of all types. Since fish do see color, it must play a fairly important role in their selection of food items.

Most of the early terrestrial patterns are relatively dull, as are many of the more modern ones. Marinaro's Japanese beetle is certainly not an attempt to duplicate the color of the natural. Neither is its smaller cousin the Jassid. Marinaro was more concerned with shape than color in both cases, and there is certainly no questioning the success of either of these patterns. He was also well aware of the insurmountable difficulties in tying patterns to deal with all types of color patterns, shades, hues, and tints for the jassids, so he didn't try to do this. There is, however, nothing wrong with tying brightly colored terrestrials, since many of them are. In some instances they seem to work better than their dully colored counterparts, so do not hesitate to experiment with different color combinations. Nature has presented the designer of artificial terrestrials with just about every conceivable color for his palette, so rejoice and be creative!

Some time ago I began tying Crowe beetles with a brightly colored rusty brown elk hair. This was done after a few autopsies revealed that brown and tan beetles made up a significant portion of the stomach contents of terrestrial-feeding trout. The pattern was fantastic! It consistently outfished comparably sized black Crowe beetles, and its success can therefore be attributed only to the color. Since then the M.P. Beetle (as it came to be known) has occupied a select corner of my terrestrial box. It is the only deer- or elk-hair beetle I fish anymore. All the other colors have been replaced by designs in closed cell foam of the appropriate color, but so far no one has yet come up with this lovely rusty brown shade for foam.
—H. R. S.

It is fun to play around with different colors for terrestrial patterns, particularly for beetles and the true bugs. For certain patterns, though, we tend to stick to rather basic colors. Crickets are for the most part black or blackish brown, and we tend to tie them that way to mimic the natural. On the other hand, hoppers range through an entire spectrum of colors, but we tend to tie them predominately in yellow. Vince Marinaro may again have something to do with this, as he is very adamant that the only color for a hopper should be yellow. His advice is to "use nothing but yellow imitations, a butter yellow or maize color." We have, however, had a great deal of success fishing hoppers in colors other than yellow—brown, tan, green, and orange, to name just a few.

Our advice on color is simply this: If Ed Shenk can fish a white cricket with great success, then you should not be afraid to experiment! Also, try out some of the newer materials in fluorescent colors. More and more evidence indicates that fish are sensitive to and respond to ultraviolet radiation. They also have been shown to respond to polarized light. Scientists are just beginning to gather information on these subjects, so we don't know that much about it. Whatever color the fish perceive these glow-in-the-dark materials to be, we don't know yet. We have had such excellent success with terrestrial patterns that incorporate certain of these materials, however, that there seems to be no question as to their effectiveness. Do we really need to know anything more about the subject than that? Maybe so. If we knew exactly which colors in the ultraviolet spectrum were most attractive to the fish, we could certainly design more effective imitations. If we were more aware of precisely what role polarized light played in the fish's reaction to predators and prey, we could also incorporate other materials into our patterns. Let's not rush it, though. It will all come in time.

SINKING TERRESTRIALS

"Wet imitations of terrestrial flies are clearly inappropriate however."
—*Gerald Almy,* Tying and Fishing Terrestrials

In the above quote, Almy was referring to his observation of the true terrestrial land flies landing on the surface of a stream and then flying away. This does happen, but often land flies are trapped in the surface film, just like ants, beetles, and a host of other terrestrial insects. If they are not taken by a fish, then they are at the mercy of the current, and in the first fast riffle or area of broken water something happens—they probably sink.

Some terrestrials don't float at all; they sink immediately! If this sounds a bit heretical it shouldn't. You simply haven't thrown enough terrestrials into the water to see it for yourselves.

It was a wonderful opportunity for a photograph. I had laid my rod down on a moss-covered photogenic rock on the bank and a brilliant green Orthopteran, *probably a bush katydid, had perched on the grip right next to the hook keeper. Its position was perfect—it actually looked as though it were knotted to the tippet. But as is often the case, no one had a camera.*

The obvious course of action in this sort of situation was to do the next best thing, toss the varmint into the river and see if you can raise a fish! So I picked it up and chucked it about ten feet out. It sank like a rock! Miller, Steve, and I sat there and watched; the water was gin clear and only about 2 feet deep.

"Well," said Steve, "that's pretty convincing. Too bad you didn't have it on videotape."

We tried the same thing with a caterpillar about a week later. It was one of those big green jobs that we didn't bother to examine too closely, so we don't know to which genus it belonged. It didn't matter, though, because it, too, sank like a rock!

—H. R. S.

Terrestrials sink—believe it! Many of them sink the moment they hit the water, but they pop back to the surface fairly quickly. Just out of curiosity, how many of you terrestrial fisherman have noticed the very subtle riseform to your beetle a second after it hits the water? The fact that you see this type of riseform is probably due to the fish's taking the beetle while it is still just a tad under the surface. It's very similar to a fish taking an emerger, subtle but determined. Many of the smaller terrestrials, and some of the larger ones, go under when they hit the first fast riffle. They may eventually rise back to the surface, but while they are under they must be considered as *submerged* food items. Remember, they *are* lighter than water, but just barely, so they can be carried for extended distances in the current before they slowly rise to the surface again. While they are under, they represent what may be the easiest pickings of all for a hungry trout. Many of them even die while they are under. If so, the wings unfurl, the legs splay out and become limp, and the terrestrial rolls and tumbles in the current with all the "attractor" parts prominently displayed. What more could a trout ask for?

Trout streams are filled with sunken terrestrials that are never seen by the angler but that present trout with a variable menu throughout a great deal of the year. Most fishermen completely ignore this and go merrily along fishing the floating terrestrial patterns, when a whole subsurface world of terrestrial fishing is available.

John Rucker and I had been fishing Virginia's Smith River for the better part of a morning. We had, for once, brought the river to its knees fishing a firefly pattern I had designed, so we decided to have some fun. The sinking beetle patterns I had designed were relatively untested, so in an attempt to prove their effectiveness we tried the following: I left on the floating firefly, John tied on the sinking pattern of the same design, and we both began to fish up the right bank of the Fishing Shack Pool. I took the lead and John fished about thirty yards behind me, taking the water I had already covered. When we got to the head of the pool, the tally stood at thirteen fish for the floating firefly and nine fish on the sinking firefly. Did fish I had already covered with the floating pattern show a preference for the sinking pattern? We'll never know, but taking twenty-two fish in any pool on the Smith River was pretty amazing and spoke to the effectiveness of both patterns. As we sat there shaking our heads, John came out with the comment, "Harry, these aren't terrestrials, they're extra-terrestrials." And thus they were named.

—H. R. S.

This in itself proved only that the sinking firefly pattern worked at that point in time on that particular river under whatever conditions existed that day. Over the next year, sinking beetles were to prove their effectiveness again and again.

It happened on the Yellow Breeches the last week of July 1990, the last night of our annual vacation at the Allenberry Inn. Fishing conditions had been pretty bad all through Pennsylvania that week. Heavy rains had many of the streams either unfishable or barely fishable at best. Most evenings I had amused myself by walking the wall above the dam on the Breeches and roll-casting a floating firefly pattern to the few rising fish that were there. The last night, however, the water in the Breeches, although still off-color, was tempting enough for me to slip on the chest-highs and get in. There were plenty of rising fish beneath the old sycamore above the last stone house, but for some reason I tied on the sinking firefly pattern and added just a touch of soft lead a foot above the fly and a strike indicator about 2 feet above that. On the first cast, the indicator hesitated, I raised the rod tip, and was into a decent fish. This happened seventeen times over the next forty-five minutes. Three of the fish were close to 18 inches. That was all I could take, so I reeled up and prepared to leave the stream. There was a fellow from New Jersey just above me who had been watching, and as I prepared to get out, he asked me if I had finally broken off the fly I had been using. Since it was my last night, I gave him the six sinking fireflies I had left. He immediately rigged up, and as I recall he missed three fish on the first four or five casts. I've often wondered how he and his partner did after I left. Maybe he'll read this and will write and let me know!

—H. R. S.

(As a point of interest, both the sinking and floating firefly imitations in the two stories above were tied with a fluorescent yellow butt. Could this possibly have had anything to do with their effectiveness? We happen to think that it did!)

The old-timers knew the value of sinking patterns. The old lacquered red ant was a standby in many fly boxes years ago, and there was a good reason—it worked. Nowadays not many people fish it, but they should. They should also fish sinking beetles, bugs, hoppers, crickets, and the like. Some people have already figured this out. Gary LaFontaine devotes almost an entire chapter in his book *The Dry Fly* to the art of and effectiveness of fishing a sunken Joe's Hopper. If you haven't read this you should, for it's really an eye-opener. LaFontaine makes an airtight case for the effectiveness of this weighted pattern. His argument in support of fishing sinking terrestrials even extends to this comment: "If they [nymph fishermen] ever start using sunken terrestrial imitations—ants, bees and caterpillars as well as grasshoppers—those flies might eliminate the slack periods that even nymph fishermen hit, ruining any chance to keep them humble."

Well, there are certain sinking terrestrials on the market, and some of us do fish them. Ed Shenk has designed a sinking cricket that is deadly,

but it's not popular (or at least not yet), which is hard to understand. The sinking inchworm has become a standard component of many fly boxes, and then there is always the lacquered sinking ant. Newer designs for sinking terrestrials are given in this book, and our experiences with these have been comparable to those of LaFontaine's when fishing the sinking Joe's Hopper. But as LaFontaine points out, for some reason fly fishermen seem reluctant to fish sinking terrestrials, and it's difficult to figure out why. After all, fishing submerged terrestrials is a lot easier than fishing nymphs. You don't have to worry about what kind of nymph to use, what kind of drift you get, or a whole bunch of other stuff. You also don't have to learn to do things like the "Leisenring Lift." In short, anybody with an IQ approaching room temperature should be able to fish a submerged terrestrial, but most people don't.

About the only thing you could argue over is whether or not you should use an indicator when fishing a submerged terrestrial, and frankly, this is a pretty inane argument. If you like 'em use 'em, and if you don't like 'em don't use 'em. It's as simple as that.

To design a good submerged terrestrial is not as simple as it might initially appear to be. The old lacquered ant was, and still is, a very good design for a number of reasons. First of all, it is not weighted, so it sinks slowly. Second, the fact that it is relatively light allows it to drift naturally in the subsurface currents. It wafts to and fro at the mercy of every little eddy. Third, it was originally tied with soft hackle, which gave the legs a lifelike (or more appropriately, deathlike) ability to sort of hang limp and loose in the current. Finally, it had a lacquered surface that shone under the water just like the exoskeleton of a real ant!

Ed Shenk's submerged cricket is another excellent pattern. The wool head and the deer hair allow this pattern to really remain suspended in the current so that it is carried along just like the real thing. If something like Krystal Flash underwings were added, it would probably be even better! Note that no weight is incorporated into Ed Shenk's cricket. It remains suspended in the current, drifting the way a submerged terrestrial is supposed to drift, lightly and unencumbered.

If weight is indeed incorporated into the design, as in the case of a weighted Joe's Hopper, the amount of weight added is dependent on the depth of the water to be fished. You would not want to fish a heavily weighted terrestrial in relatively shallow water any more than you would fish an unweighted (but sinking) terrestrial in a pool 10 feet deep! You simply have to adjust the weight to the situation. In the long run, it is probably easier to tie all sinking terrestrials without incorporating weight into the design. You can then add whatever might be necessary, even though this tends to detract a bit from the natural drift of the imitation (and makes it a bit more difficult to cast). When adding weight, however, use only enough to carry the fly *slowly* to the desired depth. The object is for the fly to float as naturally as possible, not to streak for the bottom like a weighted stonefly nymph.

So then, what materials are available for tying submerged terrestrials, and how are you going to use these materials?

Body Materials

Kreinik Braided Metallics. Kreinik braided metallics are unequaled. This material may be used to form braided bodies, wrapped bodies, or furled bodies for both smaller hoppers and crickets. It comes in three sizes of round braid and two sizes of flat ribbon. Available colors run the full spectrum of the terrestrial world, and it has all the iridescence necessary to mimic that of many terrestrials. It is virtually indestructible (as many as three dozen fish have been taken on a single submerged Japanese beetle, and the fly is still fishable). It may also be used to form wing cases on beetles, which are used in certain designs discussed later. In short, this is an incredibly versatile material.

Wool. Wool is cheap and relatively easy to use, but it lacks the "flash" of the terrestrial exoskeleton. Once it absorbs water, the fly floats very naturally.

Open Cell Foam. Open cell foam is cheap, very easy to use, and forms fairly good bodies that allow the fly to drift naturally in the current. Color availability is quite good, but it does not have any flash to it.

Vernille. Vernille is outstanding for inchworm bodies and also works very well for furled-bodied hoppers and crickets.

Furry Foam. Furry foam can be rolled to form extended bodies for sinking hoppers and crickets. It also can be used to form beetle bodies, fuzzy bodies for sinking caterpillars, and bug bodies of all types. It comes in a good variety of colors to match almost any situation.

Wings

The best materials for wings are any of those that do not have natural flotation qualities. The Kreinik braided metallics are at the top of the list, followed by Krystal Flash, strands of plastic canvas yarn or macramé cord, and Z-lon.

Legs

In most instances, legs can be represented by deer, moose, or elk hair, trimmed hackle, or some similar material. Since the body of the sinking terrestrial is going to carry the artificial pattern under, you do not have to worry about any of these materials causing the fly to float. The availability of cul-de-canard now makes it possible to incorporate this into some of the smaller terrestrial designs. While we have not done this yet, it should prove highly effective.

How to Fish Sinking Terrestrials

Now that we have introduced some of the principles of designing sinking terrestrials, is there anything special about how you should fish these designs? First of all, keep in mind that a sunken terrestrial is more likely to be found in certain portions of a stream than in others. One of the most productive methods of fishing these patterns is at the head of a pool or run. Cast the fly up into the chute, and let it follow the natural drift into the pool. It really is no different from fishing a nymph. Add weight if necessary to carry it to the desired depth. Sunken terrestrials are also extremely effective in any broken-water situation with scattered holding stations, such as boulders or logs. Again, fish the imitation like a nymph under these conditions. The point is simply this—just because you get into a little fast water, don't shut up the terrestrial box! The sinking terrestrial can be absolutely deadly under these conditions!

Sinking terrestrials are also very effective when fished along scum lines or in backwaters where debris tends to collect. Fish are constantly cruising these areas for food, and not every food item is going to be found on the surface. Remember, these areas are rich in submerged food items and in most instances will be loaded with drowned terrestrials.

Just as with floating terrestrial imitations, fish to the bank. We recommend using as small a strike indicator as possible and placing it only far enough up the tippet to keep the fly from hanging up if the water is rather shallow. Even if the water is deep, the indicator should usually be no more than 18 to 24 inches above the fly. Believe it—if there is a fish present and he wants that fly, it won't sink more than a few inches at most.

Sinking terrestrials can also be fished effectively in flat or still water. Those that sink slowly are recommended under these conditions, and smaller patterns seem to produce better than larger ones. A good time to try a sinking pattern under these conditions is when fish tend to refuse the floating imitation. They often can be tempted into accepting a smaller sinking version of the floating variety. Cast well above the fish, and again, keep the indicator as small as possible.

In actuality, the sinking terrestrials can be fished anytime and anyplace that the floating terrestrials can be fished. At times, such as during slightly high or off-color water conditions, they seem to outproduce their floating counterparts. More than anything else, try experimenting with them. If you encounter a really difficult fish (particularly if it is a large one), give the sinking terrestrial a try. Use a small sinking beetle or ant, or even a small hopper tied to sink. Be prepared to hang on! If, while sneaking along the bank of your favorite creek, you spot a fish in a hold-ing lie, try one of the sinking terrestrials before you try anything else. The results may really surprise you. Finally, if you encounter one of those days when nothing seems to be happening, go to the sinking terrestrials. Fish them into the bank and into the runs leading into pools. We have had many a successful and rewarding day doing this while others tended to pack up and go home.

A friend of mine, Gary Griffin, was recently fishing a river here on the East Coast that is known locally for large trout. It isn't widely known, and for that rea-son I won't mention the name of the river. Anyway, Gary happened upon a bait fisherman who told him that the week before he had caught a very nice brown in the pool Gary was fishing. When questioned about the method used, the fisher-man told Gary that while sitting on the bank, a horse fly had landed close by and he had reflexively swatted it. He apparently didn't swat it hard enough to mash it badly. He reeled in his line (spinning gear), put the horse fly on the hook with a small split shot above it, and chunked it out. The fly was taken within seconds. Forty-five minutes later the man netted (and killed) a 28-inch brown.

—H. R. S.

Does that convince you of the effectiveness of a sinking terrestrial? How many of you have ever caught a 28-inch brown? How many of you would like to?

4

The Terrestrial Attraction

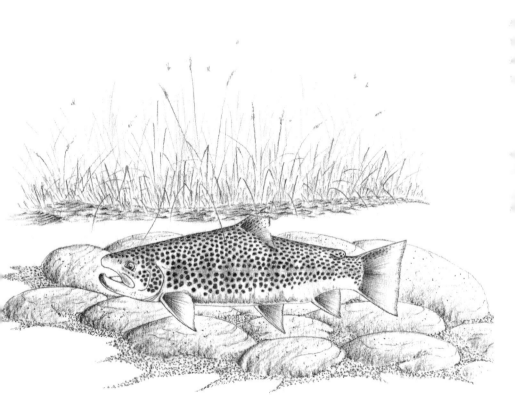

IT IS OBVIOUS that trout eat terrestrials. To learn firsthand about the tremendous variety of terrestrials the average trout will gulp down, kill a trout someday, cut open the stomach, and examine the contents. Don't stop there. Slit the intestine open and take a look at what's in there, too. If you are squeamish about killing the fish, then the next best thing to do is to try a stomach pump, but this won't really give you an idea of the full range of the trout's diet—you can't suck up a large hopper, cricket, or beetle with one of these little bitty syringes. You really do have to autopsy a fish in order to get a true picture of the number and variety of terrestrials they take. What's truly amazing is the size of some of the terrestrials even a small fish will manage to ingest.

What's in it for the trout when it eats a terrestrial? The terrestrial represents a great deal of nourishment for very little expenditure of energy. It's like breakfast in bed. Would you rather have your meal served to you or chase it down, kill it, gut it, and cook it? The terrestrials are easy pickings! No more chasing mayfly nymphs and duns or frantically scrambling after those pesky caddis that pop off like Roman candles. Granted, there are plenty of times a trout can take a station and suck down certain aquatic and terrestrial stages of both of the preceding. At those times, little energy is expended for a pretty good nutritional return. But that only occurs during certain periods. With the terrestrials, however, this is the case most of the time, and in many instances the amount of food taken in with one gulp of a terrestrial is tremendous. Whether the trout realizes all this on a conscious level is open to debate, but they certainly take full advantage of the situation.

Another point to consider is the abundance of terrestrials during most of the year. While there is a certain seasonal abundance for many of the terrestrials, such as hoppers and Japanese beetles, there is a general abundance of many terrestrials from very early spring even into the winter months. In many regions, beetles will produce well into the winter months and will again become available very early in the spring, thus leaving just a few months during which beetles are not active.

Compare this with the mayflies. In many instances, the major hatches are well over by the end of June, particularly in the East. The hatch fisherman is then confined to fishing a narrow time frame, hoping for a few hours of a *Tricorythodes* hatch and spinner fall in the morning, or something else late in the afternoon or just before dark. This is exciting fishing, but it is terribly constraining, when you consider that you could be fishing terrestrials throughout the entire day. And, by the way, probably catching bigger fish! Generally, then, most terrestrials are around for the entire season, whereas most of the caddis and mayfly hatches are confined to relatively narrow time bands. So why limit your fishing time? To sum up, terrestrials are always around, always available, and will always be eaten by trout.

Let's now turn our attention to the nutritional value of the terrestrial. We find it hard to believe that trout consciously recognize the food value of terrestrials, but they seem to take them with relative abandon. The surprising thing is that trout will even take them during the middle of a "superhatch" of mayflies or caddis. Remember the term "breaking the hatch" or "anting the hatch"? Many of us have done exactly that. This means nothing more than presenting some off-the-wall pattern to a particularly difficult (selective) fish in an attempt to break its feeding rhythm. This is often a fish that has been cast to for quite some time, using what we consider to be very good representations of the hatching fly. It is a common technique, and the fly used to accomplish this trick is often an ant, a beetle, or something like a Royal Wulff. (While the statement has often been made that the Royal Wulff "looks like strawberry shortcake" or "dessert," it probably looks more like some goofy sort of terrestrial than anything else!) We would like to think that the trout recognizes the terrestrial as a larger, tastier, or preferred food item and sucks it in. This is probably not the case, however, but we'll say more about this later.

Comparing a terrestrial with a mayfly in terms of nutritional value is like comparing steak and potatoes with a salad. Even if the salad has some cheese and meat in it, it's still pretty low in nutritional value. A terrestrial is like a loaded grocery cart, while a mayfly is akin to a light snack. Now before you hatch fishermen blow your corks, let us explain this concept. A mayfly, in most cases, has very little substance. Even the largest mayflies such as the brown or green drakes are lacking to some degree in nutritional value. The terrestrial forms of the mayfly (the subimago and imago or dun and spinner) are made up merely of reproductive organs, some muscle (they do need to fly), and some fat and glucose to act as an energy source. They do not need extensive energy deposits since they won't be around very long. Most mayflies last only a day or two, so they won't need very much in the way of metabolites over a twenty-four- to forty-eight-hour adult life phase. They don't feed during this time and couldn't even if they tried, since they have no mouth parts. As a result, they have no digestive systems and thus lack all of the organs associated with digestion and nutrition.

But in most other creatures the digestive tract and its associated structures make up a great portion of the bulk of the organism. Since these are intimately associated with the processing and/or storage of food substances, they are themselves rich in food materials. Look at the average fly fisherman. Remove the entire digestive tract and you lose the stomach, the large and small intestine (which contains food in the process of being digested), the liver (the largest gland in the body, rich in nutrients), the pancreas, and a bunch of other stuff as well. All in all, you will lose about 33 percent of the total weight of the body. You will, however, still be left with a pretty sizable mass of material, composed mostly of muscle and bone. Terrestrials are like humans in this respect. There is a mass of tissue associated with the digestive tract, with organs comparable to those found in humans, all of which are rich in nutrients. In addition, terrestrials have large masses of muscle and accumulations of stored fat. Thus, what is inside a terrestrial insect represents a great store of nutritional elements for a trout.

The mayflies are comparatively low in nutrients. You might consider the subimago (dun) stage as nothing more than a sac stuffed with reproductive organs and a bit of neural tissue. There are certainly muscles present, but nothing like the mass of muscle present in a grasshopper or beetle. The imago (spinner) represents even less of a nutritional source. The male spinner is literally a husk of its former self, and the female spinner is about the same once it has dropped its egg mass. The only thing that's left in either case is a small mass of degenerative tissue surrounded by a chitinous exoskeleton and a small amount of muscle.

Those who believe that the chitinous exoskeleton and wings of insects represent a source of nutrition are sadly mistaken. Few, if any, organisms contain the correct digestive enzymes to break chitin down into a digestible material. It thus passes unchanged through the digestive tract and never represents a nutritionally utilizable substance. If you don't believe this, take a walk in the woods and examine raccoon and possum droppings. These animals eat a lot of insects, and their fecal material is filled with the indigestible exoskeletal remains. And mammals have a much more complex and powerful digestive system than do fish. We suggested earlier that you cut open the intestine of a fish as well as its stomach. If you do, and if it has been heavily feeding, the intestine will be packed with the undigested chitinous remains of whatever insect the fish was feeding on. The exoskeletons of scuds, cress bugs, and crayfish are also indigestible and of no nutritional value to fish.

Someone is bound to ask at this point the obvious question: "Why do trout so actively feed on spinners during a spinner fall if they are so nutritionally deficient?" Well, the trout are getting *some* nutrition from them, but they must ingest great quantities of them to derive any benefit. The trout certainly doesn't know this. The reason it feeds on them is intimately associated with certain behavioral feeding patterns linked with minimum expenditure of energy. It can take in huge quantities of spinners with relatively little effort, so it derives more energy from spinner ingestion than it expends in gathering them in. But the fish must ingest great quantities of spinners to come out ahead. Also, spinners may be the only available food source at the time.

When a fish takes a terrestrial, however, it's a different story. A minimum expenditure of energy on the part of the trout often yields a great deal of energy ingested in the form of a hopper, cricket, or beetle. For this reason, the ratio of energy derived to energy expended is much greater if a fish takes a hopper instead of ingesting a mass of blue-winged olives of equal weight to the hopper. Remember, even a trout on a feeding station must move a certain amount to take a nymph, emerger, dun, or spinner. Each movement represents an energy expenditure, no matter how small that movement is. If a trout takes three hundred blue-winged olives, it has to move three hundred times. To take a big hopper or beetle, on the other hand, it has to move only once, maybe not very far, and it gets a full-course meal as its reward.

It is very important, however, to realize that whatever a trout takes, be it a terrestrial, mayfly, or other insect, it is not a conscious, rational decision on the part of the trout. The decision to take or reject a natural is an ingrained response, a behavior pattern that has been established over millions of years and is genetically encoded. The feeding behavior of trout today has developed through millions of years of evolutionary selection for those types of behavior that offer the fish the greatest sources of energy gained for the least amount of energy expended. This is not to say that these patterns cannot be altered; they can, and we'll discuss that a bit later on. Right now, however, let's examine the attraction that terrestrials have for trout.

THE MECHANICS OF ATTRACTION

To watch a trout come from 4 or 5 feet away to take a hopper or beetle pattern is an experience everyone should have. It takes a great deal of willpower to do nothing until the fish takes the fly. Many of us give it the old, "No, you can't have that" routine and jerk it right out of the trout's open mouth. The alternative for a quick instream release is to rear back on the rod and break the fish off on the strike.

The fish has obviously been attracted to the fly, and there are a number of primary sensory mechanisms involved in this attraction. The first, vision, has been the subject of many articles in fly-fishing magazines within the past few years. These articles have been highly technical and well written, and have supplied most of us with more information on trout vision than we can digest. There is little left to say about the subject other than to reiterate that the visual senses play a major role in food gathering, the phenomenon of selectivity, and predator avoidance. It is certainly of major importance to the survival and well-being of the trout.

Other sensory mechanisms have not been treated so extensively. One of these, that associated with perception of wave motion, should certainly be examined in more detail. In humans we would call this hearing, but trout don't really "hear" in the sense that terrestrial organisms do.

In terrestrial organisms such as mammals, the sense of hearing is associated with the reception of wave motion in the air, and the ears are thus highly adapted for life on land. Wave motions in the air are captured and funneled by the outer ear, which is very visible, to the middle ear. At this point the wave motions in the air cause a thin membrane, the tympanic membrane, to vibrate, which in turn sets the bones of the middle ear in motion. The movement of the bones of the middle ear then cause pressure changes and subsequent movement of fluid in the ducts of the inner ear. It is these pressure changes or "compression vibrations" acting at different amplitudes and at different points in the inner ear that initiate neural impulses that pass to the brain. These impulses are translated as sound by a specialized region of the brain. This is an extremely simple explanation for a very complex subject.

Do fish have ears? Sure, but they are not what a mammal would call true ears since they lack the outer and middle portion. When a fly fisherman splats a beetle down in front of a trout, it is safe to presume that at least two sensory mechanisms will be stimulated. The fish certainly sees the fly, and it may also "hear" it hit the water, provided you are fishing in a very quiet pool. But what happens if you cast short and the beetle splats down behind the trout? Hopefully it will turn, streak for the fly, and take it. Most of us have seen this happen on many occasions. In this case, two sensory mechanisms may still be operative. If the pool is quite still and there is no excessive background noise, such as the rushing of a nearby riffle or waterfall, the fish may indeed hear the beetle hit the water. The mechanism of hearing in the fish is elegantly explained in *Trout* (Stackpole Books, 1991). We refer you to Frederic Johnson's "Senses and Taxes" chapter not only for a discussion of hearing, but for all of the sensory mechanisms of trout. More important than hearing however, for it is questionable as to how important this sense is in trout, is the sensory mechanism that is often defined as "distant touch." This is an extremely sensitive mechanism in all fish and is associated not only with feeding but also with many other behavioral responses. The sense of distant touch is the responsibility of the lateral line system and allows the fish to detect pressure waves generated in the water. These may be caused by other fish, obstacles, predators, wading fishermen, and prey items that land in the water with enough force. What probably happens when a trout turns for the fake beetle that splats down behind it is that he has actually felt it hit the water rather than heard it. It is therefore advantageous in certain situations to forget the delicate cast and really let the fly slam down on the water. In many instances, a terrestrial imitation landed hard behind a trout will elicit an immediate and violent response. This technique works quite well in those situations where it is impossible to either get a good drift over the fish or even cast to the water above the fish.

Cliff and I were fishing above the hatchery on Falling Springs Creek near Carlisle, Pennsylvania. We were moving carefully, as all fishermen should do on any water but particularly on water like this. Just above the dam that controls water to the hatchery, there was a large mulberry tree, hanging low over the water and with its branches extending well out past the middle of the stream.

You guessed it! Right under the tree, in an impossible lie to cast to was a very nice rainbow, periodically rising to something. The fish was too far under the tree to get a cast over it, and moving above the fish surely would have spooked it. The only alternative was to try to set the fly down close enough to the fish, somewhat behind it, and in the process put enough oomph into the cast to alert the trout to the presence of the fly. The fly in this case was a size 12 foam-bodied firefly pattern that had produced splendidly on many other streams. It's what I have termed a "confidence" pattern.

The first cast was too short and too far to the right. The second was just about on target but didn't really hit the surface of the water with enough oomph. The third was just right. The fish turned to its right, came downstream a good 3 feet, and took the fly as though it had been waiting for it all day. Cliff and I wound up netting a beautiful 16-inch rainbow, admired it, and then released it.

—H. R. S.

You should be fairly careful, however, not to let the fly slam down too hard. If the fish is fairly far away from the fly, it won't make much difference, but if you smack a fly right down on the head of a fish, you probably will spook it, even if it doesn't see the fly land. A strange reflex mechanism is operational in this circumstance, and it's one over which the fish has no control.

There seems to be some critical threshold of "sound" reception. If the stimulus surpasses this threshold, it causes the rapid firing of neural cells (termed Mauthner cells) that control the contraction of muscle cells along the sides of the fish, and the fish reacts negatively to the stimulus and streaks away. The Mauthner cells, located on opposite sides of the brain, fire alternately, and not together. The end result is that first the muscles along one side of the body contract, and when they relax, the muscles on the opposite side of the body contract. This all happens very quickly, and the end result is a rapidly departing fish. There is nothing the fish can do to control this reaction, and it's a great reflex mechanism that enables the fish to avoid predation. So be a little careful in your presentation of the larger terrestrial patterns!

There are other sensory mechanisms associated with the feeding response of trout, which have long been overlooked. Bass fishermen and other warm-water anglers have long known about these and taken advantage of them, but fly fishermen (trout fishermen in particular) have pretty much chosen not to take advantage of them. These are the sensory mechanisms associated with taste and smell. Those individuals who fish for catfish, buffalo, carp, and yes, even bass, use all sorts of concoctions associated with the senses of taste and smell on their baits or lures. Bottom-feeding fish rely almost totally on these sensory mechanisms for food gathering. In the fish that feed primarily by sight (trout included), these senses are much less important but are still operative. Many fly fishermen have probably considered at one time or another the results that might be obtained by smearing beetle juice on their artificial. How many have ever done this? What, for example, would happen if you put a few drops of essence of hopper on that Whitlock hopper that was just refused for the third time by a 20-inch brown? Perhaps a little eau de *Baetis* might just turn the trick for a confirmed dry-fly fisherman, or extract of nymph for the underwater specialist. It's a point to consider.

The oral cavities of most vertebrates are well supplied with taste buds, and trout are no exception. These are scattered along the outer and inner surfaces of the trout's lips. They may not be as extensive as they are in other organisms, but they are certainly there for a reason. Though the sense of taste (gustatory chemoreception) may not be as well developed in trout as in other fish, it is fairly obvious that trout possess the ability to taste substances.

What about the sense of smell? In many of the salmonids this is a highly developed mechanism. The ability to "smell" chemical differences between rivers and their tributaries is the mechanism that allows spawning salmon to return to the exact stream where they were born. This highly refined sensory mechanism (olfactory chemoreception) must also operate, albeit to a somewhat lesser extent, in the nonmigratory salmonids. This mechanism depends upon the stimulation of receptor cells in the inner portion of the fish's nostril by chemical substances that are soluble in water. This stimulation initiates a nerve impulse that travels to the brain.

What do the senses associated with taste and smell have to do with a trout taking a terrestrial? Perhaps more than we realize. Many of the terrestrial insects produce chemical substances known as pheromones, which act as powerful attractants. These substances, associated primarily with sexual reproduction, diffuse great distances through the air. Certain female moths, for example, produce pheromones that can attract males from upward of a mile away! It is reasonable to assume that if the chemical substances that produce odors are water soluble, they can diffuse through water as well, although over a much shorter distance. A fish with a highly developed sense of "smell" should certainly be able to detect these substances as they diffused from a terrestrial that had inadvertently landed in the water. In addition to pheromones, there are many other odoriferous substances produced by insects. The odor emitted by the stink bug is a great example of this. Other chemical substances are much more subtle but nevertheless present. June bugs have their own distinctive odor, as do Japanese beetles, crickets, and hoppers. If these odors diffuse through water, then why would they not act as a stimulant or attractant for a hungry trout? They probably do, and many of us may have seen this mechanism in operation, but it is hard to prove unless one sets up rigid laboratory experimentation procedures. Field observations, such as the following, are intriguing but not definitive proof of anything.

Mossy Creek, Virginia: The brown rose to a furled-bodied yellow hopper for the third time but again refused to take. In each instance it had followed the fly for a distance of about 4 feet, eyes locked on the artificial, fins working to maintain an exact distance from the fly. On the fourth cast, the fish rose again, followed the fly for about 2 feet, then nosed the fly out of the water. It was almost as though the fish was looking for some final confirmation that this particular hopper was not a fake. The shape was very close to the natural, as was the color. The drift was excellent. The fly had even been given a few subtle twitches at the most opportune moments in the hope of eliciting some sort of reaction, but no luck. What in the hell was this fish looking for? Could it have been that the trout was looking for some sort of taste/smell confirmation? Could that last rise have been the final attempt of the trout to "smell" the fly and thus gain enough confidence to accept it as a natural? I wonder. It looked that way to me, for after that last rise, when the fish nosed the

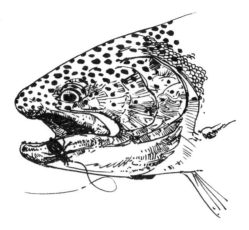

fly, it refused to show itself again. It was almost as though the fish had said, "You came close, old friend, but something didn't smell right to me."

—*H. R. S.*

Fortunately, a good bit of research has been done regarding this topic (in *Trout* and elsewhere), and there is no question that trout, as well as the migratory forms of the salmonids, are capable of detecting odors. There is also a great deal of evidence showing that the trout's sense of taste is relatively well developed. From the layman's point of view, why else would a trout reject a leaf bud, hemlock needle, or any other bit of detritus, if not for the reason that the taste was not right?

We believe that fly fishermen have ignored incorporating these two stimuli into effective fly design because "it just isn't good form." There seems to be something inherently distasteful about smearing hopper or beetle extract on our imitations. Perhaps we shouldn't feel this way, but we bet a lot of our friends would call us down if they caught us soaking our hopper imitations in a vial containing "slurry of hopper."

But attitudes may be changing. If any of you missed it, check page 69 of the September 1993 issue of *Fly Fisherman*. The Cortland Line Company is now advertising a "scented dry fly spray," which is touted as a "pharmacological replica of the body odor of mayflies." Can body odor replicas for terrestrials be far behind?

5

Terrestrials and Selectivity

All discussions about selectivity are only superficial.
　　　　　—*Vince Marinaro,* In the Ring of the Rise, *1976*

MARINARO MADE A strange statement in his 1976 book. Some twenty-five years prior to the preceding quote, he had come very close to outlining the crux of selectivity in the opening few pages of *A Modern Dry Fly Code.* Why, years later, did he dismiss the problem of selectivity with such curtness? One can only speculate.

A CASE STUDY

Pete Bromley and I had been fishing Mossy Creek for most of the day. I guess Mossy Creek is Virginia's answer to the Letort. It has many of the same character-istics. It too springs from underground aquifers of honeycombed limestone, it has similar weed and cress beds, and it has the same convoluted and contorted currents. It also has an abundant supply of hoppers during the late-summer months, and that's what Pete and I were there for. Our success had been about what we'd expected. We had taken a few, missed a few, and risen a great many that simply refused the fly.

At this point in the day we resorted to what many of the regulars do—the old chum trick. We had been grabbing a bunch of hoppers, flipping one in the water, and locating a trout. One of us would then slip downstream, well away from the bank, and sneak up within casting range, while the other would continue to run a chum line of hoppers to the unsuspecting fish. We had met with a modicum of success, but we were really struck by the number of refusals that had occurred.

We had located a fairly good fish and Pete had tried for it, but he continued to get nothing but refusals. Different patterns, lighter tippets—nothing seemed to make any difference. We switched places, and for some reason, as Pete was moving back upstream (well away from the bank), I cut off the hopper I had been fishing and replaced it with a size 10 black Crowe Beetle. Pete drifted two more live hoppers over the fish, and it took both without hesitation. I worked out enough line to cover the fish and was lucky. On the first cast, the fly landed about 6 feet above the lie of the fish, curled perfectly to the left, and made an ideal drift right over the fish's nose. I watched as beetle and trout converged on each other. The fish rose without hesitation and sipped in the beetle, and I was fast to a good 15-inch brown.

Why did that fish, which had refused all sorts of hopper imitations, suddenly decide that black beetle was exactly what it had been looking for? It was a question that begged for an answer.

—H. R. S.

In order to try to answer that question, we must do a little digging for some applicable information. That fish exhibited what most of us would consider some sort of selectivity. It was definitely selecting natural hoppers over artificial ones. Anyone with any observational powers could figure that out. But the fact that it took that fake beetle without hesitation was what was so intriguing. The Crowe Beetle had presumably acted as a stimulus of some sort, the trout had been sensitive to that stimulus, and the stimulus had been strong enough to trigger a reaction in the fish. In this case, the reaction was to eat the beetle. Was the stimulus presented by the fake beetle different from the stimulus of the fake hopper? If so, in what way? Would a fake cricket also have turned the trick? Perhaps a Royal Wulff would have given the same result, but we will never know, for this was a one-shot experiment.

Now, though we can never exactly duplicate this sort of experiment, we can certainly try to logically figure out some sort of explanation for events like this. In order to do so, however, we have to delve a little into fish behavior and try to figure out what makes them tick. To keep it simple, let's just say that "behavior" can be defined as the way organisms act. But what prompts them to act in certain ways and to act differently under different circumstances?

THE EVOLUTION OF BEHAVIOR

It's obvious that fish are sensitive to certain stimuli. It is also obvious that fish react to certain stimuli. We can then come to the conclusion that fish behavior patterns are initially determined by their sensitivity to different stimuli, and then by their response to those stimuli. This, then, would be the crux of fish behavior, but it doesn't tell us anything about _why_ they behave the way they do.

We have to go back in time to begin to figure all this out. The first fish appeared in the fossil record half a billion years ago. They didn't look much like the fish of today, but they were nevertheless the ancestors of today's bony fish (class Osteichthyes), which reached prominence 400 million years ago. Modern fish are therefore the end product of 500 million years of evolution. During that 500 million years, a lot of things happened to make fish what they are today.

Take a look at any group of organisms of the same species. No two individuals are exactly alike; even "identical" twins aren't exactly alike. If you compare the spot pattern on browns or the vermiculations on the backs of brookies, they are very different from fish to fish. These external (phenotypic) variations are easy to see in most cases. What causes them are internal or genetic (genotypic) variations from organism to organism. Behavior patterns, like anatomical patterns, are also genetically determined to a great extent.

The behavioral characteristics of today's fish, like the anatomical (and physiological and biochemical) characteristics, are the end product of half a billion years of evolution. During that long period of time, the genetically determined characteristics (behavioral, anatomical, or whatever) that best allowed fish to survive and reproduce have been retained. Those that did not were eliminated from the gene pool. Those individuals that had the most favorable genetic variations lived to survive and reproduce, and they passed these favorable characteristics on to their offspring. And so it has gone for 500 million years.

Fish behavior, then, is the end result of 500 million years of genetic selection. They behave the way they do because it means the difference between life and death, a full stomach or an empty stomach, a maximum amount of energy gained for a minimum amount of energy expended. And this evolutionary process is still ongoing today. The trout a million years from now (if there are any left) may be quite different from the ones we know today, both anatomically and behaviorally.

Let us give you an example of fish behavior that you can easily see. Walk into a pet shop and sneak back to one of the fish tanks, but don't let the clerk see you do this. Rap smartly on the side of the tank with a coin or ring and watch what happens. If you could see it in slow motion, you would see all the fish first arch their backs, and then swim to the other side of the tank. All you will see is a blur of motion as the fish streak away from you. This is a behavior pattern. The *proximate* cause is the sequence of physiological events that causes this behavior. In this case, it is a relatively simple interplay between sensory reception, neural transmission, and muscular contraction over which the fish has no control. It is a bit like your knee-jerk reflex when the doctor whacks your knee with the little rubber hatchet. The *ultimate* cause of this reaction is that it has definite adaptive value. It prevents the fish from getting eaten in many cases, or at least causes it to try to escape from anything that creates a disturbance in the water. This reaction has definite survival value and has been selected for during the evolution of the fish.

FISH BEHAVIOR PATTERNS

Behavior patterns in fish don't differ in principle from behavior patterns in other organisms. But all behavior patterns are certainly not the same. While all ultimately are genetically determined, many may be modified with age and experience. Most biologists seem to have finally agreed on this.

Let's take a look at some of these different behavior patterns and see how they might apply to fish, and more particularly to the way fish feed.

Fixed Action Patterns

Fixed action patterns probably could best be described as "instinctive" patterns. They develop with a minimum amount of experience (or with no experience at all). A fingerling trout strikes at everything that goes by or moves, provided that the presumptive food particle is small enough. Mommy fish doesn't teach it to do this; it's an instinctive response. What initiates this response? A stimulus, and in this case the stimulus is whatever the particle might be that floats by. This type of stimulus is referred to as a *sign stimulus,* and the behavior of the fingerling is blocked until a sign stimulus triggers it.

As time passes, however, the response of the trout changes. Only certain sign stimuli will elicit the feeding response, in most cases. Pieces of wood, grass, buds, and so forth usually will no longer elicit the response. This fixed action behavior pattern has been modified by experience. There is a selective advantage for this: The fish no longer wastes valuable energy and time chasing after detritus.

With certain types of fish behavior, however, the fixed action patterns remain rigid, predictable, and stereotyped. Fixed action patterns associated with reproductive behavior are good examples of this. For example, male stickleback fish will show aggressive behavior toward anything with a red underside during the breeding period. Its reaction toward a block of wood with a red belly will be pretty much the same as its reaction to another male stickleback. In this case, the sign stimulus is the color red, not the form of the object at all. There is a selective advantage to this type of pattern remaining fixed, but that's another story.

Learning

Technically, learning indicates that an organism's responses become modified by experience, but it's a little bit different from simply modifying a fixed action pattern. In the first place, it seems that the capacity of an organism's ability to learn is determined by both how complex its nervous system is and how long the organism lives. On the scale of neural complexity, we could rank the following organisms from most complex to least complex as follows: human, dog, fish, mayfly.

It's obvious that most humans are considerably more intelligent than other organisms, and this is because of our neural complexity and development. A ten-year-old human is a great deal smarter than a ten-year-old dog, and a ten-year-old dog is certainly smarter than a ten-year-old fish. To keep everything in perspective, a ten-year-old mayfly has been dead for about nine years, eleven months, and twenty-eight days. It doesn't have time to learn anything. Even if it lived longer, it probably couldn't learn anything, because its "brain" just isn't complex enough. The fish, the dog, and the human, however, have had the same timespan in which to learn things. Let's hope that the ten-year-old human knows more than either the ten-year-old dog or the ten-year-old fish! It's obvious that some species are just smarter than others.

The most common type of learning process is probably what is known as *habituation*. In effect, habituation means that an organism comes to ignore a persistent stimulus. Nothing is gained by reacting to the stimulus, so the organism learns to waste neither time nor energy in a response. Can fish become habituated? Of course! On really heavily fished water, it is obvious that fish have become habituated to the presence of fishermen. It is possible to get very close to them without having them take flight. While you may not be able to get them to take a fly, they will sit right in front of you and feed all day long, as long as you don't really cause some great commotion. This can be seen on Armstrong's Spring Creek, the Yellow Breeches, Henry's Fork, or any other water that is inundated by fishermen. In contrast, the most difficult type of fishing can be in those

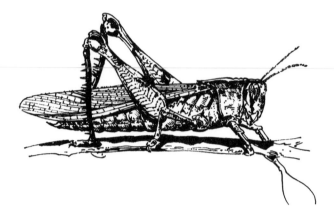

streams where very few fishermen go. The fish are wild, spooky, and skittish. They will flee at the shadow of the leader, a careless footstep, or the panicked flight of another fish through the pool. Anything out of the ordinary is perceived as a threat. On hard-fished water, on the other hand, fishermen are no longer perceived as a threat, but rather as a natural occurrence.

We also believe that habituation can occur when it comes to flies. A fish comes to your fly on the first cast but refuses it. Have you ever noticed that the second drift over him may bring him up again, but that the second response seems rather less energetic than the first? The third response will be even less so, and finally the fish simply ignores your fly. It doesn't always work that way, of course—sometimes he'll charge it on the fourth or fifth cast—but in general the fish will become less interested rather than more interested.

CONDITIONED SELECTIVITY

Another type of learning is termed *associative learning*. In this case, one stimulus comes to be linked through experience with another. The classic case is the conditioning response of Pavlov's dogs. A bell is rung, meat powder is blown into the dog's mouth, and the dog salivates. After a few trials, the dog will begin to salivate at the ringing of the bell. He expects to taste meat. The second stimulus is lacking, but the first stimulus triggers the response. Can you see this in fish? Without question.

Hans Rott and I stood on the edge of the pond. It was a beautiful spring-fed pond, with lovely, big, fat healthy rainbow trout cruising throughout. The only problem was that they weren't wild. This pond happened to be one of those pay-as-you-go ponds; you fished, you caught, you paid.

"Watch this," I said to Hans, and I began to make sweeping motions with my hand, mimicking the motion made when the hatchery manager throws food in the water.

There was a massive rush of trout to the water directly in front of us. They swooped, they swirled, they struck at nonexistent pellets on the surface. It was re-markable. They, of course, had come to associate the movement of the hand with the presence of food.

"I'll be damned," said Hans.

—H. R. S.

"Well," you might say, "that's in a hatchery, and we don't fish in hatcheries. It doesn't happen in natural situations." Sure it does, and in many instances, if you know what to look for, you can see this type of *positive response conditioning.*

I have watched the following on Armstrongs Spring Creek in Montana. An angler enters the water and begins to work his way upstream, casting to rising fish. He never looks behind him. If he did he would see a line of fish all queued up behind him, happily feeding away on all the stuff he kicks up as he wades. They will even bump into your legs at times trying to get some choice item. They will take advantage of every angler who comes along. What is really interesting is that these fish will line up behind you even if you are not moving around and kicking up food. It is as though they actually are anticipating being fed. Trout on Falling Springs Branch in Pennsylvania will do the same thing when the cows at a local dairy farm enter the water. Both are cases of conditioned response. The fish have come to associate the presence of large objects wandering around in the stream with the presence of food, and they react accordingly.

—H. R. S.

Now, we know that we can elicit a positive response through condition-ing, so it logically follows that we can elicit negative responses to stimuli as well. If you ring a bell and then hit a dog with a stick, it won't take many trials before simply ringing the bell will result in a rapidly disappearing dog! Can you do the same thing with fish? Sure. A pike is a predaceous fish and will charge almost anything. Put a hungry pike in a tank and drop in a stickleback. The pike charges, engulfs the stickleback, but doesn't eat it. It spits it out. The stickleback is given its name for a good reason. All of the fin rays, particularly the ones on the back, are elongate, very stiff, very hard, and very sharp. When the pike clamps down, it's not a pleasant experience. The stickleback may suffer some severe damage in the process, however. After a few trials like this, the pike will leave stickle-backs alone, no matter how hungry it may be. Are there examples of this sort of conditioning in the world of the fly fisherman? Very probably.

On Virginia's Mossy Creek, for example, hopper season is a big event. By the time hopper season is over, the fish have seen just about every conceivable pattern in the book, and many of them have been jerked around a number of times by a fake hopper. They have learned to associate hoppers not only with food, but also with an unpleasant experience. But they are not terribly smart and are torn between two possible reactions to the hopper stimulus: They get enough live hoppers to keep their interest up, but they get enough fakes to make them highly suspicious. As a result, every hopper that passes over is regarded somewhat cautiously. Those that act and smell like a real hopper are taken, and those that don't are given very close scrutiny (often using the senses of smell and taste) and usually don't pass the test. In effect, then, these fish have become *selective,* and it is to their advantage, from a survival point of view, to remain that way. For-tunately their memories are short, so when the next hopper season rolls around, we can have a lot of fun for the first few weeks.

With respect to fish and fishermen, this should probably be referred to as *conditioned selectivity.* It is probably the type of selectivity that most terrestrial fishermen encounter, particularly on hard-fished streams during terrestrial season. Is there anything that can be done to override this type of selectivity?

Earlier we discussed the sign stimulus—a stimulus of some type that initiates an action pattern. In the case of a fish feeding on terrestrials, the terrestrial itself acts as a sign stimulus in various ways—the general body outline, the motion or lack of motion, the wings outstretched in a futile attempt to take off. This may be why hoppers tied with legs can be more effective than hoppers tied without legs. It may also explain why a twitched terrestrial often elicits a strike when the same terrestrial pattern brings no response when dead-drifted. It may explain why certain terrestrial patterns tied with wings produce better than those with no wings. In other words, a terrestrial pattern may well be refused by a fish simply because some element in its makeup is lacking or deficient. Particularly if that fish is exhibiting conditioned selectivity. This probably accounts for the trout's behavior toward the fake hopper in the opening anecdote. When the beetle imitation was presented it represented a totally different picture (sign stimulus) and was therefore readily accepted.

But if we assume that the sign stimulus in this case is totally visual, we are in danger of making a grave error. While that may be the initial case, there are undoubtedly other sign stimuli that play a role in acceptance or rejection of the fly. One other sign stimulus that may be of major importance is the ability of a fish to "smell." (This was discussed in depth in chapter 4.) Suffice it to say that while vision is undoubtedly the most important of the sensory mechanisms a trout employs in feeding, it is by no means the only one. Smell, taste, and sensory input from the lateral line system all play major roles, and to exclude these is to commit an unpardonable error.

BEHAVIORAL PRISONERS

There is a second type of selectivity, one that the terrestrial fisherman encounters relatively infrequently. This type of selectivity occurs when trout are feeding exclusively on a single type of terrestrial to the exclusion of all others. We will term this *hatch selectivity*. It happens with annoying regularity during mayfly and caddisfly hatches, but though it does occur with terrestrials, it is not that common. It happens on occasion with ants, has been described for beetles, and may be encountered now and again with hoppers (but there have to be a tremendous number of hoppers around, and a fairly stiff breeze).

Since it can occur with terrestrials, albeit infrequently, we will examine the phenomenon. During this type of selectivity, most of us have seen

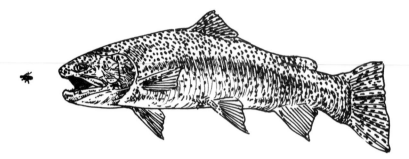

what happens. We stand there in frustration, while patterns are refused or, worse, totally ignored. We change flies. We try different ties—thorax, haystacks, hairwings, cut-wings—but they are all refused. What the hell is going on?

To make the problem relatively simple, let's assume that all the fish you can see are actively taking duns, even though they probably aren't. The natural dun (or some portion of its anatomy) is the sign stimulus that initiates the feeding response. Granted, before feeding occurs, there are many other things that must be considered, such as the water temperature, its pH, and the blood glucose levels of the fish (has it fed recently?). These all contribute to what is termed the *motivational state* of the fish. But again, let's assume that the fish is in a highly motivated state and is actively taking duns. It has taken up a feeding station and become "locked in" to that station and to that fly. It shows very little deviation from the parameters it has established for itself. It moves very little in any direction and remains more or less fixed in position, rhythmically rising and taking in flies. Sometimes this rhythm becomes so well established that there seems to be no deviation at all, particularly during a heavy hatch. The term "locked in" is a very accurate description of the fish's behavior at this time. What has happened is simply that by taking in a number of duns, the fish has established what is termed a *search image*, the image being determined by certain anatomical characteristics of the insect on which the fish is feeding at the time. When the fish's eyes send the appropriate signal to the brain, the fish takes the insect. Note that the signal must be *appropriate*. No other signal will work, and the signal is dependent upon the search image. Thus, if the search image is established as "blue-winged olive, size 20," a sulfur dun just won't do the job! What's going on? It may best be expressed by diagramming the whole process as follows:

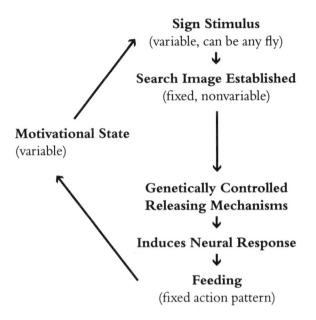

Sign Stimulus
(variable, can be any fly)
⬇
Search Image Established
(fixed, nonvariable)

Motivational State
(variable)

Genetically Controlled Releasing Mechanisms
⬇
Induces Neural Response
⬇
Feeding
(fixed action pattern)

The sign stimulus in this diagram can be any fly or any portion of a fly. The wings may be the predominant stimulus, or in spinners it may be the egg sac. If the motivational state is not high, however, the trout will not feed, no matter how many sign stimuli are floating over its nose, so that's a variable that must be considered. Have you ever encountered a heavy hatch during which very few fish were feeding? Well, their motivational state was probably very low; maybe they had fed heavily before you got there, or maybe the water temperature was wrong. In the above diagram we can say that during a hatch when fish are actively taking duns, the sign stimulus is the dun, the motivational state of the fish is good, and that both of these have triggered some genetically controlled mechanism that prompts the fish to feed.

But notice that feeding in this case is designated as a fixed action pattern, and by definition a fixed action pattern is one that can at times be quite rigid and unalterable. Why would feeding under these conditions constitute a rigid fixed action pattern? Simply because this is the most efficient type of behavior pattern for this situation. It allows the greatest amount of energy uptake with the least amount of energy expended. This type of feeding behavior has been genetically selected for over a period of about 400 million years. Since it's genetically controlled, it is rigidly adhered to. As long as the same sign stimulus is presented to the fish, the fish responds in the same manner. The fish have in effect become imprinted and operate like a loop tape—they play the same song over and over again and will continue to do so as long as the hatch continues or until they become satiated and their motivational state declines.

Under these conditions, the refusal of your fly indicates that it does not meet the criteria of the correct sign stimulus. In other words, you don't have the right combination to turn on the machine that runs the tape.

In the final analysis, fish that exhibit hatch selectivity are _behavioral prisoners_ because of their genetic makeup. Once this feeding pattern is established, it's tough to break the rhythm. The fish are programmed to react this way, and it's to their advantage to exhibit this type of behavior. They are locked in and very limited in their ability to change the response.

The best the fisherman can do is to search for some fly that comes close to meeting the criteria of the correct sign stimulus. Sometimes we get it, sometimes we don't. It might be said that all the flies ever tied to imitate hatches have been formulated in the search for the correct sign stimulus for different situations.

This behavior pattern can sometimes be broken. An ant, a beetle, a Royal Wulff, a larger size dun than the natural will all work sometimes. Why they work is beyond the scope of this book.

Luckily, the terrestrial fisherman encounters hatch selectivity only rarely. There are quite a few recorded instances of this type of selectivity for ants and some of the smaller beetles, and perhaps even for the Japanese beetle during its heyday some forty years ago. But most of the time the terrestrial fisherman does not have to deal with it. There are usually not enough terrestrials of the same species falling in the water at the same time. Because of this, the trout is essentially incapable of forming a search image for any one particular species. In order for a fish to form a search image, quite a few naturals of the same species must pass over the fish in a given period of time. Only then will the fish react to these sign stimuli by forming a search image for that particular insect. How many and over what time period are at present unanswered questions, but we have some intriguing information on the subject. Kurt Fausch (*Trout* magazine, Winter 1992), in his article "Life as a Trout Predator," cites experimental work done by N. H. Ringler showing that between 25 and 250 mealworms had to be drifted by trout that had been "taught" to feed on brine shrimp before they were accepted as food items. The time involved ranged from five to twenty-five minutes. After six days, the fish were "still learning to forage efficiently on these organisms even after 800 to 1,200 prey had been captured." Could this possibly give us a clue as to why you can sometimes break the feeding rhythm of a selective fish with an off-the-wall pattern? The point is simply this: A lot of insects over a variable period of time seem to be necessary to induce the phenomenon of hatch selectivity.

Why then will a trout attack a beetle, hopper, or cricket imitation with such abandon when it obviously does not see enough of these on most occasions to form a search image? There must be something else going on. It may be nothing more complex than a basic instinctive response to these large prey items that triggers an immediate and visceral reaction—something that says to the fish, "Eat, eat, for Pete's sake grab that thing before it gets away!" Some genetic mechanism that controls a simple stimulus-response reaction is triggered by the appearance of a large, helpless terrestrial in the interface. This might best be described in the vernacular as a "gut reaction" on the part of the fish. This is the best we can do at present. New information may provide us with a better answer in the future.

6

Order Coleoptera: The Beetles

If I had to pick one dry fly to use on spring-creek waters, without hesitation I would choose a black beetle. Even though I have seldom encountered situations where I knew trout were actually feeding on beetles, I have probably caught more fish on beetle imitations than on any other fly.

—*Mike Lawson,* American Angler and Fly Tyer, *Fall 1990*

Just how many beetles are there? There is no way to tell. Biologists can't even give you a really accurate estimate as to how many species of beetles there are, much less a count of the entire number.

There was, however a distinguished biologist, J. B. S. Haldane, who in a single remark managed to succintly indicate the vast quantity of beetle life, which permeates every ecological niche of this planet. And he did it without using any numbers.

As the story goes, Haldane was once asked by a somewhat pompous theologian if he could conclude anything about the nature of the Creator from a study of His creation. It was reported that Haldane's answer was "an inordinate fondness for beetles."

—H. R. S.

IN SHEER WEIGHT of numbers of species, the beetles are the kings of the terrestrial domain. They are one of the earliest of all terrestrials to appear in the spring and one of the last to disappear as the weather grows colder. They occupy all sorts of different habitats; come in all shapes, sizes, and colors; and probably (along with the ant) are found in the most prominent position in the confirmed terrestrial fisherman's fly box. They likewise hold a prominent position in the trout's menu, and it's a rare summer day when fish cannot be enticed to accept some form of artificial beetle.

It's probably a safe bet to say that most fly fishermen can recognize a beetle. One of the most distinguishing characteristics of this order is the modification of the first pair of wings to form the hard "wing cases," or elytra, which act as protective covers for the second pair of wings. The hind wings are therefore the only ones that function during flight. When the beetle is at rest (or at least not in flight), the second pair is folded up and tucked under the elytra. All beetles have well-developed mouth parts for chewing, and in some the mandibles are exceptionally so in order to deal with hard plant materials such as seeds or wood.

The life cycle of the beetle is one in which complete metamorphosis takes place: Eggs are laid, and the larva develops from the egg and then undergoes a complete and radical change (pupation) to the adult stage. There can be as many as four generations produced in a year in some groups of beetles. In others a period of several years may be required for a single generation. The average is about one generation per year, with the larva overwintering as pupae in soil, bark, or some other protected area.

DESIGNING BEETLE PATTERNS

There are all sorts of beetles. On the North American continent, there are approximately 23,700 species of beetles that have been described, so it is not surprising that many of them find their way into streams inhabited by trout. This abundance of beetle species would at first glance appear to represent an insurmountable problem. That is, how would you ever pick out a pattern to use? The average angler is accustomed to matching the hatch for mayflies, which is a relatively easy problem to solve. There are not that many species of mayflies, and at the risk of oversimplification, there are many instances in which a box filled with generalized shapes and colors of duns will work quite well. Caddisflies, while more numerous than mayflies, may also be matched well with a relatively few good generalized patterns. Can the same be done for beetles? The answer is an unequivocal yes! As a matter of fact, tying beetle imitations is a much less rigorous and demanding process than tying mayfly or caddisfly imitations.

This needs some explanation. How could it possibly be easier to tie imitations for almost 24,000 species of beetles than for 600 species of mayflies? Or for the 1,200 species of caddisflies found in North America? First of all, the shapes of beetles fall into only a few generalized categories and have been classified as follows according to Borror and White (*Peterson Field Guides, Insects,* Houghton Mifflin, 1970): elongate-slender, parallel sided; elongate-slender; elongate-oval; elongate-robust; broadly oval. There are, of course, variations of these forms, but the variations are subtle, for the most part. Most of the beetles we tie will probably be oval or rectangular. These two general shapes have served anglers well for years, and the subtle differences from one beetle to the other do not seem to make much difference to trout, which don't bother to classify too many beetles according to shape.

On the other hand, the size of the imitation is very important, and the closer you come to matching the exact size of the natural, the better your results will be. Japanese beetles, for example, are best duplicated on a standard #12 dry-fly hook, so you would not fish a size 6 if there were many naturals around. The size of beetles is highly variable, ranging from about 2½ inches for the largest to ⅛ inch for the smallest.

Color is just as important as size. The predominant colors of beetles are black, iridescent black, brown, tan, green, metallic green, gray, and combinations thereof. If you really collect a lot of beetles, you'll see many more colors than this, but these are the major colors you will have to deal with.

The main components in beetle imitations, then, are the characteristics of shape, color, and size. Using these three characteristics, we could probably narrow our beetle selections down into the following two categories: (1) More or less rectangular to square—black, brown, tan, or gray; sizes 10 to 18. (2) Oval to elongate-oval—black, brown, tan, gray, or green; sizes 10 to 20.

And really, why bother to go any farther? This selection would take care of just about anything the average angler would run into along a stream, yet represents far fewer flies than most of us carry to cover the major mayfly and caddisfly hatches.

The beetle selection is so wonderfully simple because we don't have to deal with nymphal stages, emergers, duns, and spinners, each of which has its own unique characteristics. There are a multitude of designs available to cover all of those life cycle stages. A beetle is a beetle, however—it's that easy. Getting the general shape and color is all that counts. You don't have to worry about the hatch, selectivity generally does not play a major role, and because the larval and/or juvenile stages are usually unavailable to the trout, you don't have that sometimes perplexing problem of trying to figure out what stage in the life cycle the fish is feeding on. In short, fishing beetles is marvelously simplistic. As a matter of fact, if you could peer into the fly boxes of most terrestrial-oriented anglers, you would probably find only black beetles in different sizes and materials.

FISHING THE IMITATIONS

When a beetle hits the water it usually goes *splat*. Beetles are for the most part far from graceful in flight, resembling lumbering transport planes rather than jet fighters. As a result, a flying beetle hits the water with all the grace of an overweight opera diva doing a belly flop in her swimming pool. Many times, beetles hit the water without ever having been airborne. At such times the beetle makes a considerable disturbance on the surface, and any self-respecting trout will certainly key in on this telegraphic message.

Now this doesn't happen all the time, but it happens frequently. Sometimes it happens more frequently than at other times, and that's when the terrestrial fisherman can really cash in his chips!

Time of Day

A good terrestrial fisherman soon learns when to expect fish to really key in on the beetles. There are certain times of the day, for example, when terrestrial beetles are more active. An early summer morning may be great for Tricos, but beetles (and most other terrestrials, for that matter) will not usually be active at 6:00 A.M. So unless you are expecting a Trico hatch, you can eat a leisurely breakfast, take your time getting the gear in the car, pick up a couple of friends, and still arrive at the stream in plenty of time. As a matter of fact, getting on the water too early can frequently result in a couple of hours of frustration, until the sun warms the beetles enough to get them moving.

In July on the Yellow Breeches in Pennsylvania, for example, the terrestrial fishing really gets going about 8:30 A.M., continues to get better throughout the day, and begins to taper off in the late afternoon. There are, however, rivers where fishing early-morning terrestrial patterns can pay big dividends. On the Smith River in Virginia, many good fish (in the 16- to 20-inch range) can be taken here fishing beetle patterns quite early in the morning. But this is a very different type of fishery. The Smith is a tailwater stream, but unlike most tailwaters its aquatic insect life is rather poor, and the fish probably rely on terrestrials throughout the summer and on into the fall. On the Smith, large (#12) beetle patterns fished early in the morning can be deadly! In other words different rules apply to different streams, so get to know those in your area intimately, and you will soon figure out the best times of day to fish the beetle imitations.

Weather Patterns

Windy days and just after a rainstorm are usually good times to fish terrestrials in general, and this certainly applies to fishing the beetle imitations. Many beetles are blown into streams or are pummeled during a heavy rain and eventually fall in. The water at these times can be covered with beetles, and the prepared angler can have a field day. The same wind that drives the hatch fisherman back to his vehicle can be a most welcome sight for the beetler. At such times, shorten the casts, shorten the leader, and keep on fishing. This is a time of plenty for the trout, so take advantage of it.

Techniques

Here are a few points to keep in mind when fishing beetles.

When fishing beetles blind, concentrate on the banks. During terrestrial season, many fish hold tight against the bank, and a beetle plopped down just inches from the bank is a deadly technique. We have watched many fisherman move up a pool, casting toward the bank but not close enough to it. By close we mean *really* close. If you don't hang a fly up in the streamside vegetation every now and then, you aren't fishing close enough to the bank.

Don't be afraid to set the beetle down with authority. A soft cast under these conditions is usually not necessary, and a good, hard *splat* tight to the bank can draw fish from a surprising distance. We have seen fish come from many feet away to take a beetle presented in this manner.

Don't make only one cast to a likely looking spot and then move on. A fish may be attracted to the noise of the fly hitting the water the first time but may be unable to pinpoint the source exactly. A second or third cast may be necessary before a fish homes in on the beetle. Remember, that fish may have been 10 or 15 feet away when you made the first cast.

When you cast to a likely looking spot along the bank, let the beetle take a natural drift as far as possible, even if you don't like the cast. You may have attracted the attention of the fish of the season, and he is coming to investigate. What's he going to think if suddenly the beetle takes off in a shower of spray? Leave the cast alone and be patient. You'll be able to make another cast soon enough. In other words, hoard the drift. We have seen fish, time after time, follow a beetle for a long distance before taking it. They don't always rush the artificial and gulp it down. If you allow the beetle to drift only a short distance, you are not taking advantage of the deadly effectiveness of this fly.

After you take a fish from along the bank, don't immediately move to a new spot. You'd be surprised how often the hooking of one fish induces another to take the fly in almost exactly the same place. They often move in, apparently prompted by either curiosity or a competitive desire to also get something to eat. This is a common reaction among fish—the feeding activity of one elicits the feeding activity of others. So try at least a few more casts into the same general area, both above and below where you took the first fish. The beetle is a wonderful fly for this technique, as it is an excellent attractor.

It happened one afternoon in the Mirror Pool on the Smith River in Virginia. It had been one of those great beetle days. The multiflora rose and grapevines along the bank were alive with Japanese beetles. Fireflies were in profusion during the warm, damp evenings along the river, and it seemed as though every fish in the river had beetles on the brain. It was almost time to leave, but a dimple along the far bank postponed my departure for a few more minutes. On the first cast, a nice 12-inch brown inhaled the firefly imitation and was soon brought to hand.

As I was releasing the fish, a movement along the bank caught my eye. A barely perceptible disturbance, a slight bulging along the old log—or was it just my imagination? I had just taken a 12-inch fish from a spot not 5 feet above that point, but what the hell, just one more cast. The firefly had floated only a short distance before it disappeared in a soft, gentle dimple of a rise, so delicate that it masked the true size of the fish. When I raised the rod tip it was immediately apparent that this was no 12-incher. The fish ran a short distance upstream, turned, and then bored downstream for deeper water. Once there it stayed deep, shaking its head and sending that delicious throbbing up the rod. I really wanted to see that fish! After about ten minutes, I brought to net a personal best for me on that river, a 20½-inch stream-bred brown. As usual, I had no camera, but I admired the fish, holding it gently in the water while fixing its size and color in my mind before returning it to the stream.

—H. R. S.

When fishing beetles to fish rising away from the bank (toward the center of the stream), use a beetle one or more hook sizes smaller than the one you would generally use along the bank. Sometimes the same size as that employed along the bank works fine, but often it seems to spook these actively rising fish and you'll have to use smaller beetles and finer tippets.

Don't be afraid to experiment with color. Basic black is fine, but other colors work too. A few years ago, we experimented with a deer-hair beetle tied with a beautiful red-brown elk hair. There was no question that it outperformed the basic black beetle. This beetle, christened the M. P. Beetle, continues to be a top producer. Remember, beetles come in many different colors, so why limit yourself? Besides, *everybody* fishes black beetles, and we can't help but think that on heavily fished water, fish become wary of this color beetle.

If you miss a "bank" fish with one beetle pattern, wait a few minutes and try the same place again with one of a different size and color. Don't immediately start casting over that spot again—give the fish enough time to return. He's not spooked; he'll be back, and he's probably going to be even more primed to take the second beetle pattern.

Don't overlook the opportunity to fish beetles in fast water. During terrestrial season, pocket-water fish are not going to be picky about what comes along. A good-size beetle imitation can be deadly fished in those areas normally associated with weighted nymphs and streamers. Rock-strewn glides, fast chutes leading into pools, boulder fields in rapid water, exposed rocks with holding water behind them—all these areas are rich in fish, many of which will go out of their way to take a beetle imitation. In situations like this, bigger beetles are easier to see, so don't hesitate to use them in sizes 10 and 8.

There will be many times you will actually see a fish following your beetle. Believe it or not, these may often be goaded into striking if you move the beetle a bit. We've all heard about drag, but in many instances a little twitch or drag on the beetle imitation will prompt an immediate and violent response from a reluctant fish. It won't work all the time, but it works often enough to make it a valuable technique. If a fish has followed your beetle a couple of times but refused at the last second, try giving the beetle a twitch, or even let it begin to drag. We have had fish take a "waking" beetle too many times for us to regard this as an unusual event. Perhaps it's something like salmon taking a waking fly—it may trigger their most predatory instincts and induce a truly savage charge at the lure.

These techniques all have a place, and they all work. Try them out when you have the opportunity.

Basking in the success of the jungle-cock Jassid pattern, Charlie and Vince set about working on a Japanese beetle. The meadows of the Letort were a lush growth of grasses, hay, multiflora rose, domestic roses, honeysuckle, grape vine, willows, oaks, maples, and buttonwoods—not as well manicured as their English counterparts by far, but every bit as abundant in terrestrial populations, and probably more so. There had to have been millions of beetles in that mile and a half of meadow riverbank. From the first sightings in May or June on through September or October, the angler was certain to encounter numerous "beetle eaters" (as the locals called them) most any day on the river. To encounter was one thing, however; to deceive them was another!

The earliest pattern Vince came up with was a real concoction—a coffee bean glued to the shank of a size 14 hook. It was strange—not the pattern, but the fact that Vince even considered using it. You see, Vince was a purist of the first order. He fished only dry flies of natural materials and upstream only to rising trout. No fishing the water, EVER! He frowned on, growled at, and associated with no one, regular or visitor, who even dared to admit to using wet flies or nymphs.

The coffee bean beetle was a bear to cast; it probably weighed five or ten times as much as the same size dry fly. It would twist and spin during the cast, making the 6X tippet look like a coiled telephone cord. It did not land gently on the water but dragged drastically in the different currents of the Letort and sank almost instantly. If I had been Vince, I would have gone to trying the cricket, hopper, or ant patterns, and the coffee been beetle pattern would have become history then and there. The beetle pattern that finally evolved was a tribute to Vince's tenacity and problem-solving abilities. This pattern had a finely dubbed body, palmered hackle, V clipped top and bottom, and two green ring-necked pheasant feathers cemented together and trimmed oval in shape, tied flat over the crook shank. It was identical to the Jassid tie except larger and almost black.

The anticipation of putting each new pattern to the test was no less disturbing than with the Jassid. Again Charlie was "spotter" and Vince was the "pursuer." Success was almost immediate as with the Jassid. Vince took four to six trout in succession. Again the trial ended with congratulations, jubilance, satisfaction and relief.

—*E. K.*

Another story involving beetles needs to be told at this time, for there is a lesson to be learned.

Don DuBois, author of the Fisherman's Handbook of Trout Flies *(A. S. Barnes & Co., 1960), was a psychologist with the federal government and lived in Virginia just outside of Washington, D.C. Don became a regular along the Letort early in the terrestrial game. He invented the first silicone dry-fly floatant, silica gel powder for cleaning dry flies, leader straightener, hook and hackle gauge, and shock absorber leader. Don was a man ahead of his time in the fly-fishing fraternity. Others were concerned with catching trout, while Don was concerned with solving problems.*

Don arrived at the Letort one Saturday morning, opened the tailgate of his station wagon, and broke out his fly-tying gear. He called Charlie, me, several regulars, and some visitors over. "I've got a great beetle imitation!" he exclaimed, bubbling with enthusiasm. He picked up a sheet of black foam rubber, grabbed his scissors, and hastily cut out several oval shapes. Picking up a size 14 hook and a spool of heavy black sewing thread (not fly-tying thread), he proceeded to tie the foam body for all to observe, as he extolled its virtues. "Look at the silhouette from underneath. It floats like a dream and is durable as hell," he proclaimed. He tied about half a dozen and offered them to the group to try. A few took them, myself included, but most passed up this opportunity.

When Vince and Ernie Schwiebert showed up, Don couldn't wait to confront them with his new beetle pattern. What a mistake! Vince howled, growled, swore, ranted, and raved! "A damnable rubber fly—NEVER!—it's a sacrilege!" he said, chewing nervously on his cigar. Ernie graciously declined the offer to try this new beetle imitation. Don's rubber beetles led to many lively conversations that summer.

—*E. K.*

Rubber bass lures with rubber bodies and rubber legs were in use way back then and were readily accepted. Fly fishermen just weren't ready for the change. What a turnabout thirty years later! How many hoppers, crickets, beetles, ants, and bees are out there today with foam bodies?

It was mid-August and I couldn't contain myself any longer. I decided to fish the "deep water," as it is known, above the dam at Allenberry on the Yellow Breeches. The water is waist- to chest-deep and about a quarter mile long. There are hundreds of trout in this stretch that lie just beneath the surface and sip and feed, sip and feed, cruise and sip and feed all year long. It may seem like an exaggeration, but it's true.

I slipped in at the lower end of the dam, waded toward the middle, and stood watching as the river's surface settled down. By the time I tied a foam beetle to the 6X tippet, the trout were up and working. These trout are used to people and it is a no-kill stretch. They are wary but not spooky if you are careful in your approach. Being waist-deep in the water, there is not much of the angler above the surface, but walking along the bank it is a different story.

A trout was working about 15 feet upstream and 3 feet out from the right bank. I've fished this water for thirty-five years, so judging casting distance has become second nature. I could see the trout holding 6 inches below the surface. The first cast landed about 6 inches in front of the quarry and a few inches to his left. The beetle landed gently on the surface. It hadn't drifted 3 inches when the trout came to the fly, nosed up, and inhaled the synthetic imitation without hesitation. The rod tip rose sharply, and I felt the weight of the brown immediately. "I'll be darned," I mumbled to myself. A few minutes later, I gently removed the barbless beetle from the trout's jaw.

False casting, I searched for another riser. A foot from the bank and in line with number one, a dimple broke the surface film. I sighted the trout immediately. Cast number two was on the mark, not 6 inches from the quarry. The beetle dropped, and instantly the trout turned, came to the fly, and inhaled. "Hmm-m," I thought to myself, "is this for real?" I was in for a big surprise. During a two-hour period, I rose, hooked and released, or missed thirty-seven trout with the synthetic beetle and hadn't covered 70 yards of water. By the time I finished, I was soundly convinced of the beetle's success.

The highlight of the morning was the third to last trout. I had hooked a trout about 20 feet upstream toward the left bank, and while playing the trout I spotted a soft rise a few feet ahead of where the present trout had taken the synthetic beetle.

The beetle landed close to the left bank and to the left of where I had seen the trout turn. The beetle hadn't drifted but a few inches when I saw the trout turn, follow the beetle downstream about a foot, and ever so delicately sip in the imitation. I struck, and the line stopped dead for a few seconds. Then all heck broke loose. The trout headed for the middle of the river and the bottom. I hadn't been expecting anything like this. After six or seven minutes, I slid the shallow bag net under a magnificent, brightly colored 20-inch brown! The beetle was firmly embedded in the upper jaw of the trout. I hadn't changed the original beetle that entire morning!
—E. K.

There are a number of limestone streams in Central Pennsylvania within an hour or two of my home, and I fish each of them as often as I can July through October when the Tricos are on the water. This was my second trip that season to the "Tulley," a limestoner and tailwater fishery with a fantastic Trico hatch. I arrived early enough to be on the water well before the hatch would start. Already there was a gentleman on the river whom I had met several seasons earlier, Alex, a school administrator from Delaware who fishes the Tricos religiously from July through September.

We chatted awhile and a few early Tricos started. It wouldn't be long before there would be thousands of flies in the air and hundreds of trout making the surface boil with gluttonous rises. We each took fish regularly for twenty minutes or so, and then suddenly it stopped—not the hatch or the feeding trout, but the taking of trout. The spinners were there, the rises continued, but suddenly we couldn't buy a taker. We looked at each other and remarked simultaneously, "Time to change!" We both changed flies and started again on the feeding browns. For another fifteen minutes we took trout on every other cast. Then the catching died again as suddenly as it had earlier. "OK," Alex called, "back to the spinners!" We changed and instantly we were into the Trico feeders again. This weird, selective feeding frenzy will change three or four times during the two or three hours that the hatch lasts.
—E. K.

What happened and why does it happen? I have talked to dozens of competent fly fishers and have yet to find anyone with a reasonable explanation, much less a final answer to this phenomenon.

What fly did we change to when the Trico takers stopped? A synthetic

Japanese beetle! Hard as it is to believe, it is true. With thousands of Trico spinners on the water and the trout feeding frantically, they will eat the beetle imitation as readily as they had the spinners just moments before. Is it the conditioned response theory we discussed earlier? Any readers who have experienced this type of phenomenon during a mayfly, caddis, or terrestrial hatch, please write and let us know.

For most of twenty-five years I fished conventional beetle patterns—the original pheasant feather and the clipped deer-hair patterns. More and more, however, I was becoming impressed with the synthetic patterns. Bill Skilton, a well-known local fly tier and angler, gave me several foam beetles he had developed. His work with foam-bodied flies has proven itself, and Bill now has a commercial business as a supplier of synthetic foam body materials. His list of clients is impressive indeed.

During one of Harry's trips in 1992, I had asked him if he had ever found or fished the Codorus, a small tailwater about 17 miles from my home. "No, where is it? Let's give it a try," he replied. "Beetle water?" he then questioned. "Don't know, only ever fished it with dries and midges," I answered.

Eight thirty the following morning found us standing on the second bridge about a mile below the dam looking upstream over 300 yards of placid surface. Though we were on a freestone stream, it looked more like a limestoner. The water was waist-deep and full of weeds, which made it impossible to wade. You could get in the water perhaps a foot or two from the bank, and that was it. Trout were dimpling as far upstream as we could see. We headed for the left bank to work into position for the closest trout, which was rising about a foot from the bank. Harry gingerly edged his way down the bank and into the water.

Neither of us could find any insects on the water. My first thought was to use a tiny midge, dry, size 20 or 22, or a size 18 or 20 pupa emerger. No hesitation for Harry; he was tying a size 14 firefly to the 6X tippet. Watching the trout, he stripped out line and false-cast to get the distance. I had moved upstream along the bank on my knees until I could see the trout. Harry's first cast was right on the mark. He made his cast turn over about 4 feet above the surface. The leader straightened out perfectly, and the beetle gently touched water about 2 feet ahead of the brown. The beetle hadn't drifted a foot and it must have entered the trout's window. He moved toward the surface, getting ready to intercept the imitation.

Then his head angled up, jaws opened, and gills flared as he inhaled the beetle. *"You got him!"* I yelled. *No need; Harry's instinct started the reflex action the instant he saw the trout's nose break the surface film. His quarry felt the bite of the beetle and headed for the weeds. It took Harry about five minutes before he released a heavy-bodied brown to tempt another angler another day.*

"That was beautiful," I remarked. *"He never hesitated. It was as though he were just waiting for that beetle to drift by."*

"I know, it's the darndest thing! It happens that way all the time whether there are beetles on the water or not," he replied. *We let things settle down and watched for another rise. We didn't have to wait long. A trout rose about 6 feet ahead of the first brown. Harry worked out line and made a cast far to the right of the trout to be sure of the distance. I hadn't moved and was unable to see the trout. Harry's second cast appeared to be right on the mark. His fly hadn't floated 2 feet and a telltale dimple broke the surface. He struck and was into his second trout on the Codorus. Two casts, two takes, two trout. "Not bad for his first time on this water," I thought to myself.*

Harry crawled back onto the bank and we worked upstream watching for another rise. We hadn't gone 15 feet when another ring broke the surface. Harry eased back into the stream and watched. The trout rose again about 10 feet out from the bank. He made another cast. This time the fly landed about 2 feet to the left of where the ring had appeared and about even with where the trout should have been. No sooner had the beetle dimpled the surface then a wake appeared headed toward the bank with the fly. A take, and Harry was into his third trout in three tries. This one was a respectable 14-inch brown.

"Your turn," he told me.

"That was impressive. Does it happen often?" I asked.

"Most of the time, and I'm not kidding," he said.

We found two more feeders. I didn't take them as readily as Harry had, but I finally managed to release both browns after a half dozen or more casts to each.

We worked upstream about half a mile, each taking several more trout. Ahead, the stream ran into several large boulders. The rocks forced the stream into a hard right turn, where it gouged a huge hole in the gravel, churning the water for a 10-foot length of broken water.

"See that?" Harry asked.

"Yes, why?" I questioned.

"Trust me. Put on a sinking beetle and start fishing the tail of the fast water. Work up through it and into the hole where it churns around the rocks," he instructed.

I did as he told me, and started working the tail of the pool. I had cast the beetle and it would disappear, drifting for 8 or 10 feet each time. I couldn't see it and felt frustrated fishing it like a nymph.

"Keep trying," Harry encouraged. *"Watch the leader for a telltale twitch or sudden stop."* Starting to work again and watching the leader where it entered the water, I had no idea whether the beetle was just a few inches beneath the surface or down a foot or two.

Then I thought I saw the leader stop, instinctively struck, and all hell broke loose. The line tore upstream toward the boulders, and I just held on to the rod. After a few minutes of steady pressure, I turned the trout downstream out of the torrent. It turned out to be a 10-inch brownie. Harry was doubled up with laughter over my antics trying to land the trout. Finally he said, *"See, I told you, pretty fantastic, huh? Try it again, there's more in there. You can count on it."*

Regaining my composure somewhat, I started working toward the top of the pool. In a stretch of water no more than 15 feet, I took five more trout on that sinking beetle. I couldn't believe it!

"Make a few more casts in front of the rocks, and let the beetle come down through the chute of fast water," Harry urged.

"There's no trout holding in there; it is too darned rough," I responded.

"Don't bet on it. Give it a try."

I did. The first cast hit the boiling water, and in a matter of seconds the leader stopped abruptly. I was into a trout. *"Unreal!"* I thought to myself.

"Try it again," he said.

"What for?"

"I don't know, just do it."

I made three more casts, and darned if I didn't hook another one. Releasing the trout, I heard Harry say, *"Well, do you believe me now? Stop and think about it. If beetles happen to fall into the stream 20 feet or so above those rocks, the minute they hit that fast water they are going to be sucked under, start tumbling, and not surface again until they are out of the fast water. The trout know that, not only about beetles but any of dozens of insects, terrestrials or aquatic."*

We continued working upstream with the sinking beetle. Harry would take a *fish, and then I would take a turn until I caught a fish. Back and forth we went, and in another quarter mile of water we released eight more trout. I was soundly convinced of the success of Harry's synthetic floating and sinking beetle patterns.*

We walked out to the road and headed back to the truck, as Harry continued to tell me of his success with the beetles on his home waters in the Blacksburg area of Virginia, as well as regularly fished waters in the southwestern corner of Virginia, northeastern Tennessee, and northwestern North Carolina. He's had numerous thirty- to fifty-trout days.

One river he talked about really intrigued me—the south fork of the Holston above the TVA Dam. I had fished the tailwaters below the dam in July and August over the years and had had phenomenal success with midge dries, midge nymphs and pupae, shrimp, caddis, and dry flies, but I had not fished many terrestrial patterns. Evidently I missed a good bet!

—E. K.

Most of the time, the floating beetle is fished to trout that can be seen in a feeding station in addition to rising trout. Sight fishing (working trout that can be seen even though not feeding) has added immeasurably to countless successful days astream for me over the past thirty years. Ninety percent of my beetle fishing is done upstream. Logical enough, you might agree, since most of the beetles that get on the water from the brush along the bank are usually no more than 2 or 3 feet out. Would you believe that 90 percent of the fishermen I have talked with over the years have never fished the banks? What satisfying days astream they have missed!

One of the rewards of sight fishing for trout working upstream is the ability to get really close to the trout using careful wading techniques. The majority of my casts are from 15 to 30 feet—at times less than 15 feet, but rarely more than 30 feet. From July to October, water is usually low and gin clear. Longer leaders from 12 to 16 feet are a must, and tippet size is 6X or 7X, from 18 to 36 inches depending on the size of the fly being fished. Use shorter tippets for size 12 and 14 and longer tippets for sizes 16, 18, and 20. Do not make the mistake of fishing a size 14 beetle on a 6X, 36-inch-long tippet. The fly is too big and will not turn over properly. Size 14 is about as large a beetle I fish, although Harry uses them in size 10 and 12 regularly. Depending on what part of the country you fish, you can start using beetles as early as May or June and fish them well into October and November.

—E. K.

MAJOR FAMILIES

To try to give a brief taxonomic survey of the different families of beetles that might contribute to a trout's diet is next to impossible, as the sheer number of beetles present in the United States is mind boggling. At least a few of the most common families should be given brief mention, however.

Family Cicindelidae: Tiger Beetles

These are termed tiger beetles not because of their color, but because of their predaceous nature. Swift, often bright metallic green, they are common inhabitants of sandy areas along streambanks. You probably will not be able to catch one of these, as they are strong fliers and cannot be approached easily. You probably would not want to catch one anyway, at least not with your hand, as they can administer a painful bite. These beetles are photosensitive, being quite active on bright, sunny days but fleeing for cover the moment the sun is obscured.

Family Carabidae: Ground Beetles

There are more than 2,200 species of carabids in North America, which makes this group the third largest of the Coleoptera. Most of them are actively predaceous, but a few feed on plant material. There is tremendous morphological diversity within this group, but the great majority are rather dark in color and somewhat flattened. Most of these beetles are nocturnal, actively seeking prey at night, and are frequently attracted to lights.

Family Staphylinidae: Rove Beetles

This is one of the two largest groups of beetles, with over 3,000 species in North America. Black and brown are the predominant colors. As the name implies, they are for the most part active runners and strong flyers, so it's no wonder that they occasionally land in trout streams. Most species are predaceous, and a few can inflict a painful bite if handled. There is considerable size variation within this group, with the largest reaching about 1 inch in length.

Family Scarabaeidae: Scarabs

There is tremendous variation in size, body form, and color within this family. This is a large group, with about 1,400 species in North America. In general, the body form is rounded, rectangular, or oval in shape, and thick, giving them a characteristic heavy-bodied appearance. Many of the scarabs are herbivorous, feeding on plant materials, but some are dung feeders and others feed on carrion or decaying plant matter. Grasses, fruits of all sorts, all types of foliage, and many flowers provide fodder for the herbivorous forms in this group, so they are quite common along trout streams.

There are many subfamilies to this group, a few of which follow.

Subfamily Melolonthinae: June Beetles, Chafers, May Beetles (June Bugs).

Subfamily Rutelinae: Shining Leaf Chafers. The common Japanese beetle (*Popillia japonica*) is a member of the group, and while its numbers are no longer as great as they used to be, it can still be an important component of the trout's diet. Look for it on grapevines, multiflora rose, all sorts of fruit trees, and many other common plants along trout streams. At the right time and place, Japanese beetle imitations can still produce unbelievable results. They even work well as a general searching pattern when no Japanese beetles are present.

Subfamily Cetoniinae: Flower Beetles. The green june beetle, a common beetle that feeds on corn, grapes, and ripening fruits, is a member of this group. These are large, reaching about 1 inch in length, with characteristically metallic green elytra and a dark metallic green underbody. Everyone has seen them, and in areas where they reach high populations, they are certainly taken by trout. We have a recorded instance in which one 15-inch rainbow had ingested sixteen of these beetles. Why it took the proffered nymph is anybody's guess!

Family Buprestidae: Metallic Wood-boring Beetles

Represented in North America by almost 700 species and up to four inches in length. Most of these are, however, ¾ inch or less in length. Many inhabit dead or dying timber, fallen logs, or slash areas following logging operations. Others are common inhabitants of foliage. They are strong flyers and runners, which makes them rather difficult to catch.

Family Elateridae: Click Beetles

Probably one of the easier beetles to identify, particularly those that have "eyes" on the pronotum. When placed on their backs, these beetles are capable of righting themselves through a complicated anatomical maneuver that results in the beetle flying into the air with a loud clicking noise. If it doesn't land on its feet, it tries again until it does! About 900 species are found in North America, with a few reaching 1½ inches in length.

Family Lampyridae: Lightning Bugs or Fireflies

How can anyone miss these? At certain times during the summer months literally thousands of these can be seen winking and blinking along trout streams at night and in the early evening. The different species of this family are all found east of the Rocky Mountains, with the two most common being the Pyralis firefly *(Photinus pyralis)* and the Pennsylvania firefly *(Photuris pennsylvanicus)*. Even though they are nocturnal beetles we have had tremendous success fishing a firefly pattern (Steeves' Firefly) throughout the day. Indeed, we consider it to be one of our most productive beetle patterns. We have also had numerous reports from fellow anglers out west that it is a top producer there as well, regardless of the fact that fireflies are not indigenous to the area.

Family Melyridae: Soft-winged Flower Beetles

Over 500 species are found in North America. These reach a size of about ½ inch in length and are often brightly colored with black, red, or brown patterns.

Family Coccinellidae: Ladybird Beetles, Mexican Bean Beetles, and Squash Beetles

The latter two groups can cause serious damage to garden plants. There are about 475 species of coccinellids found in North America.

Family Tenebrionidae: Darkling Beetles

These represent the fifth-largest group of beetles, with over 1,000 species in North America. They are much more important in the western states than in the East, where only about 140 species are found. Most are herbivorous, black, and relatively smooth, resembling the ground beetles. If you ever find a beetle colony in your flour sack, it is probably one of the tenebrionids, the common mealworm.

Family Meloidae: Blister Beetles

A few of these might be important to the trout fisherman. Over 300 species occur in North America, with the most well known being the potato beetles. These, as the name implies, are common pests of potato plants, but they also feed on tomato plants and probably any other close relatives of these two. One of these, the black blister beetle, *Epicauta pennsylvanica,* is commonly found on goldenrod, which is frequently encountered along meadow streams. It is black and reaches a length of about ½ inch.

Family Cerambycidae: Long-horned Beetles

These beetles, with their extremely long antennae, are quite easy to recognize. This is a large group, with over 1,000 species in North America. Many are brightly colored, most are elongate in shape, and many are herbivorous, feeding on flowers. Some are quite large, reaching a length of over 2 inches.

Family Chrysomelidae: Leaf Beetles

About 1,500 species are found in North America. Most of the chrysomelids are less than ½ inch in length, and many are rather brightly colored. One of the most commonly encountered is the Colorado potato beetle, *Leptinotarsa decemlineata.* It was brought to the United States on potato plants imported from Mexico and rapidly became a pest for the commercial potato growers. This beetle also feeds on nightshade, which is often found in meadows and pastures bordering trout waters. Another of these, *Labidomera* sp., is a vividly marked red and black beetle that feeds on milkweed. The metallic blue beetle, *Phratora* sp., feeds on willow and poplar, and another genus, *Calligrapha* (off-white with dark spots and streaks), is commonly found feeding on willow and alder. Other members of this group are the cucumber beetles, flea beetles, and leaf miners. One species of leaf miner, *Odonto dorsalis,* has caused serious damage to the American black locust. Anyone traveling in the East can view the sickly, yellowish brown foliage of these locusts along the highways, the result of this beetle's activity. When infestations are extremely heavy, early defoliation of the infested tree may result. This is a rather handsome beetle, yellow-orange with a black stripe down the middle of the back.

Superfamily Curculionoidea: Snout Beetles

There are over 3,000 species represented in this superfamily, which makes it one of the largest groups. They are commonly know as snout beetles because the anterior portion of the head is elongated into a snoutlike protrusion. The most easily recognized members are the weevils, many of which are of considerable importance because of the damage they do to commercially grown crops (either in the field or in storage). Due to the tremendous size of this group of beetles, it is impossible to give any generalizations regarding shape, size, or color. If you run across any beetles with a long "snout" on the front of the head, you can probably assign them to this group.

BEETLE PATTERNS

There have already been so many publications describing how to tie the more common beetle patterns that there is no need to reiterate those procedures. If we feel that there is enough general knowledge concerning any of the following patterns, we will simply list the materials necessary to tie the pattern and eliminate the tying directions.

MARINARO'S JAPANESE BEETLE

Hook: #16 standard dry-fly hook.
Body: Black or any dark hackle put on as for a ribbing hackle, then cut away above and below.
Wings: The largest jungle cock nail or two medium-sized nails tied flat on the back.

This fly has lost none of its effectiveness over the years. Since jungle cock is rather high priced these days, we suggest substituting some other feather. Many types are acceptable, particularly if they are reinforced with Flexament.

THOMPSON'S FOAM BEETLE

Hook: #8 to #22 standard dry-fly hook.

Thread: 6/0 on larger sizes, 8/0 on smaller ones. Color to match that of the body "shell."

Body: Dubbing blend of fur and sparkle yarn on larger sizes; thread only on the smaller sizes.

Legs: Palmered hackle, one size smaller than normal. Palmer the hackle only on the front half of the hook shank. Trim bottom hackle so the fly rides flush in the surface.

Shell: Closed cell foam. The original pattern called for the use of white foam, which was then colored with permanent markers. With today's colored foams, this is no longer necessary.

There are excellent directions for tying this beetle in Gary Borger's book *Designing Trout Flies.*

CROWE BEETLE

Hook: #8 to #22 standard dry-fly hook.

Thread: 6/0 or 8/0 depending on the size of the fly. Color same as body.

Body: Deer, elk, or caribou hair. Black, brown, olive, yellow, tan, and rust at the tier's discretion.

Legs: Formed by separating a few of the body hairs on either side of the beetle, bending them to the rear and finishing the head.

This has been one of the most widely used beetle patterns, and tying directions may be found in practically any book dealing with fly tying.

CORK BEETLES

These patterns have a loyal following. The shape of the cork body is easily controlled, they may be painted in any color to match the natural, they are relatively tough, and they certainly "float like a cork." They are, however, rather tedious to construct, and losing one to either a fish or a tree is a real disappointment. When you can construct foam or hair beetles so rapidly that losing one is relatively painless, we see little reason in laboring over a cork-bodied beetle. If you still desire to produce cork-bodied beetles, we refer you to Gerald Almy's book, _Tying and Fishing Terrestrials,_ which gives an adequate presentation of the techniques involved.

CLIPPED-HAIR BEETLE

Hook: #8 to #18 standard dry-fly hook.

Thread: 6/0, same color as body hair.

Body: Spun deer or caribou hair, color at tier's discretion.

This is one of the simplest of all patterns to construct. The hair is simply spun on the shank of the hook and then clipped to the desired body shape. Wings or legs may be added in the form of cock hackle, Z-lon, Kreinik braid, or whatever. Although we have seen none of these constructed with cul-de-canard wings (legs), there is no reason why they could not be. The smaller sizes, in particular, would lend themselves well to a little finishing with CDC.

This pattern has the advantages of being not only simple to construct but almost indestructible. While the Crowe Beetle looks like a mess after only a few fish, the Clipped-hair Beetle retains its sleek good looks for quite some time. It will also float forever if occasionally dried and redressed with a good floatant.

HERL BEETLE

Gerald Almy gives complete directions for tying this pattern in _Tying and Fishing Terrestrials._

Hook: Almy gives no specifications, but any standard dry-fly hook is probably acceptable.

Thread: 6/0 on larger patterns, 8/0 on anything smaller than #18.

Body: Peacock herls with palmered hackle.

Overwing: Raffia (Swiss straw) or section of mallard wing quill.

A somewhat modified version of this pattern is tied and marketed by Herb and Kathy Weigl of Cold Springs Angler. This version is termed the Hi-Viz Beetle and is tied with a goose biot forming the overwing. No hackle is palmered through the herl body.

FUR BEETLE

This is a very easy pattern to tie. It consists of nothing more than a dubbed body with palmered hackle. The hackle is trimmed flat on top and bottom and then contour-trimmed along the sides to fill out the body form. This pattern lends itself well to tying the very smallest of beetles (#22 to #24).

STEEVES' JAPANESE BEETLE

Hook: #12 standard dry-fly hook.
Thread: 6/0 olive
Body: black, closed cell Larva-Lace foam, cut into ⅛-inch-wide strips.
Underbody: peacock herl, three strands.
Wingcase: copper-colored Swiss straw.
Wings: Kreinik ⅛-inch flat ribbon, mallard, #850. Use about a 4-inch piece.

Tying Directions

1. Wrap first half of hook shank with thread. Tie in Swiss straw, and continue tying it down to the bend of the hook.

2. Wrap thread forward two-thirds the length of the hook shank, and tie in the foam body material. Continue tying the foam down to the bend of the hook shank. If the foam is tied in in this manner, the body will not rotate on the hook shank.

3. Tie in peacock herl and wrap thread forward to a point about ¹⁄₁₆ inch back from the eye of the hook.

4. Wrap peacock herl forward, tie it down, and cut.

5. Wrap the thread backward through the peacock herl and then forward again. This will reinforce the herl and prevent it from breaking loose.

6. Fold foam body material forward, over the eye of the hook and tie it down about ¹⁄₁₆ inch back from the eye. Do not stretch the foam during this procedure. Trim the forward-projecting foam even with the front of the hook eye.

7. Tie in the winging material at the junction of the head with the

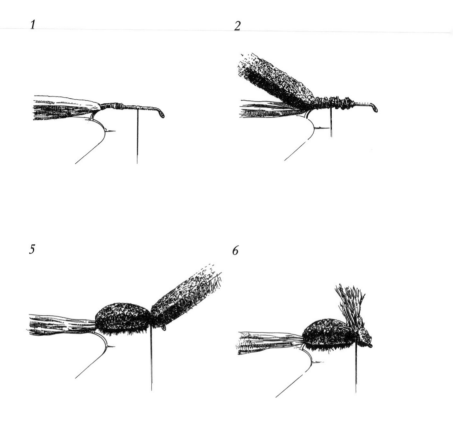

3 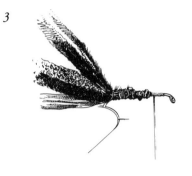   *4*

7

STEEVES' JAPANESE BEETLE

body. The wings should be as long as the body. Trim the forward-projecting winging material even with the front of the head.

8. Separate the winging material into two even portions on opposite sides of the foam body. Fold the Swiss straw forward between the wings and tie it down. Trim the forward-projecting Swiss straw even with the front of the head.

STEEVES' FIREFLY

Every now and then a fly comes along that just seems to have something going for it. This firefly pattern is one such fly. We have caught fish consistently with this pattern from Tennessee to New York and have reports on its success from many different areas of the country. We do not know what characteristics of this design make it so successful, but it sure works!

Hook: #12 to #16, Mustad 94831, Orvis 1638, Tiemco 5212.

Thread: 6/0 black or orange.

Body: ⅛-inch-thick black closed cell foam, cut into ⅛-inch-wide strips.

Underbody: two to four strands of peacock herl, depending on hook size.

Butt: Kreinik fluorescent medium round braid, yellow, #054.

Wings: Kreinik ⅛-inch flat ribbon or heavy round braid, 6-inch piece, mallard, #850.

Wing Case: Kreinik beetle black, ⅛-inch-wide flat ribbon, #005HL.

Tying Directions

1. Wrap first half of hook shank with thread, tie in 6-inch piece of wing case material to the bend of the hook. Wrap thread forward two-thirds the length of hook shank.

2. Tie in body foam and continue to tie it in back to the bend of the hook. This will prevent the body from turning on the hook shank.

3. Wrap thread forward about ⅛-inch and tie in a 6-inch piece of

butt material. Form the butt on a #14 fly by wrapping the butt material three times and tying it off. Remove excess. On a #12 fly, four wraps of butt material are necessary. On a #16 fly, only two wraps of butt material are called for.

4. Tie in peacock herl just ahead of butt, and wrap thread forward to ¹⁄₁₆ inch behind hook eye. Wrap peacock herl forward and tie down. Wrap thread back and then forward through the herl to reinforce it.

5. Fold body foam forward and tie it down about ⅛ to ¹⁄₁₆ inch behind the hook eye (depending on the size of the fly). Cut the forward-projecting foam even with the front of the eye to form the head.

6. Tie in a piece of winging material projecting backward to the fluorescent butt. Trim the forward portion flush with the front of the head. Separate the winging material into equal portions on either side of the body.

7. Fold the wing case material forward between the wings and tie it down. Trim excess flush with the head of the fly. Whip finish.

When tying this fly (and others such as the Japanese beetle or sparkle beetle) save all trimmed pieces. You can tie a lot of beetles with 6 inches of the Kreinik winging material, butt material, Swiss straw, and others.

STEEVES' SPARKLE BEETLE

Hook: #10 to #16. Mustad 94833, Orvis 1509, Tiemco 100.
Thread: 6/0 black.
Body: ³⁄₁₆-inch-thick Larva-Lace closed cell foam, black.
Underbody: Peacock herl, two to four strands, depending on size of fly.
Wings: Kreinik ⅛-inch-wide flat ribbon or heavy round braid, mallard, #850. The Kreinik peacock, #085, is also good.
Wing Case: Kreinik ⅛-inch-wide flat ribbon, peacock, #085.

Tying Directions

Essentially the same as for the Steeves' Firefly but without the fluorescent butt. There are many variations on this pattern as far as color choices are

1

2

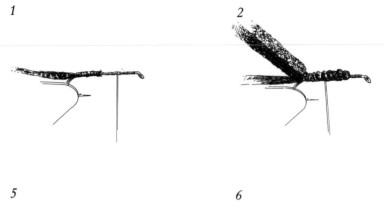

5

6

9

10

STEEVES' FIREFLY

3

4

7

8

11

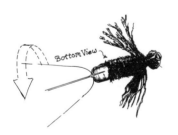

concerned, and you might want to experiment. Bodies can be tied with many different colors of foam, and the color of the wing case material can be varied as well. The Kreinik materials are available in a whole spectrum of colors, so don't be afraid to experiment. Likewise, the underbody may be tied with ⅟₁₆-inch Kreinik flat ribbon material in all sorts of different colors. We have tied these in many different color combinations, including those with fluorescent (glow in the dark) wing cases and underbodies. They are all very successful patterns. Those tied with the fluorescent materials work particularly well under low-light situations, or even after dark, when priming them with your flashlight makes them stand out like a white cat in a coal bin. One of the most spectacular after-dark patterns is the Catskill Ghost, which is tied with a white foam body, and with the underbody, wings, and wing case tied with Kreinik fluorescent white flat ribbon (#052F). Even on the darkest night, you can see this thing from 30 feet away after shining a light on it for a few seconds. This pattern has even worked during White Fly hatches!

REXRODE'S BASIC BLACK BEETLE

This is a modification of the Steeves' Firefly that was first tied by Cliff Rexrode. In this pattern, no butt is tied on the fly, and the wings are tied with Kreinik ⅛-inch beetle black ribbon instead of the mallard. On bright sunny days, this fly can be a killer! The firefly may be just a bit too sparkly, and if so, then turn to this pattern. You won't regret it!

TIGER BEETLE

Hook: #14, Mustad 94831, Orvis 1640, Tiemco 5212.
Thread: 6/0 green.
Body: Green closed cell foam, ⅛ inch thick, cut into ⅛-inch-wide strips.
Wingcase: Kreinik ⅛-inch flat ribbon, green, #008.
Underbody: Fluorescent green thread or Kreinik ⅟₁₆-inch flat ribbon, green, #008.
Wing: ⅛-inch-wide Kreinik flat ribbon, mallard, #850.

Directions for tying this pattern are the same as those given for the Sparkle Beetle.

STEEVES' SINKING JAPANESE BEETLE

Hook: #10, Mustad 3906, Orvis 1641, Tiemco 3769.
Thread: 6/0 olive or green
Body: Kreinik heavy braid, mallard (#850) and emerald (#009HL). One 9-inch strand of each will be enough for three beetles.
Wing: Kreinik ⅛-inch-wide flat ribbon, mallard, #850. Do not use the Kreinik round braid for wings on this pattern, as it does not tie in flat enough.
Wing Case: Copper-colored Swiss straw.
Thorax: Kreinik fine round braid, caddis larva green, #015.

Tying Directions

1. Wrap hook shank with thread to one-half the length of shank. Tie in a 4- to 6-inch piece of Swiss straw. Continue tying in the Swiss straw to the bend of the hook.

2. Wrap thread forward to the middle of the hook shank. Tie in the strands of body material on alternate sides of the hook shank, with one tied in slightly behind the other so that a forward taper is produced. Tie both strands down rearward to the same point as the Swiss straw. Wrap thread forward to the hook eye, whip finish, cut, and remove thread.

3. Use the overhand knot technique to form the body. On the #10 hook, seven knots will give the correct size body. After forming the body, reattach the thread, tie down the body cord, and trim.

4. Tie in the winging material equal to the length of the body. Tie it in forward, but not to the eye of the hook—leave some space! Trim forward-projecting excess and save.

5. Tie in a 6-inch piece of thorax material on the side; tie it down and backward to the base of the winging material.

6. Separate winging material into two equal portions on either side of the body, and fold Swiss straw forward and between the wings. Tie it

1

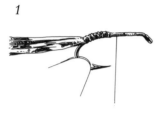

2

5

6

9

STEEVES' SINKING JAPANESE BEETLE

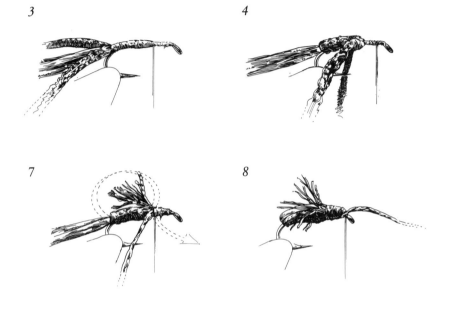

3

4

7

8

down, starting at the wing butts, and wrap the thread forward to just behind the hook eye. Wrap the thread well over the Swiss straw. This will eliminate the tendency of the thorax material to slip forward. Trim the Swiss straw to leave a small "shelf" extending forward.

7. Wrap thorax material forward (three to five wraps, depending on how far back you started the body). After the last wrap, pull the thorax material under the hook shank and into the rear of the hook eye. Tie it down with two or three tight wraps.

8. Cock the fly at a 45-degree angle in the vise, pull the thorax material backward and over the top, and tie it down with a few good wraps. Trim the excess, and finish the head with thread wraps. Whip finish.

This all sounds terribly complicated, but it isn't. After a little practice, you'll be able to turn these out a lot faster than it takes to write about it! This is one tough fly. There is one in our collection that was retired after taking more than thirty fish, and it's still fishable. The Swiss straw has broken away from the butt, but it doesn't seem to matter. As a matter of fact, it may even add to the effectiveness of the design, since it now looks like a dead Japanese beetle with the elytra open and the wings extended. Maybe we should start tying them this way on purpose!

STEEVES' SINKING BLACK BEETLE

Hook: #10, Mustad 3906, Orvis 1641, Tiemco 3769.
Thread: 6/0 black.
Body: One 9-inch strand each of Kreinik beetle black (#005HL) and emerald (009HL), heavy braid.
Wings: Kreinik ⅛-inch flat ribbon, mallard, #850.
Wing Case: Black Swiss straw.
Thorax: Kreinik fine braid, beetle black, #005HL.

Tying Directions

Follow the same procedure as that outlined for Sinking Japanese Beetle.

The above two patterns represent only a few of the possible designs using this technique. Since the Kreinik materials are available in such a wide variety of colors and sizes, it is possible to tie anything, depending on what might be prevalent in your area of the country. Some suggested color combinations for the body are black and bronze; black and peacock; black and mallard; peacock and mallard; and black and purple.

With minor modifications, it is possible to tie many different colors and sizes of sinking beetles. For example, sinking braided (or rather, knotted) body beetles can be tied down to #18 using the Kreinik fine braid for the body, eliminating the thorax material, and using Kreinik $\frac{1}{16}$-inch flat ribbon for the wings and wing case.

7

Order Hymenoptera: Ants, Wasps, Bees, and Sawflies

WHERE DOES ONE begin with this order of terrestrial insects? You can go all the way back to the third-century writings of Claudius Aelianus, who spoke of bee/wasp imitations in his *De Animalium Natura*. You could begin with Dame Juliana's "waspe flye." Or you could begin within the last year or so by simply picking up one of the more popular fly-fishing magazines. It's a safe bet that there will have been at least one article published about some member of this order, how to tie it, and how to fish it.

The order Hymenoptera is a never-ending source of speculation, wonder, and frustration for the fly fisherman. There are probably very few serious members of the fraternity who do not carry at least a few patterns for these insects (probably ants) in their fly boxes. Why is this so? The answer is simple—they are effective. Indeed, they are so effective that virtually every top gun in the sport includes ants in their selection when asked to give their "If you could only fish X number of patterns" list. But this only holds true for ants—not for wasps, bees, or sawflies, which never make anyone's top ten list! There are probably some good reasons for this, and we'll discuss that a bit later on.

From the biological point of view, the Hymenoptera is without question one of the most interesting groups of terrestrial insects. It contains a host of what might be termed beneficial insects, culminating in the bees, which are the primary pollinators of plants. The members of the order occupy a tremendous variety of habitats, occur in very large numbers, and in many instances exhibit what is termed *eusocial organization,* which means that they live in colonies and exhibit complex behavioral characteristics. The fact that they live in colonies, which range in size from a few to thousands of individuals, is very important to the fly fisherman, because it guarantees a large number of insects concentrated in a small space. If that concentration happens to be an ant colony in an old sycamore whose branches just happen to reach out over a good trout stream—well, you can figure out the consequences. A good breeze whistling through the branches is going to guarantee a pretty steady supply of fodder to any trout downstream. It is also quite common to find wasp, yellow jacket, or hornet nests in overhanging branches along streambanks, and though these terrestrial insects are probably not found as frequently on the surface of streams as ants, there is no question that they are on occasion dumped unceremoniously into the water.

ANTS

If I were to make a selection of the most productive and consistent trout-taking patterns of the terrestrials, I suppose it would have to be the ants. All round, I don't think they can be beat.

            —Ed Koch, Terrestrial Fishing, *1990*

I don't necessarily agree with Ed, or with others who tout the ant so highly. Give me the beetles any day. Trout are suckers for beetles in all sizes, but if a beetle won't work I'll sure as hell try an ant before anything else.

        —Harrison Steeves, after a double vodka on the rocks, 1992

  Within the order Hymenoptera it is only logical to begin our discussion with the ants (family Formicidae). They are certainly the ones that have attracted the majority of attention from fly fishermen and those who write about the sport. There is a good reason for this—ants are everywhere! They are among the most successful group of insects on the planet, terrestrial or aquatic. There are incredible numbers of ants, surpassing any other group of animals on the face of the earth, and they are found in all terrestrial habitats. What this means to us as fly fishermen is that there is always going to be a pretty good supply of them being dunked into trout streams. The trout are certainly going to take advantage of this food supply, and as a result we can then take advantage of the trout with a well-placed imitation.

  There is no question then that ants make up a portion of the trout's diet. Just how important they are is debatable, however. In *Tying and Fishing Terrestrials* Gerald Almy states that "in point of sheer numbers ants surpass all other kinds of trout food." That's correct but somewhat misleading, for in making this statement Almy is not saying they constitute the bulk of the trout's diet. All he is saying is that there are more ants around than anything else. Anyone who has ever dissected the stomach of a trout that has been feeding on terrestrials will certainly find a mixed bag. The majority of what is found is no doubt dependent on what terrestrial is present in the greatest number at the time, so it's difficult to generalize. We've dissected trout stomachs in which beetles were the predominant (and sometimes the only) food item. On other occasions, ants comprised the greatest number of terrestrial food items, but whether they made up the bulk of the food is open to question. It takes a lot of ants to equal a few june bugs!

There are certain times when ants will indeed make up the bulk of the trout's diet, and in order to explain this we have to take a quick look at the life cycle of an ant colony. Notice that we did not say "ant" but "ant colony."

In most ant colonies there are hundreds or thousands of individuals. Within this general population, there are usually at least three different categories of individuals: queens, males, and workers. The queen is responsible for laying eggs, which most of the time will develop into sterile, wingless females. These females are the workers and make up the majority of the population of an ant colony. What we see most of the time in our own backyard or along the banks of a trout stream are ant colonies made up of possibly a few queens and many sterile female workers. The individual ants that drop or are blown into streams during most of the year are then these hapless sterile females. The unwinged standard ant pattern represents an attempt to imitate this member of the ant colony, and anyone who has tried it knows that it is a very effective pattern.

At times, however, there are true ant hatches that cover the water with helplessly struggling morsels. The biological mechanism that causes this is the annual mating flight of ants from the nest. At this time of the year, large numbers of both winged males and queens are produced. The exact timing of this mating swarm is governed by many factors, but the swarming occurs simultaneously in different nests over a wide geographic range. There are advantages to this synchronization. First, it is easier for individuals to find mates when there are larger numbers of males and queens present. Second, it helps to ensure the continuation of genetic diversity.

On August 16, 1992, Miller Williams and I were returning to Blacksburg after a somewhat frustrating day on the Jackson River. We reached the little town of Fincastle, Virginia, and turned to take the back road home. We had gone no more than a quarter mile when the appearance of sizable spots on the windshield indicated that a hatch of something was in progress. There was no water to speak of nearby, so we reasoned that there was no way it could be anything like mayflies or caddisflies. Traveling at any speed over 5 miles an hour makes it difficult to exactly identify anything, but just looking out the window told us that there were a lot of fairly large insects in the air.

As a matter of fact, there were two different types of swarming insects we kept running into. So employing the old "hat out the window" collecting technique, we grabbed some of the smaller insects from the next swarm we came to. They turned out to be gnats. A hundred yards down the road the hat technique pulled in what we were really interested in—a number of the larger guys. They proved to be large, winged red ants, and there must have been hundreds of thousands of them. Why do we put the numbers estimate that high? Simple—we encountered these insects in huge swarms for a 15-mile stretch along an entire valley! Until that time, I had never seen a really extensive and synchronized ant hatch. It gave both of us a new appreciation for the magnitude of the populations of these insects. Now, if only that hatch had been about 40 miles farther to the north, a little closer to the Jackson, it could have been a very different day!

—H. R. S.

What we had witnessed were synchronized swarms of winged fertile males and queens engaging in their mating flights. They were obviously from many nests along the entire 15-mile floor of the valley and were widely dispersed. After these mating flights, the males die and the queens shed their wings. The queens then set out to find suitable locations in which to set up housekeeping and lay the first brood of eggs. These eggs hatch to give rise to the first generation of sterile female workers, which then take over all the housekeeping chores while the queen settles down to producing more eggs.

When the fly fisherman encounters this phenomenon on a stretch of trout water, the results can be spectacular. Trout rise to this hatch of ants with absolute abandon, and even the most hardened water weasel will develop a bad case of shakes, be unable to tie knots, wrap his line around the rod, and develop bird's nests in the tippet without making a single cast. The phenomenon is well known, and fly-fishing literature is filled with descriptions of ant hatches.

It sounds great, but many times it's tough to duplicate the original with a pattern, since most of us do not carry a terribly extensive catalog of ants (particularly the winged phase) in our fly boxes. Furthermore, these hatches are relatively unpredictable and last only a few hours at best, so they may end before you can beat feet back to the car and tie up the appropriate pattern (assuming that you have had the foresight to bring your kit with you). But occasionally you hit it right, and the fishing can truly be spectacular!

The Ant Mystique

There has been a great deal of speculation on exactly *why* trout take ants under certain conditions, notably during a heavy hatch of mayflies. Quite a few authors have offered explanations for this phenomenon, and most have concentrated on the assumption that ants "taste good" to trout. We don't know this, and we can't prove it. We can only draw conclusions from what they taste like to humans, and it's dangerous to extrapolate our perceptions of taste to those of trout. Nevertheless, the literature is full of articles describing the taste of ants and carrying these observations over to the preferential taking of ants by trout. There's no doubt that ants have a powerful taste—at least to humans. What do you expect from an insect that's loaded with formic acid (hence the name Formicidae for the order) or some other equally obnoxious substance? Lots of us have experienced this taste, and if you haven't, you should eat an ant someday—it won't hurt you.

I've eaten a lot of ants. Big ones, little ones, red ones, black ones, and in-between ones. I was at one point intrigued with the idea of the taste of an ant being a major factor in the selection of ants by trout as preferential dietary items. The more ants I ate, however, the more I began to realize that different species of ants tasted differ-ent. Carpenter ants, for example, taste nothing like citronella ants, and other species of ants taste decidedly different from these two species. Some ants had no taste at all! The more ants I ate, the more I became convinced that taste as we de-fine it for humans does not apply to trout.

I killed some fish at one point, examined the stomach contents, and found many different ant species. From my own experiences, I knew that the species I found in the trouts' stomachs tasted different (at least to me). The trout showed no preference as to species that I could tell. They took whatever ants were available, and the predominant species in their stomachs reflected the predominant species on the water at the time. Ants, then, are nothing more than an accepted food item to be ingested along with whatever else may be floating by.

—*H. R. S.*

Most of the authors who theorize that ants are a tasty gourmet food item for trout are basing this assumption on the fact that ants will work when trout are selectively feeding on mayflies during a heavy hatch. Their reasoning is that the ant must be a very tasty item in the trout's menu, is recognized as such by the fish, and is immediately sucked in. Maybe it really doesn't work quite this way, however. A small Royal Wulff will often accomplish the same result, and it doesn't have any taste at all! So will a beetle. Even small hopper and cricket patterns will work at times, as will other patterns.

But though other patterns will also work, they have never attained the popularity of the ant for "breaking the hatch." There undoubtedly are multiple reasons for this. The major reason is probably that the ant patterns were the first ones to be widely used to break the hatch and were therefore the first ones to be written about. The idea that ants tasted good to trout was a more or less logical assumption that followed, and people began eating ants to find out what they tasted like. If beetles had been employed before ants, there undoubtedly would have been some adventurous souls who would have begun to eat beetles. The wonder of this whole process is that very few people have ever experimented with the taste of terrestrials other than ants. Why haven't fly fishermen tried leafhoppers, crickets, grasshoppers, and many of the beetles that abound along streams? The answer is probably relatively simple—ants are compact, small and relatively innocuous critters when compared to the rest of the terrestrials. It's not all that hard to pop one in your mouth and bite down.

The fact remains that ants *are* choice food items in a trout's diet. They work magnificently on many occasions, such as "anting the hatch" or on highly selective and difficult fish. They work so well and so frequently that they do indeed appear to be a preferred food item, but to attribute this to their taste, which is only apparent after crunching down on one, may be a mistake. Something else may account for it, and that something else might be intimately associated with the fact that ants are social organisms, live in organized communities, and communicate with each other. The method by which they communicate is through the secretion of different types of chemical substances termed *pheromones*. There are different types of pheromones that regulate different behavior patterns. Certain pheromones are secreted when ants lay down a trail for other members of the colony to follow to a food source. Other pheromones trigger agressive behavior for protective purposes, and still others regulate other activites, such as mating. It may be that it is not the taste of an ant that is so attractive to trout, but the smell of the pheromones it is producing. Pheromones do diffuse through water and are pretty potent chemical substances, even though they are produced in small quantities. Think of them in terms of a woman's perfume. It only takes a small quantity to exert a pretty potent effect! We are not saying that this is the answer to the mystique of the ant, but it may be somewhat closer to the truth.

On the other hand, maybe ants aren't really any more attractive than any other terrestrial! That's going to be a pretty heretical thought to many people, but there just aren't any controlled scientific studies to show that they are. Terrestrial-feeding trout are at best opportunistic and take whatever comes along that suits their fancy. If there are more ants than anything else, trout will consume a proportionally higher number of ants than any other food item. Since there are so many ants, it stands to reason that they will make up a numerically greater portion of a trout's diet than other terrestrials. Also, on any given day there are probably more ants on the water than any other terrestrial insect. The result of this would be to intensify the establishment of a stronger or more well defined search image for this particular prey item, and fish would take them more readily or indiscriminately than other terrestrial food items on most days. But on the basis of total dietary bulk (dry weight, or wet weight of the stomachs' contents), the ants will probably take a backseat to all the other terrestrial insects consumed on any normal day.

As far as the mystique of the ant is concerned, most of it seems to be based on nothing more than field observations (which in many instances can be highly suspect), supposition on the part of outdoor writers, and speculation by untrained individuals. Fantasy often comes to be regarded as fact due to reinforcement. For example, one outdoor writer uses an ant in a number of situations to catch selectively feeding fish during a hatch. It's a great technique! It works! He writes about it. Others try it and it works for them as well. So suddenly ants are irresistible to selectively feeding fish, and it becomes fly-fishing dogma. What would have happened if that author had originally used a beetle instead of an ant? We know that beetles will work under these situations, because we have used them. What if he had used a Jassid? They will work, too. Next time you are tempted to try an ant to break the hatch, give some other terrestrial pattern a try. You might be pleasantly surprised.

Designing Ant Patterns

Ants, because of their rather simple structure and lack of frills, are pretty easy to tie, although much time and effort has gone into the design of successful ant patterns and the materials have been chosen with some care.

Basic Anatomy. The shape of an ant's body is really quite simple. It is basically composed of three portions—the head, thorax, and abdomen—which are relatively distinct from one another. Most ant patterns, however, are tied with only two "humps" rather than three. This design seems to work very well, so why bother complicating matters by tying three humps? Besides, a three-hump design seems to crowd the rest of the fly too much and cuts down on the characteristic thin "waist" of the imitation. This reduction in the conspicuous waist really does appear to decrease the effectiveness of the pattern. (Most authors have historically considered the "two humps and a waist" design to be crucial, and we are not going to argue with them about that!)

The legs of an ant are six rather spindly structures that can be represented in a number of ways. Some patterns give an impressionistic representation by a simple winding of black hackle between the two body portions. In other patterns, a more realistic representation is attempted by tying in six legs (three per side) using moose, elk, or deer hair or one of the latest synthetic fibers available for this purpose. Both designs seem to be equally effective, so we leave leg representation to the discretion of the tier.

Other anatomical characteristics that might be represented are the antennae and mouth parts (mandibles). The antennae are so short and clubby, however, that their inclusion does not seem necessary. And even though the mandibles may be rather prominent, their lack seems to make little difference in effectiveness, so we see no reason to include these in our imitations.

Color. The traditional colors for ant patterns are black, brown, and cinnamon (red-brown), but there are many other colors present in the ant kingdom. Ants range in color all the way from a pale golden to a deep jet black. There are even two-toned ants and multicolored ants. Black and cinnamon are the two most widely encountered colors, however, and should serve well for the majority of ants you encounter along trout streams. If you find a preponderance of ants of some other color along a stream and have the wherewithal handy to duplicate that color, then by all means do so. Color seems to make a real difference in ant imitations, particularly since they lie so low in the surface of the water.

Pete Bromley and I were fishing a small, nameless stream somewhere in Virginia. It was one of those rare occasions when we decided to kill a couple of fish apiece for the pan, and we both headed upstream to do whatever damage we could. I stopped at a favorite run and was delighted to find fish rising. As a matter of fact, there were so many fish rising that I found it hard to believe there could be that many fish in such a small stretch of water.

Knotting an elk-hair caddis onto the 6X tippet, I stepped into the water with all the confidence of the American basketball Dream Team entering the court against Angola. Boy, was I ever wrong. Thirty minutes, three thousand casts, and a dozen patterns later, I finally did what I should have done initially—put my nose to the water and looked. Even with bifocals it was easy to see what was going on. The water was covered with size 16 winged cinnamon ants, which by some miracle I happened to have in my box of patterns. And not only did I have the right pattern, I had six of them! What had begun as a frustrating morning ended as one of the most satisfying days I have ever had with the ant patterns.

—H. R. S.

Another factor to consider is the proper translucency of the color you choose for the body material. Other authors, such as Marinaro, have discussed this extensively, so we will give it only a cursory examination here.

Black seems to present no problem, as most black ants are opaque. But cinnamon (red) ants and others may be far from opaque, some even aproaching a degree of translucency that could almost be considered as transparent! If you don't believe this, the next time you capture a flying cinnamon or yellow ant, hold it up to the light and look *through* it rather than at it. The body in many instances is indeed translucent, allowing a great deal of light to pass through and lightening the color considerably. In many instances the body even seems to glow. Thus, the dubbing used for certain ant patterns should be chosen carefully to give the finished imitation this desirable quality.

Something else about color: In the past few years, some rather unusual colors have been used to dub ant bodies. The two that seem to be employed most often are bright orange and lime green, and believe it or not they can be real producers! Why these two colors should give such excellent results has yet to be explained, but people are catching on to this. We fully expect that in the future dubbed-body ants will be tied with purple, white, green, and other colors as well, and there is no reason why they should not work.

Using "off-the-wall" colors for ants is really not that new. In 1983, Art Lee wrote in *Fly Fisherman* about the new McMurray patterns ("The McMurray Flies—II"). In this article are pictures of McMurray ants tied in all sorts of colors and combinations of colors. There are blue, olive, tan, white, yellow, gray, and two-toned ants either pictured or listed in the article, so Ed Sutryn—the designer of the McMurray patterns—was thinking well ahead of most of us when it came to color. Gerald Almy (*Tying and Fishing Terrestrials*) was even ahead of this. Back in 1978, he mentioned the effectiveness of different colors for ant patterns and specifically pointed out the value of ants tied with "hot orange dyed fur." But many fly fishermen have not caught on to this yet!

Materials. In the past, the materials of choice for ant patterns were relatively simple. Nothing more than the correct dubbing, thread, and hackle have been necessary to tie very successful imitations. If the tier was so inclined, the judicious use of deer hair also could produce very effective ant patterns. To this day, these simple materials are probably used by more fly fishermen than anything else, and for a very good reason: Patterns tied with these materials work. No muss, no fuss, no strain. Just sit down at the bench and crank out a couple dozen, and you're in business. You want to add wings? Tie in a couple of dun or grizzly hackle tips or a bit of duck quill, some Z-lon, or one of the other synthetics. What could be easier? These are great patterns, and they are just about as simple a fly to tie as you could ask for. They are also so terribly effective that every fly-fishing guru will always include the ant in his "top ten list," and it's usually going to be a dubbed-body ant.

But times change, and today we have many different materials to play with. One of the first questions we have to ask, though, is whether these new materials produce imitations that are any more effective than the old ant patterns, and that is a difficult question to answer. Maybe they do and maybe they don't. You just have to decide that for yourself!

It was a difficult fish in difficult water, and it would have nothing to do with the little Blue-Winged Olive Comparadun I was using. I switched to a tiny hairwing dun, but the fish thumbed its nose at me again. Six patterns later, I tied on an old standard, size 18 black ant to a new 4-foot section of 7X tippet, and on the first drift the brown came up and gave it a good, close look. Frustrating, to say the least.

Steve Hiner caught up to me about that time, and I pointed out the rising fish. Steve is a superb fly fisherman, one of the best I've ever run into, and like all of them he is supremely confident that he can catch any fish. What really makes you mad is that he is right most of the time. Our conversation went something like this.

"That's a catchable fish," said Steve.

"Yeah? OK, let's see you do it," I challenged.

"What have you tried on him?"

"None of your business."

"OK, he'll take this."

"What is it?"

"None of your business!"

So Steve tied this fly on and dropped it nicely about 3 feet in front of the brown, and the damn thing (all 16 inches of it!) swam up and took it.

"OK," I said, "what did you use?"

"A size 16 black McMurray ant."

I knew when to quit, so I let it go at that.

—H. R. S.

Does this prove anything? No, not really, but it's interesting. Most of us have experienced something like this or at least have had those days when one type of ant has appeared to work better than another. But we really cannot say that the new patterns work any better than the old. Some guys swear by the McMurray ant and argue convincingly that the balsa body makes all the difference in the world, and it might. After all, many people do not use McMurray ants but prefer the old dubbed-body style. On those streams where dubbed-body ants are used by most fishermen, the McMurray pattern may be just different enough to account for its great success. Others tout the foam ant or the Hi-Viz ant or the para-ant. They are all excellent patterns, and they all catch fish. New materials such as closed cell foam and balsa wood bodies allow us to create *different* patterns, but whether they are *better* or not is going to be very tough to prove. And in the long run, they all catch plenty of trout, so it's really up to the individual to pick what he likes the best and stay with it.

There is one new material, however, that we think is really worth mentioning. When tying dubbed-body ants, the dubbing material of choice is usually some natural fine-fibered fur. The synthetic polypropylene dubbings work fairly well for the larger sizes. Even then, though, the body must sometimes be sheared to obtain the desired effect. We have never really been that happy with any of the synthetic dubbings for ant bodies, but (like everyone else) we have used them and they seemed to do fine. There is, however, a new dubbing material that should be readily available by the time this book is published. This new dubbing material is a silk fiber dubbing produced by the Kreinik Manufacturing Company of Parkersburg, West Virginia, and we are confident that it will cause quite a stir in the fly-fishing fraternity. This dubbing is made of unbelievably fine, highly flexible silk fibers and has a lustrous sheen unlike that of any other dubbing. Those of us who have tried it have been amazed at its properties and are now spoiled rotten! We routinely employ it to tie everything from size 16 to size 28 flies of all sorts. For ant patterns, it allows us to tie even the smallest sizes with relative ease. Size 28 ants can be perfectly tied with the two humps and constricted waist so characteristic of this group of insects.

The Sinking Ant

No discussion of ants is complete without including the subject of the sinking ant. Like all terrestrials, ants *will* sink. OK, some (or many) might rise back up to the surface after being under for a while, but they don't pop up like corks out of a champagne bottle. They rise to the surface very slowly if the tracheal system has not filled with water. If water has entered the tracheal system, they are going to stay under, whether they are in heavy water or not. If you don't believe that there are subsurface ants, just stretch a catch net about 4 inches under the surface and let it sit there for a while. We think you'll be convinced! Remember that these relatively small terrestrials will be rapidly sucked under in broken water. They are then at the mercy of the current, and many of them are held under for quite some time. If they don't die from drowning, they will probably die in the digestive tract of some opportunistic trout. As we have said before, sunken terrestrials are easy pickings, and ants are no exception.

Whether or not the "old-timers" collected sunken ants doesn't really matter. They certainly recognized the effectiveness of the pattern, and they fished it extensively. Bob McCafferty is generally considered to be the originator of the "modern" sinking ant pattern, and there are many references concerning the use of this imitation. Ernie Schwiebert, for example, has a delightful little essay in *Trout Strategies* on fishing a sinking ant in the company of Charles Wetzel. Gerald Almy likewise speaks to the effectiveness of this pattern in his book *Tying and Fishing Terrestrials*. We particularly like the story told by Fran Betters in *Fly Fishing, Fly Tying and Pattern Guide* (1986). Betters tells of an old gentleman he met fishing the Flume pool on the Ausable who was "casting his imitation ants into the foam and letting them swirl around and sink down below the foam."

The sinking ant is obviously an effective pattern. A hell of a lot of fish have been taken with it, so why it remains largely overlooked by modern fly fishermen is a mystery.

The original McCafferty lacquered ant is probably as good a pattern as any. It has stood the test of time well. It is worth mentioning, however, that the Kreinik silk dubbing is excellent for tying sunken ants; all you need to do is to coat the body with clear fingernail polish, and the fly sinks beautifully. One advantage to this is that the dubbing retains its natural color even when treated. The use of different colors of lacquer is thus eliminated.

Classification of Ants

All ants belong to the family Formicidae, which is placed under the super-family Vespoidea (the vespoid wasps). The ants were derived from the wasps in the course of evolution and are similar to these insects in many respects.

There are really only two groups of ants of interest to the fly fisherman.

Subfamily Myrmicinae. This is the largest subfamily, with over 300 known species in North America, yet they are probably not as important to the angler as those members of the second-largest subfamily, the Formicinae. This widely distributed group includes the harvester ants of the genera _Pogonomyrmex_ and _Pheidole_. The harvester ants feed primarily on seeds and rely on stored seeds as their food supply. Harvester ants are all capable of delivering a nasty sting, so if you are inclined to collect ants of any type, be careful! Unless you are an accomplished entomologist, you should assume that any ant can hurt you and act accordingly. This subfamily also includes the leaf-cutting ants, genus _Atta,_ which cut and store bits of leaves in their nests and then feed on the fungi that grow on these leaves. The fire ants, _Solenopsis_ sp., are likewise members of the Myrmicinae but because of their distribution are probably of no consequence to trout fishermen.

Subfamily Formicinae. This subfamily of ants is probably the most important group of ants to both trout and trout fishermen. While there are only 200 species of these ants on the North American continent, their habits put them near, and in many cases over, trout streams. The carpenter ants, members of the genus _Camponotus,_ are on a day-to-day basis the most important of all. These ants excavate their nests in wood and are extremely common in the vegetation along trout streams. These are most likely the large black or brownish ants (some reaching a size of $\frac{1}{2}$ inch) that most anglers have encountered swarming over tree trunks along streams. They are frequently dislodged by rainstorms, wind, predators, or even squirrels and birds simply creating a commotion in the branches. As such they are often found in large numbers floating (or sunken) in trout streams. Mound-building ants of the genus _Formica_ are also included in this subfamily, but unless they are swarming, their importance is probably minimal.

BEES AND WASPS

Many people think that trout won't take a bee or a wasp, but that's just not so. Their thinking is probably based on the assumption that if the insect can hurt them, it's going to hurt the trout too, and after a couple of bad experiences the fish will turn down any more bees or wasps that come along. This might be true if the things were constantly falling into the water and the fish were thus supplied with a continual stream of these stinging insects. Under these circumstances, fish that were stung a few times would probably become conditioned to turn these offerings down. But at most a trout might see only a few of these insects during an entire week, and it's doubtful if it would remember its unpleasant experience longer than a few hours without constant reinforcement. So even though there are reported cases of trout refusing these insects (Alfred Ronalds, Charlie Fox), we among others, have often seen trout readily accept them.

Most bees and wasps are very good fliers, and because of this they do not often wind up in the water. When they do, many of them are probably taken by trout. Please notice we said *taken,* not *eaten!* There's a big difference.

There is no question that there are plenty of wasps and bees along the banks of trout streams. We often see yellow jacket, wasp, or hornet nests in the branches of trees overhanging the water. We hope we see them before it's too late, but that's not always the case, as many of us can testify. What we usually don't see are the myriads of these insects that are more or less solitary but are nevertheless present. Both the visible and the invisible

members of this group of insects undoubtedly play a role in the trout's diet, but it is probably very minor, with the host of other terrestrials available. Nevertheless, wasp and bee patterns have been tied for centuries (Dame Juliana's "waspe flye" for example), and the fascination with these insects still persists.

It was the last week in July 1992, and Ed Koch and I had been fishing Pennsylvania's Clarks Creek for the better part of a morning with mixed success. We had both tried a number of different patterns, and while each accounted for a few fish, none had proved to be what we considered a "winning pattern." As I recall, we had tried ants, beetles, inchworms, midges, midge larvae, and small scuds. We had met with mixed results for all. I had hesitated in trying a pattern that had worked well the previous year on the same water (because I was testing some new patterns) but I finally broke down and tied it on. The pattern is a cinnamon ant, but one that is tied with a duck quill wing and six or eight long, trailing legs (three or four on each side). I had obtained the original some four years previously from Stuart Asahina (legendary light line fisherman and part owner of the Spinner Fall Fly Shop in Salt Lake City). I have no idea who originated this pattern, but it can be deadly at times. It proved its worth that day on Clarks Creek, so much so that I had to give Ed a couple to fish with.

On the drive back to Carlisle, we began to speculate as to why that particular pattern worked so well, and Ed made a comment to the effect that it might look like some kind of little wasp. Indeed it does! When you really examine this pattern, it looks much more like a wasp than an ant. I think what does it are the long, trailing legs along the side of the fly; they are distinctly wasplike in character. Whatever it might resemble, it works well not only on Clarks Creek, but also on many other streams.

_—H. R. S._

Nevertheless, even though imitations of wasps and bees (particularly the latter) have been tied and fished for years, they are not generally popular patterns. Anglers, however, do fish them. Schwiebert in _Trout Strategies_ makes the comment that "on the limestone streams of Pennsylvania many anglers swear by bee imitations in hot weather." He further states that clipped-hair patterns of the honeybee, sweat bee, and bumblebee "have often proved themselves on selective trout." Gerald Almy has indicated great success using certain imitations of these insects along the Yellowstone River. Dave Whitlock has also pointed out that wasp and yellow jacket patterns are quite productive along Arkansas's White River, particularly in October "after frosting begins." Fran Betters has mentioned that "a few of the other terrestrials I have found quite productive are bee imitations." Finally, Ed Shenk ("'T' Time," *Fly Fisherman,* September 1986) makes the statement that "house fly and bee imitations, while not absolutely necessary, can sometimes catch trout that see many other patterns." We would almost guarantee, however, that if you examined the fly boxes of twenty anglers picked at random, not more than one would have a true wasp or bee pattern in their collection. If they did, it would probably be an old McGinty that belonged to their father or grandfather and they have kept it for sentimental rather than practical reasons.

In actuality, there are very few wasp or bee patterns on the market. We have seldom (if ever) seen them for sale in fly shops. If an individual develops a lust for such an imitation, he must tie his own. It also seems that the only two patterns that have ever had any following at all are those tied with clipped deer hair in the appropriate colors. We really cannot include Almy's deer-hair wasp as an accurate imitation—it looks more like a cricket than anything else!

Is there anything we can do about this? Sure, we can come up with some reasonable imitations, test them out, and see what kind of results we get. After all, it's not very difficult to do!

Steve Hiner and I had been talking about the firefly pattern one day. As usual the conversation centered around why this particular pattern works so well and so consistently. We've never been able to answer that question, but it's fun to talk about stuff like this. At any rate, Steve told me that a mutual friend of ours thinks that trout take it for a wasp of some sort—after all, it does have this wonderful, glow-in-the-dark yellow butt. But that's all the yellow on the whole thing, and it really is not shaped very much like a wasp at all, so I disagreed.

Well, then Steve said, "There aren't any good wasp patterns on the market. Why don't you come up with something?" About that time, Ed Koch's comment about the cinnamon ant we had fished on Clarks Creek came rolling out of the fog of my memory. Yes, by damn, that pattern does look like a wasp, but to make it really look like a wasp, it needs a lot of work. So I went home that evening, hauled out the fly boxes, and took a look at the ant. The design is a good one, no question about it.

A few hours later (nothing comes quickly when you are fooling around with a new pattern), I had what I thought was a pretty acceptable wasp. A little black foam, some fluorescent yellow poly-floss thread, a bit of duck quill for a wing, some moose-hair legs, and a little black dubbing was all it took. I had to admit, I was excited. The things lay there on the tying table, and they just looked good. Every now and then you come out with something that you simply know is going to be a winner, and I had that feeling about the Turbo Wasp.

The pattern had its baptism of fire a few weeks later on Virginia's Smith River. I like this river. If a pattern is accepted by the trout population there, it will usually be an outrageous success anywhere else.

The weather was not the best that day—partly cloudy but very windy. Steve was guiding a couple of people from northern Virginia, and I was more or less along for the ride (and trying to stay as far away from them as possible). For once the firefly seemed to have lost its magic, but tucked away in the corner of the terrestrial box were half a dozen of the wasps. What better time to test them; if they could produce when the firefly didn't, it would be worth knowing.

A few hours and twenty-six fish later I had my answer. It was deadly, and I have a couple of witnesses (Blaine Chocolate and David Garst from Roanoke) just in case. The Turbo Wasp was a real winner!

—H. R. S.

Again we have the problem of deciding whether the trout really thinks it's a wasp or something else, but does that really matter? What we care about is whether it fools them or not, and this wasp pattern definitely does. It doesn't look like a beetle, it has plenty of bright yellow color to it, the general shape comes reasonably close to that of a wasp, and it catches a lot of fish. So what we are going to do is call it a wasp and leave it at that. That's probably good enough!

Classification of Wasps and Bees
Superfamily Vespoidea. This superfamily contains the family

Vespidae, which includes the common yellow jacket (*Vespula maculifrons*) and the bald-faced hornet (*Dolichovespula maculata*). These both are social insects and construct the typical "paper" nests that are often seen in the bankside foliage (although most species of yellow jackets prefer to build an underground paper nest). Do we need to warn you about these? Probably not. All we can say is to simply keep a sharp eye out for both types of nests. Those that are underground are particularly insidious, since the only way they can be spotted is by the comings and goings of the inhabitants.

Superfamily Apoidea. All of the common bees belong to this superfamily, and although there are somewhere in the neighborhood of 3,500 species, only a few are of importance to the fly fisherman on a regular basis. The common honeybee, *Apis mellifera,* is the only species of the subfamily Apinae found in North America, but its numbers and habits are of great importance. The most important of all the bees in the pollination of plants, it can be expected along any trout stream where there is a profusion of plant growth. On a historical note, the honeybee is not native to the United States but was introduced from Europe. Whereas most of the colonies are domesticated, many have escaped and established themselves in the wild. Compared with wasps and yellow jackets, the North American honeybee is a comparatively mild-mannered and nonagressive insect. Not so its cousin the "killer bee," which is a particularly agressive strain of *Apis mellifera.* This strain was originally imported to South America (Brazil) from Africa. It is a better honey producer than the European strain, and the initial idea was to cross-breed the two strains for greater honey production. Its escape from domestication and its rapid colonization of South and Central America coupled with its recent appearance in the United States are certainly cause for alarm. Colonies of these bees will attack at the slightest provocation and do not give up easily. They will chase the intruder for hundreds of yards and have been the cause of numerous deaths of both humans and livestock. Fortunately, trout fishermen have little to worry about yet.

The bumblebees are members of the subfamily Bombinae. The common bumblebee, *Bombus pennsylvanicus,* is probably the one most familiar to anglers and does occasionally manage to blunder into trout waters. We do not consider it a steady dietary item for trout, but because of its relative rarity on the water, it could be the very thing that big brown is looking for. A couple of imitations of these in the terrestrial box could pay a big dividend some day!

SAWFLIES

Sawflies are wasp- or beelike members of the suborder Symphyta. Most of the ones encountered by fly fishers are probably members of the family Tenthredinidae, of which there are 790 North American species. Others, such as the conifer sawflies (family Diprionidae), may be occasionally encountered. In some instances the larvae of sawflies, which look a great deal like caterpillars, might occur in enough numbers to warrant fishing an imitation.

I have been a fly fisherman for over forty years, and I have never been in a situation where I found the need for a pattern to imitate either the adult or the larval stage of a sawfly. I have none in my fly boxes, so if I ever run into a bunch of these critters, I guess I'm just out of luck. But on the other hand, I have plenty of terrestrial patterns that would probably come close enough to work, so I'm not going to lose any sleep over it

—H. R. S.

ANT, WASP, AND BEE PATTERNS

Just as for the beetles, we feel that in-depth tying instructions are unnecessary for patterns that are well known and have been described in other literature. For those patterns we will therefore list only the materials used. Stewart and Allen's book *Flies for Trout* has excellent color illustrations for many of the patterns listed.

Floating Ants

For the first six patterns listed, we recommend following Marinaro's advice of removing a broad V-shaped region of hackle from the undersurface of the fly. As he (and many other later authors) indicated, this allows the ant to ride flush in the film rather than high on the surface as do most standard dry patterns.

FUR ANT

Hook: #12 to #26 standard dry-fly hook, Mustad 94833, Tiemco 100 or 101, Orvis 1509.

Thread: 6/0, 8/0, color to match that of the dubbing used to form the body.

Body: Larger sizes: natural fur dubbing or polydubbing in black, cinnamon, tan, brown, red, or white. (Yes, white ants work wonders at times.) Also, try tying some ants in bright orange, lime green, and other highly visible colors. Small sizes: We strongly recommend the use of the Kreinik silk dubbing on any ant smaller than a #16. It is clearly superior to anything else available.

Legs: Good-quality dry-fly hackle, usually black. If necessary, match the color of the hackle with that of the body.

FOAM BODY ANT

Hook: Standard dry-fly hook in desired size, Mustad 94833, Tiemco 100 or 101, Orvis 1509.

Thread: 6/0, 8/0, color to match that of the body.

Body: Preformed or flat piece of closed cell foam in appropriate size and color (usually black, brown, or cinnamon). The new high-visibility (white-tipped) foam bodies are an excellent choice for those who have problems keeping track of the fly (Orvis Quick-Sight Ants).

Legs: Good-quality dry-fly hackle, usually black.

There are many variations of the basic foam body ant, to say the least! There are the Hi-Viz Foam Ants, tied using a foam body on which there is either a red or white foam patch on the apex of the head. These are much easier to see under low-light conditions. Bill Skilton has designed his beautiful Hard-Shell Foam Ant and the flying variation of the same using his own particular brand of foam. These are quite realistic and highly effective

McMURRAY ANT

Hook: Standard dry-fly hook in desired size to match pre-
    formed body, Mustad 94833, Tiemco 101, Orvis 1509.
Thread: 6/0, 8/0, color to match that of the body.
Body: Preformed, color as desired. (Black and red are most
    commonly used.)
Legs: Good-quality dry-fly hackle. Black is the usual choice,
    but the color can be matched to that of the body if
    desired.

ROD'S BLACK ANT

This, like the McMurray ant, is tied with a balsa body but is a much
more realistic pattern. The average tier is not going to spend a great deal
of time producing this pattern at the bench, but the end result is lovely, to
say the least!
Hook: #12 to #22 standard dry-fly hook.
Thread: 6/0 or 8/0 black.
Abdomen: Balsa wood formed to correct shape with monofila-
    ment connection to shank of the hook.
Thorax and head: Spun died black deer hair, trimmed to the
    correct shape and then lacquered black.
Legs: Three strands of black deer body hair, figure-eight
    wrapped and trimmed to correct length.

DEER HAIR ANT

Hook: #14 to #20 standard dry-fly hook.
Thread: Black, 6/0 or 8/0.
Abdomen: Deer or elk hair. While the color is usually specified
    as black, rusty brown, tan, brown, and other colors will
    work just as well (and sometimes even better).
Head: Formed by pulling the hair used to form the body
    forward, tying it down just behind the eye of the hook,
    and trimming the butts.

Legs: Three strands of hair pulled out on the sides and trimmed to correct length.

SILK ANT

The silk ant is tied using the same procedure as that employed for the fur ant. The only difference is the type of dubbing used. With Kreinik silk dubbing, you can tie beautifully shaped and tapered bodies on the smallest of hooks. The flotation properties of silk are equal to those any of the natural or synthetic dubbings. When forming the body of an ant using silk dubbing, wind the material in a manner similar to that of a level wind casting reel. In other words, do not build up the body in one place. Wrap the dubbed thread back and forth, progressively decreasing the number of wraps as the body is built up.

BORGER'S PARACHUTE ANT

Hook: #12 to #28 standard dry-fly hook.
Thread: 6/0, 8/0, color to match body.
Abdomen: Fur and sparkle yarn, blended. Color at discretion of tier.
Thorax: Same as abdomen
Hackle: Dry-fly quality. Color to match body. Tied in at rear of thorax and wound parachute style, one or two turns, around base of thorax.

BORGER'S WINGED PARACHUTE ANT

Hook: #12 to #20 standard dry-fly hook.
Thread: 6/0, 8/0, color to match body.
Abdomen: Fur and sparkle yarn, blended. Color at discretion of tier.
Thorax: Same dubbing as the abdomen, wound parachute-style around the base of the wing.
Wing: Gray sparkle yarn (BCS 108) tied in at the thorax. Borger apparently ties this in as a parachute post.

Hackle: Good-quality dry-fly hackle, same color as the body; wound parachute-style (one or two turns) around the base of the thorax.

FRANK ANGELO'S PARACHUTE ANT

Hook: #12 to #20 standard dry-fly hook.
Thread: 6/0, 8/0, color to match body.
Abdomen: Fur or poly dubbing. Color at tier's discretion.
Thorax: fur or poly dubbing, built up evenly on both sides of the parachute post.
Wing (post): White calf tail, tied upright.
Hackle: Good-quality dry-fly hackle; color to match body, wrapped twice around base of the parachute post above the dubbed thorax.

SCHROEDER'S PARACHUTE ANT

This pattern appears in the 1993 catalogue of the Fly Shop, Redding, California. It appears to be almost identical to Frank Angelo's pattern described above, except that grizzly hackle is used to form the wing.

WESTERN ANT

This is a pattern we have used with great success, even in the East! In Stewart and Allen's book *Flies for Trout* (Mountain Pond Publishing, 1993), the Western Ant is tied with red fur dubbing forming the body, but we have tied this with black, cinnamon, and other colors as well. The cinnamon body variation seems to be particularly effective.

Hook: #10 to #18 standard dry-fly hook.
Thread: 6/0 or 8/0, black.
Abdomen: Dubbed fur, color of choice (red, black, cinnamon, tan).
Thorax: Dubbed fur, color to match that of the abdomen.
Outriggers: Stewart and Allen indicate that only a single strand of moose or elk hair is employed. We, however, tie ours

with three strands on each side to simulate the long, trailing legs of small wasps or large ants.

Wing: Pretreated section of gray mallard wing quill, tied in flat and projecting rearward over the abdomen.

Hackle: Black or dark dun, wrapped in front of the point at which the outriggers and wing were tied in.

Flying ants, or the winged stage of the life cycle, are easily tied by incorporating wings into many of the preceding patterns. This is commonly done for any of the dubbed or foam body ants, the McMurray ant, or the deer-hair-bodied ants. We have found the following winging material to be useful: hackle tips in white, grizzly, or blue dun; Z-lon or any other similar synthetic; nylon organza (beautiful); pearlescent mylar gift wrap; Z wing material.

Sinking Ants

In the past, the body of the sinking ant was usually formed with thread and then lacquered to give the appropriate color. An alternate and probably faster method is to form the body using the Kreinik silk dubbing in the appropriate color and then treating it with either Hard as Nails clear fingernail polish or clear lacquer. The body colors of choice have usually been black, red (cinnamon), and brown, but you should also experiment with some of the colors used to tie the floating patterns. White, bright orange, lime green, and other colors can really produce at times when nothing else seems to work. The hackle used to form the legs on sinking ants should be fairly webby and soft. Starling feathers (hackle), if you can find them, are ideal. Hen hackle or poor-quality Indian cock will do if you can find it small enough. Black is the usual color of choice, but other colors may be used at the discretion of the tier.

GENERALIZED SINKING ANT (BOB McCAFFERTY)

Hook: #12 to #20 standard nymph hook, Mustad 3906, Tiemco 3769, Orvis 1641.

Thread: 6/0, 8/0, color to match body.

Body: Thread built up and lacquered (McCafferty), or Kreinik silk dubbing treated as described above. Color is at the tier's discretion.

Legs: Indian cock hackle, starling hackle, or any other appropriately soft and webby feather. Black is the usual color, but other colors may be used depending on the body color.

TRANSPAR-ANT (HARRISON STEEVES)

Marinaro was much concerned with the property of translucency as seen in the body of ants, particularly the red and yellow varieties. As a result, he advocated the use of certain types of dubbing that would allow the passage of light and lend a special glow to the bodies of these ants. This sinking pattern was designed to produce that marvelous translucency, which it does very effectively. It is quite easy to tie, taking no more time than the old lacquered ant pattern, and is much more realistic when used to imitate ants that have a translucent body. It is also extremely effective.

Hook: #16 to #20 straight eye, Tiemco 101.

Underbody: Monocord for the larger hook sizes, 6/0 or 8/0 thread for the smaller sizes. Yellow, rust, cinnamon, or a combination of these, using different colors for abdomen and head.

Body: Devcon five-minute epoxy.

Legs: Black or furnace hackle.

Tying Instructions

When tying this fly, we suggest that a rotary-type vise be used, as this is the only way the body may be formed easily.

1. Build up a small underbody for both the thorax and the abdomen, using monocord or thread in the color of choice. Leave a portion of the hook shank bare between the two underbody portions. The abdomen should of course be somewhat larger than the thorax. A little practice is all that is necessary to achieve the correct proportions.

MacHopper

Foam Grasshopper

Shenk's Letort Hopper

MacCricket

Letort Cricket

Black Ant

Hard Shell Foam Ant

Red McMurray Ant

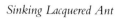

Winged Hard Shell Foam Ant

Sinking Lacquered Ant

E-Z Sight Foam Ant

Cinnamon Fur Ant

Black Fur Ant

Black McMurray Ant

Japanese Beetle

*Floating Foam
Japanese Beetle (top view)*

*Floating Foam
Japanese Beetle*

*Steeves' Sinking
Japanese Beetle*

Sinking Black Beetle

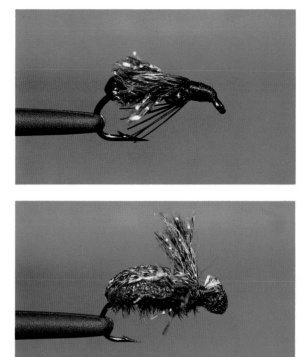

Sparkle Back Beetle

Grass Bug

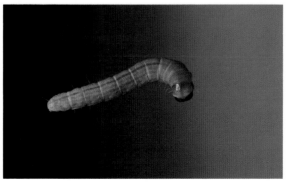

Inchworm

Firefly

Steeves' Floating Firefly

Steeves' Sinking Firefly

Steeves' Honey Bug

Steeves' Turbo Wasp

Bumblebee

Bivisible Beetle

Ghost Beetle

Black Barking Spider

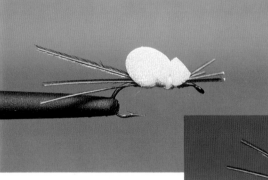

Yellow Barking Spider

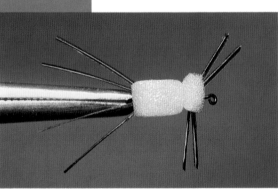

*Yellow Barking Spider
(top view)*

Jassid

2. Mix a small amount of five-minute epoxy, and using a needle, apply an appropriate amount to both the abdomen and thorax. The advantage of a rotary vise for this operation is obvious. As you apply the epoxy, the vise may be rotated and the body built up and tapered as desired. By rotating the vise slowly for a few minutes, a perfectly shaped and even body can be obtained. Continue rotating the vise until the body has partially hardened (it only takes a few minutes).

3. Remove the completed body from the vise by grasping the eye of the hook with a fine-pointed pair of forceps so as not to touch the still tacky body.

4. Place the bend of the hook on a magnetic strip cemented to a block of wood so that the body will contact nothing until it is completely hardened. Bodies may be produced fairly rapidly using this procedure.

5. Allow the completed bodies to cure for a few hours. Tie in the appropriate size hackle between the abdomen and head, give it a few turns, and tie it off to form the legs. If you do not want to use hackle, three strands of moose body hair may be figure-eight wrapped between the thorax and abdomen and then trimmed to form the six legs.

Wasps and Bees

STEEVES' TURBO WASP

Hook: #14 or #16, Mustad 94831 or equivalent.

Thread: 6/0 or Danville polyfloss, fluorescent yellow. If the polyfloss is used, then the head must be treated with head cement.

Body (abdomen): ⅛ inch black foam cut into ⅛ inch-wide strips.

Thorax: Black dubbing, either natural fur or poly dubbing, or a strand of black extra-fine Easy Dubbing (Orvis Co.).

Wing: Mallard wing quill sprayed with Tuffilm.

Legs: Six moose body hairs.

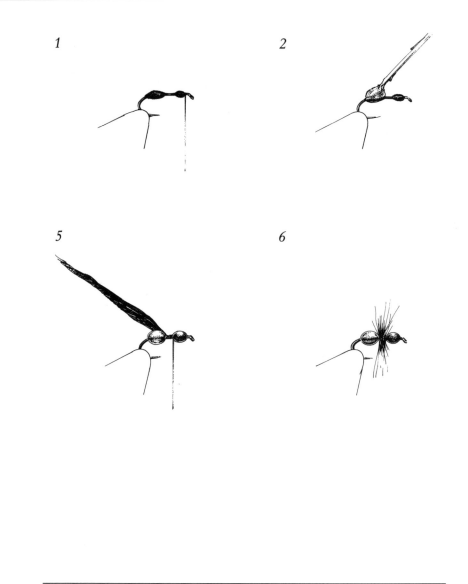

TRANSPAR-ANT

3

4

1

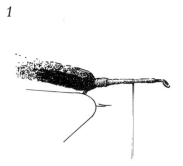

2

5

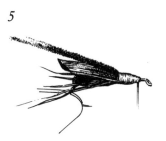

6

STEEVES' TURBO WASP

3

4

7

© CREED TAYLOR 1993

STEEVES' TURBO WASP

Tying Instructions

1. Wrap the shank of the hook with tying thread to a point behind the barb of the hook. Tie in the body foam close to the hook bend and wrap down with the tying thread until none of the foam is visible. This should form a slight enlargement at the rear of the hook shank. Wrap the tying thread forward about two-thirds the length of the hook shank. The thread should cover the hook shank completely to give the underbody color.

2. Fold the foam body material forward, and tie it down to form the abdomen. Trim the excess that projects forward, and save it for more bodies.

3. Tie in the six moose body hairs so that three lie along each side of the body and extend a short distance past the rear of the abdomen. A single figure-eight wrap will serve to separate the hairs nicely into two bunches. Wrap the thread backward to the forward portion of the body. Trim away the forward-projecting portions of the hairs.

4. Tie in the duck quill wing so that it extends slightly over the butt of the fly. Trim the forward portion off, and cut the rear portion on each side to form an angle.

5. Wax the tying thread, and apply dubbing. Wrap the dubbed thread to form the thorax. If you use Easy Dubbing for the thorax, simply tie in a 6-inch piece and make three to four wraps. Tie it down and trim away the excess. Save the leftover piece for more flies.

6. Form the head with the tying thread, and whip-finish.

The Turbo Wasp is also very effective when tied with fluorescent green or fluorescent red polyfloss. On the fluorescent red Turbo Wasp, chocolate brown dubbing or Easy Dubbing is used for the thorax.

McMURRAY YELLOW JACKET

This is essentially a McMurray ant with a different paint job. As a matter of fact, the Yellow Jacket (according to Art Lee, _Fly Fisherman,_ July 1983) is available not only in yellow and black, but also in blue and black, white and black, cinnamon and black, and green and black.

DEER-HAIR BEE

Hook: Mustad 94833 or equivalent.

Body: Spun and clipped deer hair in different color combinations (white and black, yellow and black, yellow and brown).

Wings: Polywings, deer hair, Z-lon, Kreinik braided material, hackle tips, or any other of a host of natural or synthetic materials.

There are so many variations for the spun deer-hair patterns that it is impossible to list them all!

STEEVES' BEE/HORNET

Hook: #10 to #16, Mustad 94833 or 94831, or Tiemco equivalent.

Thread: 6/0 brown.

Body: ⅛-inch thick yellow closed cell foam.

Underbody wrap: Kreinik ¹⁄₁₆-inch flat ribbon, bronze, #052HL.

Overbody material: Kreinik ⅛-inch flat ribbon, bronze.

Wings: Kreinik ⅛-inch flat ribbon, mallard, #850.

Tying Instructions

The tying directions for this pattern are essentially the same as those for Steeves' Sparkle Beetle (see chapter 6). Before bringing the overbody material forward to separate the wings, use a brown Pantone marker to form bands on the body. A very acceptable bald-faced hornet can be produced using white foam banded with a black Pantone marker for the body and thorax and black Kreinik flat ribbon for the underbody wrap and the overbody material.

TENNESSEE BEE (BRAD WEEKS)

Hook: #10 to #14 standard dry-fly hook.

Thread: 6/0, black.

Body: Yellow poly dubbing.

Rib: The original pattern calls for the ribbing material to be "black floss soaked in vinyl cement and permitted to dry before winding." A much easier method is to use small- or medium-diameter Kreinik beetle black braid, #005HL.

Head: Yellow poly dubbing.

Wing: Light elk hair.

Hackle: Light ginger or ginger grizzly.

8

Order Orthoptera: Grasshoppers and Crickets

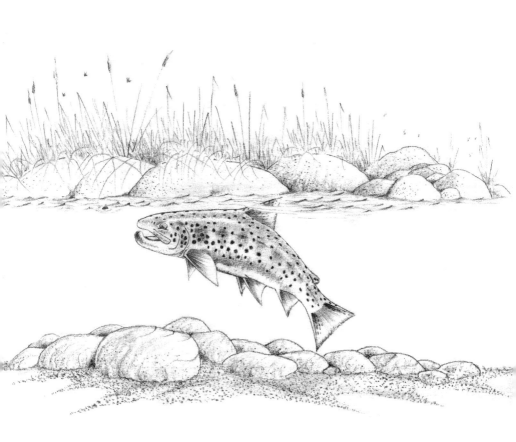

THERE IS SOMETHING about "hopper season" that elicits a primitive response in fly fishermen. One of A. K. Best's statements, with the addition of one word, seems to sum it up best: "Me fool BIG fish." We all seem to believe that this is the time of the year when we stand the best chance of taking that fish of a lifetime on a dry fly, and with good reason—many people do! When the hoppers are in the fields (and on the water), trout seem to go a little berserk. It's a period when even a misplaced cast from an inept angler can result in a frenzy of flying water, flying fish, and crying angler as the tippet parts. The experienced fly fisherman usually fares a little better, although not always, simply because he expects this to happen. He is, in short, prepared for the event even when not fishing to a rising trout.

Hopper season is a time of giant flies sometimes fished to giant fish, but not always. Sometimes the size of the fish is relative to the time and place or to the stature and mindset of the fisherman.

It was a blue 1937 Ford, the year was 1949, and it was my first "trout trip." Through north Georgia (I wonder if Wildcat Creek is still as lovely as it once was), on into Tennessee, and finally to the sleepy little town of Brevard, North Carolina. We fished along the way, streams with names and those without. It made little difference to Dad and me.

There were lessons to be learned on that trip. I learned that an early-morning stack of hotcakes and winding mountain roads don't mix; that a hellbender will sure as hell slime up your trout net; that wasps like to build their nests at eye level along the stream; that you don't laugh at your dad when he goes in up to his armpits, 'cause you're next; that country ham sandwiches taste fine when they're wet; and that being fishing tired is the best tired of all. Yes, I learned a lot on that trip. I also learned that when it comes to grasshoppers, trout are nothing but suckers.

We fished the Davidson River outside Brevard and we caught trout, but I really only remember one of them. To me it was a monster fish, forming those wonderful telltale rings in a greasy-slick glide right below a chute. I wanted that fish in the worst kind of way, but it refused the odd assortment I threw at it. Oh sure, I had lots of flies. I had a lovely little South Bend cane rod, too. But the trout didn't give a damn about that. It stayed where it was, gliding up every now and then to take something that struck its fancy. Whatever I had was not what it wanted. I knew nothing. I was not even a teenager then, and there were no books, no fancy schools, no fly-casting lessons, no streamside entomologies, no hatch charts, no nothing. My dad had put a fly rod in my hands a few years before and said, "Make the cast from ten to two and practice it." I did. I was a fairly good caster, and even though the flies I showed that trout floated true over its lie, it refused to take.

My battle with this fish seemed to last three or four years, but I was a fairly bright kid, and eventually I went up and sat on the bank. As I moved through the wet grass, a big old hopper, still chilled from the mountain night, made a half-hearted effort to get out of the way. As I said before, I was a fairly bright kid, so I grabbed the rascal and stuck him in an empty compartment of my fly box. The next step was simple logic. I needed a bare hook, and what better place to find one than under the immaculate dressing of one of the flies my dad had so carefully tied for this trip. I chose a Parmechene Belle. The hook was about the right size.

Now let me explain something to you. My dad was an architect and an artist. If he did something he did it well, and he was an exceptional tier. If he had pursued it, he would have been one of the best. His Parmechene Belle was a work of art. The wings were perfectly married. The proportions were exact. The head was carefully lacquered. It was exquisite. Did I care? No. There was a fish rising in that pool, I had a live hopper in my fly box, and I needed that hook. So I took my pocket-knife and I cleaned that Parmechene Belle off the hook in about fifteen seconds.

I moved to the chute above the fish and hooked up the hopper the same way I did when I used them for bluegills—right through the thorax. That way they kicked and bucked and raised a good ruckus on the surface. I dropped the hopper into the chute, frantically played out line to get the drift just right, and held my breath. The son-of-a-bitch took it. He took it on the first drift. He took it like a freight train.

I do not remember fighting that fish, but there it was in my net, all 16 inches. I killed it the way Dad had taught me, cleaned it, and put it in the creel with a handful of wet ferns. It was a huge fish to a young boy, and I could not quite understand that strange emotional mix of elation and regret I felt. As I sat there trying to sort out these strange feelings, Dad joined me.

"Any luck, Buster?" (he always called me Buster when we went somewhere together).

"Some." I was beginning to feel ashamed of myself.

"Let's see." He reached for the creel, opened it, and slid the great fish out.

"That is a lovely fish." He touched its purple and pink flanks, not yet faded in death.

"What did you take it on?"

"A hopper." I suddenly knew what was wrong. I had cheated. But at least I wasn't going to lie about it.

"A hopper? I didn't tie up any hoppers. Where did you get a hopper?"

"In the grass, up there." I pointed up the bank.

"You used a live hopper?"

"Yes." I was shrinking into nothingness.

"Where did you get a hook?"

"Cleaned a fly off one." He didn't ask which one. God had granted me at least one slight favor.

My father looked at me (he was no longer Dad). He touched the fish again and stared deep, past my eyes and into the mind of a very young boy.

"Did you see any other hoppers up there?"

"Yes, there were a lot."

"Well, don't just sit there on your butt. Go up and catch some more while I clean a couple of flies off the hooks."

He was again my dad, no longer Father, and I loved him deeply, for there was still enough of the boy in the man to understand the weakness of his son. Since that day, I have never again used any sort of live bait on a fly rod. But I frequently use hopper imitations, and I frequently fish them on a downstream drift. It was a lesson well learned.

—H. R. S.

Bring up the subject of hoppers or crickets to a group of fly fishermen, and within an hour everyone will have recounted his favorite "big fish on a hopper" story. For some reason you never hear any "little fish on a hopper" stories. Rest assured that there have been plenty of smaller fish taken on hopper imitations! But for some reason, it seems as though most people don't ever tell these stories. Maybe it's because almost everyone has had a run-in with a big trout while fishing a hopper pattern, or maybe it's just the old "can you top this?" syndrome. Whatever, the fact remains that "hopper," in the minds of most trout fishermen, is synonymous with "big fish." On the other hand, "cricket" usually means "a whole lot of fish," but maybe not that many big ones.

Just exactly what are hoppers and crickets, and where do they fit into the grand scheme of things? Well, to start with, the group contains some gold-medal jumpers. If you do a little extrapolation and compare them with human capabilities, it is amazing what they can do. On a proportional basis, if humans could jump as well as hoppers, they could make it a good hundred yards up and land a little less than two football fields away from their starting point. This ability is a very nice example of the evolution of a specialized mechanism to avoid becoming some predator's dinner. Over the course of the evolutionary history of this group, those that could jump a little better than others survived and reproduced. They passed those genetic characteristics associated with jumping to their offspring, some of which could jump even better than their parents, and so it went for millions of years. What we see today is simply the current result of an evolutionary process. It is not the final product. Who knows what the hoppers of a million years from now might be able to do.

Not only can the members of this group escape predators by jumping, but many of them are very nicely camouflaged. We all know the frustration of trying to catch hoppers. You watch the sucker take off, carefully mark its landing spot, and when you get there you can't see it! That is, you can't see it until it moves, and it usually moves another 5 or 6 feet at a time. You may also have noticed that even if you see the hopper, it has this frustrating habit of moving around to the other side of the plant when you reach for it. You always wind up grabbing a fistful of plant along with the hopper. In the process, the hopper seems to come out of your hand a little the worse for wear! If the hopper lands in the grass instead of on a plant, it usually seems to get away by burrowing down into the tangled mass of vegetation. Crickets, even though not as good at jumping, can be just as frustrating to catch, because of this "head for the deep cover" behavior.

There are approximately 1,200 species of hoppers and crickets in North America. Since the habitats of many of these species put them in the neighborhood of trout streams, and since they don't seem to pay much attention to the direction in which they jump, many of them land in the water. Those that choose to fly can make it over small streams without much trouble, but larger streams present them with a real problem. Other than the strong-flying migratory grasshoppers, most hoppers are pretty weak in the air. A stream the size of Henry's Fork presents a rather formidable barrier, and most of them are going to poop out before they get to the other side. The end result is *splat,* kick, and good-bye!

Not only the adult Orthoptera but also the young can provide food for trout. This is because of their method of growth and development, scientifically termed *hemimetabolous.* Don't get the idea that this process is unique to the Orthoptera; other insects (such as the Hemiptera, or true bugs) are hemimetabolous as well. In this type of development, the young that hatch out of the egg look very much like the parents. In the case of the Orthoptera, even an untrained eye can tell that the funny-looking misshapen critter is a baby hopper. This baby hopper, or nymph, will then go through a series of molts, getting larger and progressively more adultlike in appearance and behavior. When the nymphs are very small they don't represent much of a food source, but as they get bigger and begin to jump and to really move around, many of them wind up in the water. The next time you start catching hoppers along a streambank, take a careful look at the backs of some of your captives. If the wings are fully formed and encased, you have an adult. If you see some strange-looking structures that look like stumpy, fleshy, immature wings, that's exactly what they are, and you have a nymph. These nymphal or immature stages get quite large, are capable of jumping very nicely, and provide trout with handy snacks whenever they land in the stream.

Most Orthoptera, both the mature and immature stages, are plant eaters (herbivorous). Any farmer who has suffered severe crop damage is well aware of this, and those of us who have not seen it firsthand have heard reports or seen pictures of the devastation these pests can cause. If these proverbial "locust plagues" destroy all available plant food material, these insects may revert to cannibalism and feed on each other. Other members of the Orthoptera will feed on both plant and animal matter, depending on what is available at the time.

What else is interesting about the Orthoptera? Well, they have some of the most highly developed sound-producing and sound-receiving organs among insects. The production and reception of sound in this group is associated with courtship and mating. The cricket's chirp is not for your pleasure, but is the cricket's attempt to ensure the survival of the species. Sound production is accomplished in one of two ways: Either the spiny hind legs are rubbed against a vein located on the outside of the forewing, or a "scraper" on one forewing is rubbed against a filelike vein on the other wing. The method has often been compared to that of drawing the bow of a violin across the strings. Each species has its own specific song, which is produced only by the males. The females of each species thus respond only to a specific song and actively seek out the correct species of male with which to mate. Mistakes are thus neatly avoided!

The reception of sound ("hearing") is accomplished by structures termed *tympanic organs,* which are similar in function to human eardrums. They are set in motion by sound waves in the air, and their movement stimulates nerves that are associated with them. The Orthoptera are thus a rather unique group of insects, since they rely so heavily on sound production and reception for mating purposes.

THE HISTORY AND DEVELOPMENT OF HOPPER AND CRICKET PATTERNS

The fly fisherman's fascination with hoppers and crickets is obvious. Just about everyone who ties has a hopper variation that is a local or regional "killer" pattern, and we have seen so many cricket imitations that it is impossible to catalog them all. Most of these imitations are very, very good. A tremendous amount of thought, time, effort, and talent has gone into the development of these patterns, sometimes too much! Neither of us believes that it is necessary to reproduce an exact imitation of any insect in order to fool a fish, but some of the patterns seem to attempt to do just this. Any pattern that takes more than a few minutes to tie is usually too complicated to deal with; your time is better spent on the water.

It would have been an incredible experience to have been on the Letort with all the regulars during the years when the terrestrial patterns were being developed. I wasn't there, so I can only read about it and dream the dream. What a time that must have been. What a host of gentlemen, and what a giant step in the history of fly fishing for trout! Many of the regulars are gone, but their efforts and experiences are burned into the pages of angling literature, and we owe them everlasting gratitude.

Some of the streams have likewise suffered from time's march forward. The Letort may never again be as productive as it once was. Big Springs receives a fair amount of runoff from the tears of anglers who knew it in its prime, and Falling

Springs is a pale reflection of its old self. For most of these streams, time's march forward has represented nothing more than progressive abuse.

I cannot talk to you concerning what went on during the early years around Carlisle, Pennsylvania. My information has been gleaned from pages open to anyone, so those of you who read know what I know. Fortunately, many of the anglers who played a role during the early years are still around. Ed Koch is a member of that elite fraternity, and who better to tell you the stories of the Letort Cricket and the Letort Hopper.

Ed, I owe you an apology! I make you sound like an old man! For those of you who do not know this gentleman, I can assure you he is not some feeble old geezer stumbling around in his dotage. Ed is not old (neither am I, or at least I like to think I'm not). Both of us are at the age, however, when people in their twenties and thirties call us "Sir" if they don't know us. Let me tell you, the first time that happens to you it's really going to make you mad.

Anyway, Ed Koch was there, he heard it all and saw most of it. He was there with Vince Marinaro, with Ross Trimmer, and Don DuBois. He, along with Ernie Schwiebert, Ed Shenk, and others, remember those times well, and we are damned fortunate to have all of them around.

So without further rambling, I leave it to Ed to enlighten you about the development of hopper and cricket patterns on those fabled Pennsylvania limestone streams.

—H. R. S.

Satisfied with the success of the Jassid pattern, Vince and Charlie tackled the second most abundant terrestrial on the Letort—the hoppers. In those early days, hoppers were almost overabundant in the meadows of the upper mile and a half of the stream—little hoppers, medium-size hoppers, and the "big boys." I do mean big, some as long as 2 inches. We used to catch this kind when we were kids, and they would squeeze what we called "tobacco juice" all over your hands. They contributed greatly to the river's smorgasbord. They were really the "prime ribs" of the summer's offerings.

Charlie and Vince did a lot of chumming in those early years as part of the learning process. They would use a long-handled salmon boat net that Charlie had fixed a fine mesh net on. They would make a sweep with the net in the tall grass and come up with several dozen to perhaps a hundred hoppers at a time. The hoppers were put in jars and carried to the river's edge. Charlie and Vince knew *where just about every trout in the river lived as well as where they fed.*

One of them would go upstream with a jar of hoppers, and the other would hide in the grass along the edge of the stream by a trout's regular feeding station. It didn't matter whether the trout happened to be out in the feeding station.

They didn't know for sure why the trout fed when they did. Was it because they were hungry? Logical. Did something trigger the feeding instinct, such as beetles or hoppers struggling on the water as they floated helplessly downstream? Or did the trout come to a feeding station and wait in the hope that sooner or later food would come by? Did they know when a mayfly hatch was about to start or had started? When the beetles would come? When it was hopper time? When it was jassid season? When it was cricket time? These were all unknown factors in those early years. Developing a pattern solved only one part of the puzzle, but Charlie and Vince needed to understand the whole puzzle. It didn't happen overnight or during one season. Experimentation went on for years.

When "chummer" and "watcher" were ready, the upstream partner would start the parade of hoppers, throwing them on the water so they drifted downstream 2 or 3 feet apart. Oftentimes a dozen or more hoppers floated over a known trout's feeding station and nothing happened. Did he not come out because it wasn't feeding time or because he wasn't aware of the hoppers passing by? But then, as if he had received some kind of a signal, the trout would appear in the feeding lane and start gulping in the helpless hoppers.

What caused him to finally come out and start feeding? Did his internal clock strike lunchtime? Did the kicking hoppers send some kind of signal that triggered the trout's feeding mechanism? After all these years, no one can say with certainty why or what makes it happen. But it does, and we fly fishers are thankful!

Could it be the "terrestrial attraction," which equals anatomy plus food value, that we discussed earlier? I think it is. In those early days on the Letort, however, we just never applied scientific knowledge to our trouting knowledge. We were content when a trout took a well-presented fly. We didn't care why. We attributed it to a well-executed cast, proper presentation, and a perfect imitation. Was there more to it than that? You bet there was, but we didn't care—we had fooled a wise, old brown! Lots of wise, old browns!

Back to the chumming once more. Once the trout started on the line of hoppers, they would feed until there were no more. It didn't matter if a dozen drifted by or fifty or sixty, the trout ate until the hoppers stopped.

Charlie and Vince played this chumming game with every trout they knew of in the river. Not once but hundreds of times. They loved showing the regulars and visitors alike their parade of hopper-eating browns. But feeding them live hoppers was one thing; could they do it with an imitation?

During the course of the hopper chumming, Vince had located a monster brown that would eat every live hopper in sight. The brown weighed about 8 pounds; at least that's what he and Charlie figured. It was with that particular brown in mind that Vince set out to tie an imitation to fool his "monster hopper eater," as the brown became known.

It didn't happen overnight, and it never does. But one day, Vince arrived at Charlie's ready for his "monster hopper eater." They sat on the bench behind Charlie's house while Vince unveiled his creation—a pontoon hopper. A big one. A size 8 long shank to look exactly like the 2-inch hoppers they had fed the big brown so many times.

The body of the hopper was a duck wing quill clipped to length. The hole was plugged with a piece of cork and then glued. The legs or pontoons of the hopper were small wing quill points tied on and glued so that they stuck out just like the folded legs of a real hopper. The body was painted yellow, and the legs were yellow and brown banded. It really did approximate the size, shape, and color of the real thing.

After serious discussions of the strategy to be used on the "monster hopper eater," they headed upstream. Charlie gathered several dozen hoppers along the way. Vince stopped at his preselected position. He would be downstream from the brown. The brown was not out in his feeding station. This didn't bother Charlie or Vince, for there were many occasions when they had "teased" him out with live beetles or hoppers. Charlie began throwing hoppers, one at a time, into the current that would carry them to the channel the brown fed in. The hoppers kicked and struggled as they drifted downstream. The first three hoppers drifted over the trout's feeding station—nothing. Charlie was spacing the hopper parade at about 3- to 5-foot intervals. As the fourth hopper drifted into the brown's channel, the brown suddenly appeared deep in the weed, about 2 or 3 feet below the placid surface. As the fifth hopper came into his window, the brown came up to within 10 or 12 inches of the surface. He took the sixth hopper. Both men were elated, for they knew they could keep him feeding on a dozen or more hoppers.

Vince checked his imitation leader and knots. He stripped line from his reel and coiled it in the grass in front of him. There was more soft talk between the two about when and where to place the new imitation hopper.

Vince's first cast was perfect, the fly landing about 3 feet ahead of the brown. The fly drifted into the window, and the brown tilted upward and inspected the imitation, drifting back and back, until suddenly he sank into the channel. Rejection! Vince was not troubled, however. He had challenged these wise Letort browns enough to know that seldom did they ever take a first presentation. Charlie continued feeding naturals and Vince continued showing the monster the pontoon imitation. On the fifth try, the fly drifted into the brown's window. Again, up under the hopper he rose, then he drifted back slowly, checking Vince's "fake." Suddenly his nose tilted upward, jaws opened, and in an instant Vince's hopper disappeared. Vince struck.

The brown felt the sting of the hook and all hell broke loose! The brown dove into the channel and into the weed. The fight would go on for almost twenty minutes. Charlie had joined Vince with the long-handled salmon net. The huge brown finally tired, and Vince began to guide him above the weed and toward the bank. The brown was within several feet of the net's ring when, with a last powerful surge, he dove deep into the channel and weed. Just as suddenly as he had taken the pontoon hopper he was free. The hook pulled out. Neither angler was upset. Sure, they would have liked to have landed, measured, and admired him, but he would have been returned to the water. They had succeeded again with another terrestrial imitation, and they were satisfied.

Several weekends later, Ernie Schwiebert showed up with some new deer-hair patterns tied similarly to a muddler minnow. They worked well. And later that same summer, Ed Shenk tied his now famous Letort hopper with a turkey wing tied "flat" over the body, giving the fly an almost perfect silhouette.

It was turning into quite a satisfying summer for Charlie and Vince. Successful patterns were developed for the jassid, beetle, and hopper, which are the three most prolific terrestrials found along the Letort. Then Charlie, Vince, and other Letort regulars settled down to enjoy the fruits of their labor. Days, weeks, and seasons followed where fishing the terrestrials almost replaced fishing to the few mayfly hatches that exist on the river. There was, however, another little critter that fell between the cracks, so to speak, as a result of the success with the new terrestrial patterns. The youngest of the regulars at that time was Ed Shenk. He had fished the Letort longer than Vince or Charlie, having started as a youngster in grade school. He literally grew up on the Letort. An innovator, he continually looked to develop and improve new and better patterns. His cress bug, though not a terrestrial, was just as important as other patterns developed at that time.

Crickets were as prolific along the Letort meadows as the jassids, beetles, and hoppers. It was Ed Shenk who developed the Letort Cricket. At least two seasons had passed after the hopper pattern was tied. The cricket's body was black dubbed fur, with dyed duck wing for the flat wing, and dyed black deer hair for the overwing and head. He tied the pattern in sizes 10, 12, and 14.

Ed and I were fishing one Saturday morning. It started out to be a great day. I was fishing beetles and Ed was fishing hoppers, or so I thought. After an hour or so, Ed's average was probably five trout to my one. We sat along the river's edge to take a break and to locate more of the early-morning risers.

"What the Sam Hill are you doing?" I asked. "What pattern are you using?"

He looked at me with a sheepish grin from ear to ear like a kid caught with his hand in the cookie jar!

"Oh no," I thought to myself, "I've been had again." This would not be the first time with Ed!

Holding his folded hand outstretched, he opened his fingers, and there in the palm of his hand was a cricket.

"So, that's it?" I queried.

Still with the impish grin, he replied, "Look at it."

I looked at the size 12 imitation and said, "So what?"

"Look at the wing," he replied.

Examining the fly more closely, I realized the wing was tied flat over the back so that when you looked at it from the bottom it had the perfect shape of a real cricket.

"Is that it?," I asked.

"Yep," he responded. "Been tying my hoppers and crickets this way for a couple of seasons now."

"That can't be the difference," I said to myself and then out loud to Ed.

"Here, try one." He dropped a flat winged cricket into my hand.

I tied it on and we headed upstream. As usual, he was right. He was an observant angler and still is, some thirty years later. My average never quite equaled his that morning, but it sure did improve the longer I used his cricket.

We encountered several tough trout that morning that would not take our crickets, no matter how perfect the cast and the float. I had moved upstream in frustration, looking for an easier quarry. I hadn't gone 50 feet when I heard a splash. I looked around; Ed was into another trout. It appeared to be a fish we had both worked on but hadn't been able to move.

"Was that a new trout?" I asked.

"Nope, the last one we fished to," was his reply.

"New pattern?"

"No, a cricket. Wait there and I'll show you."

Ed came upstream where I was getting ready to work another trout. The brown was feeding about 6 inches from the bank.

"Go ahead," I told him.

He began false-casting to get the distance. The next forward cast, he let the line go, the leader turned over beautifully, and the cricket landed in the grass on the edge of the bank. Expecting a string of cuss words, I watched as Ed waited until the current straightened the leader and the cricket tugged on the grass. Then, with a sharp upward motion of his wrist as though he were setting the hook, he flipped the cricket out of the grass, and it landed on the water about 6 inches to the trout's right side. No sooner had the fly hit the water than the trout turned, swam to the cricket, opened his jaws, and inhaled the fly. What I thought had been Ed's mistake in putting his cricket in the grass had turned out to be the brown's demise. When Ed snapped the cricket from the grass, it hit the water just as a real cricket would have, and the trout never hesitated.

Shenk looked at me and grinned. *"Works every now and again!"*

These were the kinds of experiences I had during those early years on the Letort, and they eventually turned me into a fair angler compared to the likes of Ed Shenk, Charlie, Vince, and about a dozen other regulars of the Letort clan.

In 1962, three years or so after Shenk had shown me his first cricket, I landed a 27-inch, 9-pound brown on one of Ed's cricket patterns.

As evidenced by the number of patterns listed in this work, the terrestrials have come a long way, and we can presume they are here to stay.

—E. K.

DESIGNING HOPPER AND CRICKET PATTERNS

If you capture a live grasshopper and take even a cursory look at it, it's very easy to pick out the most prominent anatomical characteristics. On an adult hopper, for example, the abdomen and the thorax constitute the bulk of the body. The large hind legs, very specialized for jumping, are much more prominent than the other two pairs. Lying over the back of the hopper are two sets of wings: the forewings, or *tegmina,* which are thickened, rather narrow, long, and heavily veined, and the hindwings, which are membranelike structures, larger than the forewings, and folded up much like a fan until the hopper takes flight. The head in many species is not very prominent. In many instances, it is smaller in diameter than the thorax. What really draws attention to the head region of the insect are the eyes, which are quite large in some species.

So in designing a pattern, we have the following anatomical characteristics to work with: the abdomen and thorax (which we can count as a single unit), the hind legs, the wings, and the head. As far as the wings are concerned, we really only have to pay close attention to the forewings. The hindwings are rarely unfurled, even when a hopper happens to jump into the water. The hopper apparently would much rather try to swim to shore than try to fly out. It's a good thing for fly tiers, too, because the wings on most hoppers are quite large, and trying to cast a hopper imitation with wings fully spread would be a nightmare.

Most hopper and cricket imitations incorporate into their design the abdomen and thorax, the forewings and a hint of the hindwings, and the head. Some patterns also include legs. So hoppers and crickets aren't that hard to design, and as a matter of fact, they are very easy to duplicate. Many of the most successful patterns are very good impressionistic representations of the real thing, with one glaring exception: Most of them do not have eyes. As far as we know, the only well-known hopper pattern that has eyes is that tied by Rod Yerger (Rod's Hopper), and even on it the eyes are relatively small in relation to the head. Could this make a difference in a pattern's effectiveness? We have no idea, but it might, and it's worth a try. It would be relatively easy to do on some patterns. All you'd have to do is add a couple of large, black lacquer spots on the head of something like a Dave's Hopper. Better yet, glue on a couple of eyes with five-minute epoxy or Super Glue. This probably would not be worth trying on any of the deer-hair bullet-head patterns, as the heads on these fall apart rather rapidly. But gluing eyes onto any pattern with a clipped deer-hair head may prove to be a real advantage. We haven't tried this yet, but we are going to!

Basic Anatomy

Lets take a look at some of the components that have been used to assemble imitations of both hoppers and crickets.

Body. In most imitations, the body represents both the thorax and the abdomen and can be tied using a variety of materials. Bill Bennett's use of a turkey tail feather quill to construct the Pontoon Hopper (Marinaro, *A Modern Dry Fly Code*) was a classically practical approach to the problem. It apparently was a very successful pattern, particularly when two small quills were added for legs; these acted as pontoons and kept the imitation floating upright. No matter how good this pattern may be, however, most fly dressers would prefer something a little less tedious to tie. As a result, you will rarely (if ever) see this pattern in someone's terrestrial box.

At the time, however, it was a considerable improvement over the Palmer grasshopper pattern (Marinaro, *In the Ring of the Rise*), which had a cork body. The Palmer Hopper was first tied "in 1915 by M. Palmer of Pasadena, California," and although it may have been a favorite local pattern, Marinaro states that it "never achieved any popularity" in the area where he lived and fished. Indeed, cork-bodied hoppers have never achieved much popularity anywhere, although Gerald Almy includes a pattern for one in *Tying and Fishing Terrestrials.*

Let's face facts: There are much easier ways to construct hopper bodies than by using either quills or cork. Nevertheless, at the time, Bennett's Pontoon Hopper was state-of-the-art, and according to Marinaro, there was "no better imitation hopper than Bill Bennett's Pontoon Hopper." But evolution is an inexorable force, there are many very creative tiers, and the Pontoon Hopper seems to have lost out during the process of natural selection in the never-ending search for the perfect hopper imitation.

Deer hair has proved to be one of the more useful materials for constructing hopper bodies. Whoever may have been the first to use this material is unknown, but Marinaro gives credit to John Alevras of Bloomfield, New Jersey, for introducing him to a "beautifully tied sample" in which a "newer technique involving tying a bundle of deerhair on a piece of stiff wire" was employed. According to Marinaro, "the body is removed from the wire and tied to the neck of a No. 14 hook, short shank." Marinaro did not like this hopper as well as the Pontoon Hopper, but he still thought quite highly of it, commenting that "it is a worthy pattern and has many virtues." Coming from Vince Marinaro, that is high praise indeed! Today there are numerous hopper patterns with deer-hair bodies. Thumbing through catalogs, you'll see many samples of these.

Balsa wood has been used on occasion to form hopper bodies, but like cork, it has never been widely accpted. Even the McMurray patterns, which were so highly touted by Art Lee (*Fly Fisherman,* July 1983), do not seem to have become very popular. At least, we don't see them for sale in the fly shops we frequent. Why is this? Have they met with no commercial success, or are we just hanging around the wrong shops?

At least one tier, Rod Yerger, successfully combines deer hair and balsa wood to produce lovely imitations of both hoppers and crickets. These were the subject of an article in the Summer 1990 issue of *American Angler and Fly Tyer,* and we refer you to that article for details.

Other materials that can be used for tying hopper and cricket bodies include polypropylene dubbing, braided macramé cord, and plastic canvas yarn ("plastic" refers to the canvas, which is made of molded plastic, not to the yarn, which as far as we can tell is identical to that used in the manufacture of macramé rope).

One current favorite is closed cell foam, such as polycelon or Evasote. Foam is available in flat sheets of varying thickness (depending on the supplier) or in round cords such as those marketed by Rainy Riding of Logan, Utah. These foams are available in a wide variety of colors, are extremely easy to work with, and produce flies that float well and are tough. In short, they work very nicely, and more and more tiers are turning to this material for manufacturing terrestrials.

Another material that works nicely for bodies is Kreinik Micro-Ice chenille. Bob Cramer's Disco Cricket is nothing more than a Letort Cricket with a body formed of black, peacock, or mallard Kreinik Micro-Ice chenille. It has apparently been a top producer on some pretty tough water, so it's worth a try.

Wings. Most hoppers and crickets are tied with at least one of the two pairs of wings represented in some way. The standard method of representing the forewings is with a segment of reenforced mottled turkey

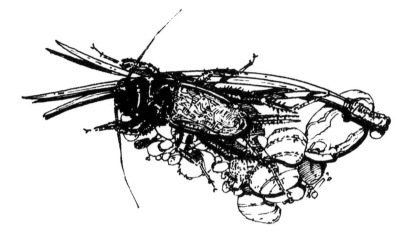

wing or tail barbs. Mike Lawson's Henry's Fork Hopper is tied with forewings formed from a pheasant feather treated with Flexament (which makes them very durable). The forewings of Roman Moser's patterns (*Fly Fisherman,* May 1986) are tied using a synthetic fabric with a printed pattern, available through the Orvis Company (or contact Umpqua Feather Merchants, P.O. Box 700, Glide, OR 97443, for the nearest dealer).

Hindwings can be represented by elk or deer hair, Krystal Flash, Z-lon, golden pheasant feathers, fibers of nylon organza, or any other translucent sort of winging material.

Most patterns seem to be tied with either the forewing or the hindwing, but very few are tied with both. Does it make any difference? We can't really say. We've done very well using all three types of imitations. Our advice is simply this: If you enjoy fishing your old favorite, consistently catch fish with it, like the way it casts, and it's easy to tie, then stay with it.

Legs. We've seen hoppers tied with legs and hoppers tied without legs. We've also heard all of the stories about how hoppers tied with legs are so much more effective than those tied without legs. Can anyone prove this?

None of my hoppers or crickets have legs. At least, they aren't tied with legs, although I suppose the long strands of elk hair forming the underwing on some of them do sort of hang down along the sides in a leglike manner. Why don't I tie them with legs? Good question. I don't know! It may be because one of my all-time favorite patterns, Mike Lawson's Henry's Fork Hopper, doesn't have legs and it produces just fine, thank you. When I started tying a furled body hopper a number of years ago, it just sort of naturally took on some of the characteristics of Lawson's pattern, and that's why it looks the way it does today. I liked Lawson's pattern from the first. It's neat, compact, and easy to tie; a good impressionistic pattern; and it casts very well and catches a lot of fish. It's a great pattern, so why do I prefer my furled body hopper? Simple—I invented it (or at least I think I did). Actually, it's more than that, but you are going to have to wait to hear the reasons why.

—H. R. S.

There is just no way, given all the variables encountered in the field, that anyone can prove that hoppers or crickets tied with legs are more effective than those tied without legs. OK, OK, all of you who prefer hoppers with legs simmer down! We know both sides of the story, and our advice to everyone is simply to fish the pattern you like. If you have confidence in it, you will probably catch fish. On the other hand, if one of your buddies is fishing a different pattern and cleaning up while you go hitless, then bum one from him. It doesn't mean it's any better, in the long run, than your favorite. It's just working better on that particular stream at that particular time. Who knows what the favored pattern for next week or even the day after tomorrow might be.

If you want to tie legs on your hoppers, the two materials most frequently used are a section of knotted turkey wing or tail barbs or a knotted hackle with the fibers trimmed to shape (Rod Yerger uses a trimmed hackle fiber that is bent and lacquered rather than knotted). Either one does an excellent job. Other materials that have been used include goose biots in the appropriate color, and rubber leg material.

Head. Up until the introduction of the closed cell foams, the heads of most popular hopper and cricket patterns were formed using deer hair. Most patterns used one of two procedures: either the hair was used to form a bullet head with the collar projecting backward, or a clipped deer-hair head was tied with a rearward-projecting collar. The second technique is a modification of the procedure used in tying a Muddler Minnow. Indeed, Schwiebert's Letort Hopper (and by the way, there are *two* Letort Hoppers, as indicated later) is nothing more than a modified Muddler Minnow! Each of these head types has its advantages and disadvantages. The bullet head is not that durable, but it presents a very nice impression and it's fast to tie. The trimmed deer-hair head takes a little more time to tie, is much more durable, and gives the fly more buoyancy. If you like the trimmed deer-hair head, we suggest you trim it smaller than that seen on many of the commercially tied patterns. You are not tying a Muddler Minnow, you are tying a hopper or cricket, and the head should be scaled to the size of the body.

A single piece of closed cell foam can be used to tie both the body and the head (see Larry Tullis's patterns in *Fly Fisherman,* March 1993, and David Lucca's nicely designed Jimminy Cricket in *Fly Fisherman,* May 1990). Other tiers use closed cell foam to form just the head. In either case, the use of closed cell foam has definite advantages: It is extremely durable, floats beautifully, is very easy to work with, and gives a very lifelike form to the finished product. In short, we like it!

Color. Vince Marinaro, once stated that the only color appropriate for the hopper body was "butter yellow." He was so adamant about this that he probably intimidated many who might have considered tying hoppers in different colors. Let's face it, Marinaro could be pretty intimidating! Well, Vince was wrong on this one. We fish hoppers in all sorts of different colors—orange, olive, tan, green, and brown, to name just a few— and they all work. Granted, some work better than others at certain times, but each has a reserved room in the Wheatley Hotel!

On the other hand, crickets seem to be destined to wear widow's weeds forever. Getting away from "basic black" on a cricket is hard to do. Maybe it's simply because patterns such as the Letort Cricket are so terribly successful that it goes against our grain to change anything about them. You really should not feel this way about the cricket at all, however. Ed Shenk fishes a white cricket with great success, but it does not seem to be very popular as a standard offering. We fish crickets in all sorts of colors and have found that they are quite effective. Olive, brown, and gray work just as well as black, and sometimes even better! We don't know why, but, who cares what the reason might be, as long as the pattern is working well.

So, our advice is simply to pick your own pattern, whatever it may be, and fish it with confidence. It's strange, but patterns in which we have a great deal of confidence seem to catch a great many fish. No one has come up with an explanation for this phenomenon, but it may be due to nothing more than the fact that you fish a "confidence pattern" with a bit more concentration.

FISHING THE IMITATIONS

Whichever pattern you fish, hopper or cricket, there are some basic methods employed. Most of the hopper and cricket patterns are relatively large flies. As such, they land with a pronounced *splat* and will immediately catch the attention of even a semialert predator. Much has been written about this *splat* presentation, and there is little point in our expounding on this phenomenon any further.

There are times, however, when this *splat* tends to spook fish, particularly in thin-water situations. At these times, a more sophisticated and delicate presentation is called for, and this requires (in most instances) a pattern considerably smaller or lighter than the commercially available giants. For example, Orvis offers Dave's Hopper and Dave's Cricket in sizes 8, 10, and 12. OK, a size 12 doesn't sound so bad, but "size 12" doesn't mean a thing unless you look at what type of size 12 hook is used. The two Whitlock patterns mentioned previously are tied on 2X or 3X long standard or fine-wire dry-fly hooks. As such, even a size 12 is a fairly large fly, but it lands much more softly than a size 8. Also, take into consideration how the fly is dressed. A size 12 Henry's Fork Hopper is much less bulky than a size 12 Dave's Hopper and will therefore allow a more subtle presentation. What we are saying is simply to match the pattern to the conditions. A size 14 or 16 Letort Cricket can, for example, be presented with a delicacy approaching that of a comparably sized Adams (provided you are a reasonably good caster).

One other note regarding size: Many of us have found that the smaller hopper and cricket patterns outproduce the larger ones in many instances, so don't be afraid to try some of these little guys in size 14 and 16. Immature forms of both insects are quite small, and imitations of them can frequently be the fly of choice for the day.

Chester sat on the bank and howled—Woody had crossed the "forbidden line," somehow established deep in Chester's doggy brain, that told him the Boss was too far away. Chester was an outsized Chesapeake Bay retriever, and Woody Wimberly was the Boss, or maybe I had it wrong and Chester was actually the Boss. Whatever, Chester was pissed and was letting Woody, me, and anyone else within 2 or 3 miles know that the Boss was more than 40 yards away from shore and should come back at least 10 feet.

"Does he do this all the time?" I asked.

"Yeah, all the time. Watch this." Woody waded 10 feet back toward shore. The sound of a soul in torment ceased, and Chester lay down with his head on his front paws, his caramel-colored eyes riveted on the Boss.

"What happens if you sort of sneak back out after a little while? You know, real slow and creepy like."

"Doesn't matter," said Woody. "He's got a damned surveyor's transit in his brain. He knows 50 yards to the inch. He'll just get pissed again."

So, shaking my head over Chester the wonder dog, I left Woody to fish the run between the island and the shore and I headed out for the flats on the far side of the island.

It was one of those magic western days, mid-August, not much wind, hoppers along the banks, and the big, bad rainbows of Henry's Fork in the cruise and crush mode. Just the day for an 8½-foot, 6-weight rod, 5X tippet, and size 14 Henry's Fork Hopper. The trout had turned on to the hoppers the day before when a good wind had sown them over the flats like so many seeds. But today there was no real wind. It didn't matter, though; the trout seemed to be cruising like so many sharks, searching for the hoppers that should have been there but weren't. It was perfect. All you had to do was find a cruiser and put the hopper down in the general direction it was headed, and a big, old white mouth would come up and suck it in.

I awoke that afternoon to a copper sunset, a sphere of reddish gold suspended somewhere between the sky and the water. In my hands I held the last fish of the day, bathed in a luminous mixture of light and water. I have no idea how large it was; it was no bigger than some of the others, certainly no smaller. Everything was great; the world was a fine place.

I waded over and joined Chester and Woody on the bank.

"Nice day," said Woody.

"Definitely a nice day," I answered.

"What were you using?"

"One of Lawson's Hoppers, size 14."

"Great pattern."

"Yeah," I agreed, "definitely a great pattern."

We sat, lost in the river, and watched the sun creeping down behind the mountains to the west. Then a duet of sandhill cranes pierced the stillness with their haunting asthmatic croaking, and the spell was broken.

"Time to go," said Woody.

"Yeah. Let's do it." I rose to my feet, clipped off the hopper, and stuck it in my fly patch.

Woody looked back over his shoulder at the river. "It was a great day," he murmured.

"Yes," I agreed, "a great day." What was I saying? It hadn't been a great day, it had been a stupendous day! It had been the Mother of All Days, it had been a lifetime of days compressed into eight hours, it had been the Day of the Hopper—the Day of the Henry's Fork Hopper. I thanked you silently then, Mike Lawson, and now, years later, I thank you again.

—H. R. S.

Different sizes of both hoppers and crickets may also be used according to what type of water is being covered. In fast, broken-water situations, it's advisable to go to a large pattern, which will float well and can be seen easily. On Virginia's Smith River, a large cricket is very effective when fished through the faster sections, but a smaller pattern is much more productive in the more gentle water. As a matter of fact, there is a local expert on the Smith, Bennie Hunley, who fishes a cricket pattern about 90 percent of the time. Does he do as well as others on this difficult river? You bet he does! As a matter of fact, Bennie probably catches more large fish than any other accomplished angler who is familiar with this water.

Hoppers and crickets are both effective patterns throughout much of the year. You don't have to wait for "hopper time" or "cricket time" to fish them. These patterns can even be successful during major hatches of other flies.

Have you ever met anyone who has gone fishless on Utah's Green River? I haven't. It's a great river to fish if you want to take a whole lot of fish, take big fish, or simply introduce someone to fly fishing and don't want them to get discouraged. Even if they don't catch many fish, they will see plenty of them and will have a lot of fun in the process. I love to fish the Green, but I like to fish it my way, with a small rod, light tippet, and tiny flies. It's a hoot!

The first time I ever fished the Green was with an old friend, Stuart Asahina, and the cicadas were on. It was awesome! Rick Lee, Cliff Rexrode, Stuart, and I were actually yanking the big macramé cord cicada imitations away from fish we thought were too small. At one point we realized we were getting low on cicadas, so I switched to a big, black cricket imitation I had with me (luckily I had about a dozen). No problem! The fish took the cricket as well as the cicada, and I continued to fish nothing but that pattern for the rest of the day.

—H. R. S.

So don't be afraid to use either of these imitations at odd times of the year; they work. They, along with the ant and the beetle, can also be employed as "hatch breakers" on selective fish, particularly when the smaller sizes are used. In short, hopper and cricket patterns are extremely versatile, much more so than the average angler realizes. Different sizes, different colors, different patterns all have a place in the fly box, and at different times and in different places they can really surprise you.

I don't remember exactly what month it was. It was sometime during the summer, prior to what could really be termed "hopper season." It was more than ten years ago, but I remember what happened as though it were yesterday.

The fish, a nice brown of about 14 inches, was holding in a pool formed by two small spring creeks feeding the upper Provo River, not far from Salt Lake City. One of these small spring creeks entered the pool through a large, galvanized drainpipe over which a farmer had built a road to the adjacent field. Stu Asahina was my partner that day, and we stood back from the bank concealed by a stand of willows.

"What's he taking?" Stu whispered.

"I have no idea," I whispered back.

At this point it dawned on me that we always seemed to whisper in situations like this, and I wondered why. The fish couldn't possibly hear us, but it just seemed appropriate under the circumstances.

"What do you have on?" asked Stu.

"An elk-hair caddis."

"Well, you found him, you try him," said Stu.

We stood behind the willows and watched. It wasn't going to be easy. The currents from the two springs met and formed the sort of swirly-twirly wash that you have bad dreams about. Besides that, in order to reach the fish, you had to crouch behind the willows, cast blind, and throw a left curve to get a decent drift.

I hunkered down behind the willows and missed the first couple of casts rather badly but on the third or fourth cast managed to salvage something fairly presentable.

Three casts later, the fish (which had come up to take a look at the first decent drift of the fly) was back on station. It was no secret that the elk-hair caddis wasn't the fly of choice.

"OK, you go for it," I said to Stu.

Stu looked at me over the top of his glasses and gave me a nasty grin. I've seen that grin before; it's more like a smirk. He does it well.

"I know he'll take a little hopper."

"Yeah? Well you might know he's gonna take that hopper, but I know what he's gonna do if he does!" I had it all figured out. But then, so did Stu.

"Yeah," said Stu. "He's gonna blow right up that drainpipe!"

So Stu knotted on this little Henry's Fork Hopper, hunkered down behind the willows, and made a good cast. That little hopper landed about 4 feet in front of the fish, and the second it hit the water the brown went stiff. The hopper made about a foot of headway, and the brown became 3 feet of blurred fish. The instant Stu raised the rod tip, the fish went straight up the pipe and the tippet separated on the sharp edge. I'll bet Stu had that fish on for maybe, just maybe, one second!

We looked at each other and grinned.

"It's nice to call all the shots right every now and then," said Stu.

"Yeah," I agreed, "even if you only fool them. Sometimes landing them isn't that important."

—H. R. S.

We have to this point discussed only the floating patterns, which are familiar to everyone. What about fishing a sinking hopper or cricket pattern? Is there any place for them in the fly box? The answer is a resounding yes. Gary LaFontaine wrote a wonderful chapter testifying to the effectiveness of the sinking hopper in his book *The Dry Fly*, but it has attracted little attention from the general angling public. Likewise, Ed Shenk has spoken on the effectiveness of the sinking cricket, but again most people seem to have passed this pattern by. Well, if anglers do not care to exploit these sinking patterns (or any other sinking terrestrial pattern), we'll just keep our little secrets and continue to chuckle all the way back to the car, even if our wrists ache.

One major problem associated with fishing sinking crickets and hoppers is simply getting them to sink. Sure, you can add a little split shot to your leader, fish a standard floating pattern, and get it under. But they never seem to float correctly when you do this. You *can* catch fish sinking a standard pattern this way, but if you design the fly to float correctly subsurface, you can catch a lot more fish. A much more effective method is to weight your standard fly with just enough lead wire to carry it under *slowly*. You don't want it to streak for the bottom like a size 2 weighted Bitch Creek Nymph. Real hoppers and crickets just don't behave this way. When they go under, they float nicely in the subsurface currents, more or less suspended between the surface and the bottom, and you want your imitation to "suspend" the same way.

If you get caught short, go ahead and add a little weight to the tippet, but experiment with the amount so that it just barely carries the fly under. You want that fly to roll and tumble in the current just like the real thing, not like some block of lead. A drowned, subsurface hopper usually won't make it to the bottom anyway. If it does, you can probably conclude that there were no fish in the neighborhood. Just like any drowned terrestrial, they are easy targets, and most fish are just going to cruise up and suck them in before they sink too far.

Ed Shenk has solved the "suspended orthopteran" problem very nicely by tying his sinking Letort Cricket with ram's wool instead of deer hair. The resulting pattern is extremely realistic underwater. It would be quite easy to modify Shenk's Letort Hopper in the same way.

Another approach would be to use the technique described by Dana Griffin III ("Great Diving Grasshoppers," *American Angler,* May-June 1992). The diving grasshopper, genus *Orchelimum* (which is misspelled as *Orchelinum* in the original article), does indeed seek the safety (?) of water when disturbed, and Griffin's patterns for this hopper are designed to go under. A little modification of the color of his patterns could give us some pretty decent "suspended" imitations of whatever the locally predominant hopper might be. If indeed you do find *Orchelimum* along a streambank in your area, fish the pattern as a sunken *but living* hopper. That is, retrieve it just as though it were swimming underwater, with short jerks to imitate the kicking of the legs.

One last word about sinking hopper and cricket patterns. These are, with the exception of *Orchelimum,* usually dead insects. As such, the legs may play a significant role. On a dead hopper or cricket, the muscles relax, and the legs trail out well behind the body of the insect, more or less dangling limply in the current. So if you are going to design a good "suspended" pattern, keep this in mind and stay away from rigid, unyielding materials for the legs (or at least tie in the material extending backward with no "joint" between the two portions). The muscles that keep the forewings folded over the hindwings also relax, and the hindwings may become exposed. We suggest using a split turkey quill wing case to imitate the forewings, and Krystal Flash or some other synthetic in the appropriate color for the underwings (a combination of pearl and either pink or orange works very nicely).

MAJOR FAMILIES

Family Acrididae: Short-horned Grasshoppers

If you collect grasshoppers along a stream, chances are that the majority will belong to this family. The antennae are typically less than half the length of the body and are described by learned authors as "horn shaped," although it takes a bit of imagination to visualize them as such. The body of these hoppers can be from ½ to 3 inches in length, so some are quite large.

Some of the more common members of this family are the spurthroated grasshoppers, or locusts, which may cause considerable damage to crops; the band-winged grasshoppers, which have brightly colored hind-wings, apparently used to startle predators as the hopper takes flight; and the slant-faced grasshoppers (on which the lower portion of the head is noticeably slanted down and backward), which are usually found adjacent to marshy areas and in wet meadows.

Family Tettigoniidae: Long-horned Grasshoppers
The antennae of hoppers in this family are equal to or longer than the length of the body, which can range from over ½ inch to about 3 inches, hence their common name. Most species are easily recognizable, not only because of the antenna length but also because of the prominent *ovipositors* of the females. These are long, swordlike extensions from the posterior portion of the abdomen that are used to slice through the plant tissues in which the female lays her eggs. The color of these hoppers ranges from brown to bright green, the green color being derived from the chlorophyll of the plants they feed on. As a result, many of the green-colored species are well camouflaged, resembling both in color and form the leaves of these plants. Most species of long-horned grasshoppers are elegant songsters, and the well-known katydids are included in this group.

The cone-headed hoppers, which are easy to recognize with their cone-shaped heads, also belong to this group, and we should warn you about these. They have powerful jaws and can give you a pretty good bite, so handle anything cone-headed with respect! They also come in either brown or green.

It took only a few experiences with cone-heads to teach my cousin and me that they could bite. Once we discovered this marvelous attribute of these little monsters, the door was opened for all sorts of boyish mischief. We would pick them up carefully by the wings, sneak up behind someone, and slap the varmint on their neck, arm, or whatever other part of their anatomy was available. We lost a few friends in the process, but the laughs were probably worth it.

We also found out that you could grab them by the wings, stick a grass stalk up to the jaws, and they would grab hold. A quick jerk on the grass stalk would then decapitate the little bastards. There is nothing like childhood cruelty, unless it's adult cruelty.

—H. R. S.

The meadow grasshoppers are also included in this family. These are small to medium sized (⅔ inch long), usually greenish in color, and common along streambanks and in wet grassy meadows. The previously discussed diving hoppers of the genus *Orchelimum* are also members of this group.

The shield-backed hoppers, which belong to this family, look more like crickets than hoppers. Not only the color (brownish to black) is similar to that of the crickets, but also the general appearance. The majority of these hoppers are western species, and some occasionally cause considerable crop damage. The Mormon cricket (*Anabrus simplex*) can be a serious pest in the Great Plains states, and the coulee cricket (*Peranabrus scabricollis*) can be quite destructive in certain regions of the Pacific Northwest.

Family Gryllidae: Crickets
Eight subfamilies of crickets are found in the United States, but only a few are of interest to the fly fisherman. The ground crickets and the house and field crickets are the two groups for which most imitations are tied. They are so like each other that there is little use in the untrained individual trying to differentiate between the two. In the eastern United States, the most commonly encountered cricket is probably the northern field cricket, *Gryllus pennsylvanicus.* Both the ground crickets and the house and field crickets are common residents in meadows, along roadsides, in the fields along streambanks, in pastures, and in woodlands.

GRASSHOPPER AND CRICKET PATTERNS
It is absolutely impossible to list all of the hopper and cricket patterns that are currently being tied. Many of the new imitations are beautifully done, there is no doubting this, but to try to catalog them would be a Herculean effort. Many of the new patterns are also extremely effective, but do they really offer any advantages over the older tried and true patterns? Do they catch more fish? Do they catch bigger fish? Do they have

the same effectiveness but take half the time to tie? Are they more durable? We considered all of these questions in compiling this list.

We have chosen to honor the classics, for the most part, and to include only those newer patterns with which we are familiar and that seem to offer some advantage, use certain unique or new materials, or offer promise for the future. With all respect to the many talented tiers out there, we apologize if your pattern is not included in the following section. There are a lot of you, and in many instances we are not familiar with what you are doing. We are also unable to read all of the current articles, particularly those included in regional publications.

As far as tying directions, we believe that for the classic patterns no directions are necessary. These have been published time after time, and most good tying manuals give adequate directions. In the case of new patterns, we will refer you to the publication in which the tying directions appear. Directions will be given only for our previously unpublished patterns.

A word of warning: Anytime you coat a section of quill or a feather of any type with something like thinned Goop, Flexament, or any other material in which an organic solvent is present, be careful. The fumes of all of these solvents are toxic (some much more so than others) and can cause all sorts of problems! Work in a well-ventilated area, particularly if you are tying lots of patterns in which this technique is utilized. Not only can breathing the solvent vapors be dangerous, but absorption of the solvent through the skin of the fingers is also hazardous.

Hoppers

SHENK'S LETORT HOPPER

This is the obvious place to start. The development of this pattern by Ed Shenk predates Schwiebert's Letort Hopper and to us represents the beginning of the modern hopper patterns.

Hook: #10 to #18, Mustad 9671, 9672.

Body: Yellow, cream, tan, or orange spun fur.

Wing: Section of mottled tan turkey feather, folded and tied flat; tip trimmed to a broad V. Tan poly yarn with dark markings from a felt-tip pen can also be used.

Hackle: Swept-back tips of tan deer hair from the head, trimmed on the underside.

Head: Spun tan deer hair.

Shenk does not specify the color or type of thread in the article from which this materials list is taken (*Fly Fisherman,* September 1986). Anytime you are going to spin deer hair, however, Monocord is better than 6/0 thread.

SCHWIEBERT'S LETORT HOPPER (ERNIE SCHWIEBERT)

Hook: #6 to #16, 2XL fine wire; Mustad 94831, TMC 5212, or Orvis 1638.

Thread: 3/0 waxed yellow monocord.

Body: Yellow wool dubbing (for a more modern dressing, use poly).

Wing: Brown mottled turkey barbs, pretreated with Flexament.

Legs: Brown deer body hair.

Head: Trimmed deer hair with the tips projecting backward.

JOE'S HOPPER

Hook: #6 to #18, 2XL fine wire, Mustad 94831, TMC 5212, or Orvis 1638.

Thread: Black or brown 3/0 waxed Monocord.

Tail: Small clump of red deer hair or thin section of barbs from a red goose feather.

Body: Yellow yarn or any type of yellow dubbing.

Rib: Ginger or brown hackle.

Wing: Section of mottled turkey wing barbs pretreated with Flexament.

Hackle: One grizzly and one brown or ginger hackle.

DAVE'S HOPPER (DAVE WHITLOCK)

Hook: 2XL or 3XL, regular or extra-fine wire. For 2XL fine
wire hooks, Mustad 94831, Tiemco 5212, or Orvis 1638.
For 3XL hooks, Mustad 9672, Tiemco 5263, or Orvis
1526.

Thread: 6/0 nylon or Monocord in either tan or yellow.

Tail: Red deer hair.

Body: Yellow poly yarn. Yellow is designated for the original
pattern, but you should try these with bodies tied to match
the color of the predominant hopper along any stream.

Rib: Grizzly or brown hackle.

Underwing: A section of turkey or peacock wing quill that has
been treated with either Flexament or thinned Goop.

Legs: Knotted turkey, pheasant, or peacock quill fibers.

Head: Natural deer hair, spun and trimmed to shape with
some tips extending backward.

Dave's Hopper has an interesting history. Dave Whitlock designed
the original pattern as a hybrid between a Muddler Minnow and the old
Joe's Hopper. In its original form, it was tied without legs, and it was the
suggestion of master tier Jay Buchner of Jackson, Wyoming, to add legs
to it. As a result, the legged pattern was for a time (and still is by some)
termed the Jay-Dave's Hopper. In most tying manuals and texts, however,
the original designation of Dave's Hopper is more often used.

WHIT'S HOPPER (DAVE WHITLOCK)

Hook: Same as for Dave's Hopper.

Thread: Same as for Dave's Hopper.

Body: Elk or coarse deer hair. Again, yellow is indicated for
the original, but do not be afraid to use other colors.

Rib: Brass or stainless-steel wire.

Underwing: Gray or pale yellow deer hair.

Overwing: Segment of turkey barbs, pretreated with Flexament
or thinned Goop.

Legs: Knotted golden brown grizzly saddle hackle.
Head: Bullet-style head formed with yellow and brown deer or
elk hair.
Antennae: Brown hackle stems.
For added durability, it is recommended that both the head and body
also be coated with either thinned Goop or Flexament.

HENRY'S FORK HOPPER (MIKE LAWSON)

Hook: #8 to #14, TMC 5212 2XL or equivalent.
Thread: Yellow 3/0 waxed Monocord.
Abdomen: Cream or yellow elk hair.
Head and thorax: Bullet-style, natural light gray elk hair.
Underwing: Yellow or olive elk hair.
Overwing: Mottled hen saddle feather or pheasant rump
feather pretreated with Flexament.

AL'S HAIR HOPPER (AL TROTH)

It's very obvious that Al Troth came up with the design for this hopper
using his very successful elk-hair caddis as a base. It's an interesting tie in
that it incorporates certain elements of the Letort Hopper and the Elk-
hair Caddis into a single entity. If it works as well as either of these, it's a
hell of a pattern! For some reason, however, this pattern does not seem to
have caught on as well as some of the others.
Hook: #10 to #16, Mustad 94840, TMC 9300, or Orvis 1876.
Thread: Yellow 3/0 waxed Monocord.
Body: Either the long hair from the base of a yellow-dyed
buck tail or long, cream elk rump dyed yellow.
Wing: Natural-color hair from white-tailed deer flank.
Legs: Red goose biots.

AUSSIE HOPPER, A.K.A. LATEX HOPPER
(BRUCE WHALEN)

Hook: #8 to #14, Mustad 3906, 9671, or equivalents.

Thread: Yellow Monocord.
Body: Yellow-dyed deer hair.
Ribbing: Latex strip.
Wing: Golden pheasant tippet.
Topping: Natural deer hair.
Head: Natural deer hair, modified bullet shape.

Since many of the most common hoppers have brightly colored underwings and are strong fliers, we have included this and the following pattern, both originated by Australian tiers. Although neither has become extremely popular, they are both highly effective when hoppers have matured and become fully winged. Those of you who have not tried them, particularly in the late summer when large winged hoppers are common, have been missing out! Complete tying directions for both of these Australian patterns are given in Jack Dennis's *Western Trout Fly Tying Manual,* Volume II.

TEVAROVICH HOPPER (DAN TEVAROVICH)

Hook: #6 to #12, Mustad 79580, 9672.
Thread: Yellow waxed Monocord.
Underbody: Yellow art foam.
Body: Chartreuse dubbing.
Wing: Golden pheasant tippets and sections of turkey barbs.
Legs: Trimmed and knotted brown hackle stems.
Head: Natural gray deer hair, spun and trimmed with tips
    extending backward.

GARTSIDE PHEASANT HOPPER (JACK GARTSIDE)

Hook: #8 to #14, Mustad 94831, 9671, or equivalents.
Thread: Yellow Monocord.
Body: Polypro yarn, yellow, gray, olive, tan, orange.
Ribbing: Badger or furnace hackle.
Tail: Dark moose hair.
Wing: Pheasant back feather.
Underwing: Deer hair, color to match that of body.

Hackle: Deer-hair tips extending back from head.

Head: Deer body hair, flared and trimmed.

BING'S HOPPER (BING LEMPKE)

Many of the current younger crop of fly fishermen have no idea who Bing Lempke was. For your information, Bing Lempke was Mr. Henry's Fork. When _Time_ magazine did an article on the Henry's Fork back in the early 1980s, Bing occupied a prominent position in the text, and even though his hopper pattern has not been overly popular, it should certainly be included for its historical interest. Bing's most interesting ties are without question the minuscule extended-body mayfly patterns, often tied on a #32 hook. They are indeed artistry, having gone far beyond the simple craft of fly tying! If you ever get the opportunity to visit Henry's Fork, stop in at Mike Lawson's fly shop and ask to see some of Bing's work. Mike used to have a little glass tube with Bing's flies on display near the cash register. If they aren't out, get on your knees and beg a little—it's worth it.

Hook: #6 to #12, Mustad 9672.

Thread: Yellow Monocord.

Body: Yellow or tan art foam.

Underbody: Yellow art foam, 30-pound test monofilament.

Ribbing: Yellow floss.

Wing: Bleached barred turkey quill or natural mottled turkey quill.

Underwing: Yellow or brown deer hair.

Hackle: Ginger.

Head: Yellow or chartreuse deer hair.

For complete tying directions, see Jack Dennis's _Western Trout Fly Tying Manual,_ Volume II.

NYMPH HOPPER (GERALD ALMY)

Hook: Mustad 94833, TMC 5210, Orvis 1523.

Thread: 6/0, color at tier's discretion.

Abdomen: Dubbed rabbit fur, color to match that of thread.

Head and thorax: Dubbed rabbit fur, color to match that of abdomen.

Wings: Natural deer body hair, separated into two bunches on either side of the abdomen.

For complete tying directions, see Gerald Almy's *Tying and Fishing Terrestrials.*

DIVING GRASSHOPPER (DANA GRIFFIN III)

Why are we including this pattern? For a number of reasons. Members of the genus *Orchelimum* are fairly common, they do exhibit some peculiar behavior, and they fall into the category of sinking terrestrials, which we like to fish. Any other reasons? Well, as a matter of fact, yes. It's a classic example of someone who can't make up his mind! The materials list is very much like someone at a fancy restaurant trying to pick out something from the dessert cart! Let's see, I think I'll try the German chocolate cake with the raspberrry icing. No, let me have the apple strudel with a bit of vanilla ice cream. No, wait I think I'll take the pomegranate flambé with the pistachio cream sauce. Please, find something that works and stick with it! Why offer all of the alternatives if one material works just fine?

Hook: #2 to #6, Mustad 9672 or equivalent.

Thread: 6/0, tan or brown.

Weight: lead wire, .03-inch diameter.

Eyes: Medium-size gold bead chain.

Tail: Yellow or orange quill fibers, bucktail, rabbit fur, or yarn.

Wing: Tan bucktail, calf tail, or rattan.

Rib: Fine gold or copper wire or monofilament.

Body: Green floss, yarn, or yarn dubbing.

Legs: Green saddle hackles or dyed rubber bands or Evasote strips.

Head: Tan floss, yarn, yarn dubbing, or wool.

Complete tying directions are given in Griffin's article, "Great Diving Grasshoppers," *American Angler,* May-June 1992.

RAINY'S HOPPER (RAINY RIDING)

Rainy Riding of Logan, Utah, is marketing a unique round Float

Foam, which is available in three sizes. Hoppers tied with this foam are durable, float well, and are extremely easy to see, as they float somewhat higher than the standard hopper patterns. Whether this high-floating quality is desirable is a debatable point. Hoppers float low in the water, as many individuals have reported, so the high-floating Rainy's Hopper may be somewhat less effective. Can this be proven? Well, not really, so we wouldn't worry too much about it!

Rainy markets her foam through various fly shops or directly. She also supplies directions for tying both the hoppers and other patterns with each package of foam. For more information, contact her at the following address: Rainy Riding, 600 North 100 East, Logan, UT 84321.

Mike Howard, one of the proprietors of the Spinner Fall Fly Shop in Salt Lake City, touts this pattern highly. It must be effective, since Mike says he orders twenty dozen every year and sells them out with no problem!

The following is taken from the directions included with each package of Float Foam.

Hook: #4 to #8, Mustad 9672.

Thread: Yellow, 3/0.

Body: Yellow Float Foam (or white, colored with permanent marker).

Ribbing: Large, brown neck hackle palmered down the body and trimmed short. (The tail and ribbing need to be tied in at hook shank before applying the body material).

Tail: Dyed crimson red hackle fibers.

Underwing: Pearlescent Krystal Flash.

Overwing: Red fox squirrel tail.

Head: Lightly dyed yellow deer hair tied in bullet-head style, or spun deer hair trimmed to square head.

Legs: Round, yellow rubber hackle tied in at each side when doing bullet-head style, or knotted lightly dyed yellow turkey round quill for trimmed deer-hair method.

MOSER GRASSHOPPER (ROMAN MOSER)

Wow! This is a pretty pattern. It appears to be one of those beautifully simple but effective patterns, and we refer you to the article by Moser in the May 1986 issue of *Fly Fisherman* for a peek at it. The materials list is taken directly from the article.

Hook: VMC 9283 B.

Thread: Galaxy Wonder Thread or prewaxed 6/0.

Thorax: Poly-Syndub-Seal.

Abdomen: Polycelon.

Body hackle: First-grade cock hackle.

Wing: Sedge Wing or Muddler Wing.

Head: Polycelon and polypropylene yarn strip.

Legs: Two primary wing quills.

If you cannot locate these materials in your local shop, they all are distributed by Umpqua Feather Merchants, P.O. Box 700, Glide, OR 97443. Contact Umpqua for the name of the nearest dealer. Some of the materials might be available through the Orvis Company as well.

No colors are specified for the materials, but this should present no problem. Just use the colors of the predominant hopper along your favorite stream!

ROD'S HOPPER (ROD YERGER)

These are beautiful little guys. Tied with a balsa core for the body and an overlay of deer hair to form an extended body, they are simplistic jewels. They are also the only hoppers we know of with painted eyes. Whether the eyes make the pattern any more effective is food for thought, but hoppers do have prominent eyes, and their inclusion might make a real difference.

The balsa cylinders for the body are available directly from Rod in two different sizes (⅛-inch and ³⁄₃₂-inch diameter). Contact him at P.O. Box 294, Lawrence, PA 15055.

Rod is quick to point out that his hoppers are not as durable as others— six to twelve fish per hopper seems to be the general case, but if those are good fish, anyone should be satisfied with that.

For complete tying directions, see Rod's "Hoppers and Crickets," in *American Angler and Fly Tyer,* Summer 1990. The following materials list is for the "natural" hopper. Different colors can be used for the predominant hopper in your area.

Hook: Mustad 94840 or equivalent.
Thread: Prewaxed 6/0, cream.
Body core: Shaped balsa cylinder.
Body: Natural deer body hair.
Wing: Mottled turkey quill section.
Rear legs: Trimmed grizzly hackle stems.
Front legs: Light moose body hair.
Antennae: Dark moose body hair.
Eyes: Red lacquer.

FOAM GRASSHOPPER (LARRY TULLIS)

All we can do for this one is to refer you to the article by Larry Tullis, "Foam Flies," published in the March 1993 issue of *Fly Fisherman*. There are some nice pictures of these hoppers and some very basic information, but no details are given as to materials or tying procedures. Too bad, they look very nice. Any good tier can probably figure out what needs to be done, however.

STEEVES' MINI-HOPPER (HARRISON STEEVES)

We have fished this pattern extensively, and it may offer some distinct advantages. It's very simple to tie, can be tied in about any color of the spectrum, floats low in the surface, is extremely durable, has great hooking properties, and can be fished as either a floating or sinking pattern with no modification. It borrows from many other patterns (after all, there is very little that's totally new) but uses some materials and techniques that are rather interesting. The Cinnamon Hopper in Stewart and Allen's *Flies for Trout* is a color variation of this basic pattern.

Hook: Mustad 94831, Orvis 1638, TMC 5212.
Thread: 6/0, color to match body of hopper.
Hook shank wrap: Kreinik $\frac{1}{16}$-inch flat ribbon, color to match body.
Body: Plastic canvas yarn, color of choice, furled to form body.
Hindwing: Rusty brown elk hair.
Forewing: Pretreated section of mottled turkey wing or tail quill.

Head: Natural deer hair, tied bullet-style.

Tying Directions

1. Wrap shank of hook with tying thread to the rear of the shank and tie in the hook shank wrap. Wrap thread forward to a point about ⅛ inch back from the eye of the hook.

2. Wrap the Kreinik material forward, tie off ⅛ inch back from the hook eye, and remove the excess.

3. To form the furled body, tightly twist a 3-inch piece of the plastic canvas yarn. Place the twisted piece of yarn over the shank of the hook, and pull it forward so that it slips over the eye and off the shank. The yarn will twist up on itself very nicely to form the furled body.

4. Tie in the furled body about ⅛ inch back from the eye of the hook. Fifteen to twenty thread wraps work nicely. Trim the forward-extending portion at an angle, and tie down to form a tapered front.

5. Tie in the hindwing material with the tips extending about ¼ inch past the furled body. Trim away the forward-projecting excess.

6. Tie in the turkey barb forewing, and trim to the same length as the body.

7. To form the bullet head, select a bunch of deer hair and stack it so that the tips are even. Trim the butts even, and push the butts over the eye of the hook. Tie the butts down at the same point at which the forewing was tied down. Use three or four loose wraps initially, and then tighten down on the thread. Continue tightly wrapping the thread forward to the eye of the hook. On the last few thread wraps, release the deer hair and it will flare nicely away from the shank.

8. Wrap the thread backward about ¼ inch, fold the forward-projecting deer-hair tips backward, and tie them down to form the bullet head. Trim away the backward-extending deer-hair tips below the hook shank. Whip-finish and remove thread.

9. For greater durability, coat the head liberally with Flexament.

If you like legs on your hoppers, then by all means add them to the above materials list, although we don't think they are really necessary. Either knotted turkey barbs or trimmed hackle stems work well.

Plastic canvas yarn is available from Rose's, Wal-Mart, Kmart, most craft shops, and many other sources. It comes in more colors than you

1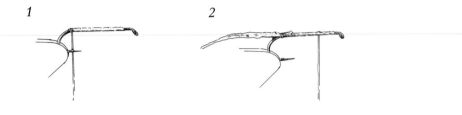

2

5

6

9

10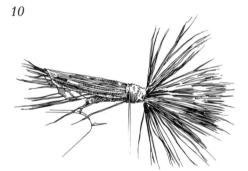

STEEVES' MINI-HOPPER

3

4

7

8

11

STEEVES' MINI-HOPPER

will ever be able to use, but at about fifty cents for 10 yards you won't go broke. You can also use it for many other applications, such as extended-body damsel flies, dragonflies, and Green and Brown Drakes; nymph wing cases; or as a substitute for Z-lon. In short, it's pretty versatile material!

One other thing about plastic canvas yarn. It comes standard as two strands and is used in this form for tying both the Steeves' Mini-hopper and Mini-cricket. If you separate the two strands, you can tie really small stuff with it, using the same furling technique. It even makes great little bodies for caddis!

If you have tied the Mini-hopper correctly, you will notice that everything is tied in at the front of the hook and that the hook hangs down and away from the body at an angle of 15 to 20 degrees. This gives the pattern superb hooking qualities. The plastic canvas yarn is virtually indestructible, and the body will last forever. The first thing to tear up on this fly will be the deer-hair head, and if that gets frizzed up a bit, it certainly does not take anything away from the fly's effectiveness.

If you want to fish the Mini-hopper dry, use a good paste floatant and grease it up. It floats beautifully and naturally, deep in the surface. If it begins to sink, squeeze the water out of the furled body (use a paper towel, chamois, shirttail, or whatever), dress it again, and go for it. To fish the Mini-hopper, wet-treat it with something like Gerke's Xink or Orvis Mud, and it will drop down nicely under the surface to nestle naturally in the subsurface currents. And, we might add, it's a killer when fished wet!

Crickets

SHENK'S LETORT CRICKET (ED SHENK)

Hook: #10 to #18, Mustad 9671, 9672.
Body: Spun black fur dubbing.
Wing: Section of black-dyed goose barbs, tied flat and
    trimmed in a broad V, or black poly yarn.
Hackle: Black-dyed deer hair tips from the head hair.
Head: Spun and trimmed black deer hair.

HENRY'S FORK CRICKET (MIKE LAWSON)

Hook: #12 to #16, TMC 5212 2XL or equivalent.
Thread: Black 3/0 waxed Monocord.
Abdomen: Brown elk hair.
Head and thorax: Bullet-style, black elk hair.
Underwing: Brown elk hair.
Overwing: Black hen saddle feather pretreated with Flexament.

SHENK'S SINKING LETORT CRICKET (ED SHENK)

This cricket pattern is tied exactly the same as the original Letort Cricket, but black-dyed wool is used in the place of deer hair for forming the head and hackle. This is a deadly pattern, as are most sunken terrestrials. If you haven't fished it, you have missed out on something! But don't overdo it. As Ed Shenk advises, keep it for an ace in the hole.

ROD'S CRICKET (ROD YERGER)

According to Rod Yerger (*American Angler,* Summer 1990), "An effective cricket imitation can be made following the basic hopper procedures and substituting all black materials. The cricket wing should be one half of the body length to give the proper silhouette. Instead of coating the completed body with vinyl cement, I use thin black lacquer or hobby paint. I make most of my crickets black but I've also made some in various shades of brown."

JIM'S CRICKET (JIM CHESTNEY)

Hook: #8 to #12, Mustad 9671.
Thread: Black Monocord.
Body: Black deer hair.
Legs: Two sections from the short side of a black-dyed goose
   feather.
Wing: The directions as published called for black goose quill,

but there seems to be a mistake here. In the illustrations, the wing is black Swiss straw.

Head and collar: Black deer hair.

For complete tying directions see Jack Dennis's *Western Trout Fly Tying Manual,* Volume II.

STEEVES' MINI-CRICKET (HARRISON STEEVES)

Hook: #12 to #14, Mustad 94833 or equivalent.

Thread: 6/0 black.

Hook shank wrap: Kreinik, beetle black, ¹⁄₁₆-inch flat ribbon, #005HL.

Body: Black plastic canvas yarn, furled.

Wing: Black or peacock Krystal Flash.

Head and collar: Black deer hair tied bullet-style.

Tying directions for the Mini-cricket are the same as for the Steeves' Mini-hopper.

JIMMINY CRICKET (DAVID J. LUCCA)

There are a number of foam-bodied cricket patterns that we know exist, and probably many more of which we are unaware. This and the following two patterns are a few that have appeared in print.

Hook: Mustad 94840 or equivalent.

Body: Black polycelon (⅛ inch thick).

Head: Black polycelon (⅛ inch thick).

Wing: Dark brown mottled turkey tail slip, and black-dyed deer or elk hair.

Legs: Trimmed black hackle stems or knotted turkey quills.

Antennae: Black-dyed monofilament.

Eyes: Lacquer.

For complete tying directions, see Lucca's article "Jimminy Cricket" in the May 1990 issue of *Fly Fisherman.*

FOAM CRICKET

This pattern appeared in the November–December 1992 issue of

American Angler. No directions are given for tying this cricket, but it is so simple that you won't have any trouble figuring it out.

Hook: Tiemco 100.

Thread: 6/0, black.

Body: Black closed cell foam, preshaped or cut from Evasote sheets.

Legs: Black goose biots swept to rear and black Krystal Flash.

Antennae: Black Krystal Flash.

Head: Black closed cell foam.

RAINY'S CRICKET (RAINY RIDING)

This materials list is taken directly from the nifty little card included in each of Rainy's Float Foam packages.

Hook: Mustad 9672.

Thread: Black 3/0.

Ribbing: Large, black neck hackle palmered down the body and trimmed short. (Tie in hackle on hook shank before applying the body material.)

Body: Small-diameter Float Foam for #12 to #14 hook. Medium-diameter Float Foam for #6 to #8 hook. Large diameter Float Foam for #2 to #6 hook.

Underwing: Black Krystal Flash.

Overwing: Black and white calf tail.

Head: Black-dyed deer hair tied in the bullet-head style, or spun deer hair trimmed to square head.

Legs: Black rubber hackle tied in at each side when doing the bullet-head style, or knotted black-dyed turkey barb sections for trimmed deer-hair head method.

Well, there you have it! These certainly are not all of the patterns available for hoppers and crickets, but if you can't find one you like in this list, then you're going to have to sit down at the vise and get busy. Again, if we have excluded your favorite pattern, we apologize.

9

Order Lepidoptera: Moths and Butterflies

WITH MORE THAN 11,000 species of moths and butterflies in the United States and Canada, the lepidopterans make up a very significant population of terrestrial insects. This group of insects is of extreme economic importance for a variety of reasons. Crop destruction by the larvae (for the most part plant eaters) causes millions of dollars worth of damage every year. Even harvested crops, such as stored cereal grains, can be destroyed by larval infestations of certain species of Lepidoptera. Woolen goods and rugs, as well as the fly tier's stored hoard of fur and feathers, can be the target of other larvae. Forested areas of certain portions of the eastern United States are currently under attack by larvae of the gypsy moth, which are causing tremendous economic damage to these areas, particularly to the timber industry. Gypsy moth larvae are also of great concern to ecologists, since the total defoliation in certain areas is extremely detrimental to local ecosystems, trout waters included! On the other hand, many adult lepidopterans are sought out by avid collectors, and unbelievable prices are paid for rare and exotic species. Wings of adults have even been incorporated into various works of art, some of which are themselves rather pricey.

Where trout are concerned, lepidopterans occasionally represent a very important food item but one that in most instances would be considered unreliable. On certain occasions, however, large numbers of the larval forms of these insects may present the fisherman with a few days (or even weeks) of unsurpassed pleasure!

The adult forms of these insects are certainly familiar to everyone. These airborne rainbows are not easy to ignore, but in actuality it is not these brightly painted adults that present the fisherman with unforgettable angling opportunities. It is, instead, the larvae, or caterpillars, that are most important in the trout's diet. This is unique! In none of the other orders of terrestrial insects do the larvae play a terribly significant role as a dietary item. OK, there may be a very, very few exceptions or isolated instances (sawfly larvae, for example), but on a day-to-day basis they are not too important. Why is this different with lepidopterans?

First of all, adult moths and butterflies often occur in huge numbers. Huge numbers of adults mean even huger numbers of larvae. There are in actuality many more larvae produced than will ever grow into adults. Many of the larvae fall victim to predators (birds and other insects, which either feed directly on them or parasitize them) or to bacterial or fungal diseases. So if you see large numbers of adult lepidopterans flitting about a stream, it is safe to assume that at one point there were huge numbers of larvae present somewhere. Somewhere! That's the key word, and that somewhere is more often than not right in the vegetation along, or at least near, the stream.

It is not only the numbers but also the habits of the larvae of certain species of lepidopterans that may be a contributing factor to their importance in the trout's diet. While many larval lepidopterans are relatively solitary and go about their business alone, others form large colonies. In many instances, the shelters of certain of these colonial larvae are readily visible as tentlike, silken nests in the branches of trees. If you encounter such a structure along a stream, it is well worth investigating. The members of these colonies leave the shelter during the day to feed in the branches of the tree. They are then at the mercy of wind, rainstorms, predators, and ultimately trout if they happen to lose their footing. Those that make it through the day return to the nest for the night. Others, such as the larvae of the gypsy moth, construct no shelter but live in huge colonies among the leaves and branches.

Other larvae are not so visible as the preceding examples but may nevertheless be present in sufficient numbers to provide trout fodder. The inchworms, or measuringworms, are good examples. Anglers frequently see members of this group suspended over the surface of a stream by a silken thread. Cankerworms (a type of inchworm) may occur in considerable numbers, in which case defoliation of the tree is common. In short, many larval lepidopterans are encountered in streamside situations, and fly fishermen should be on the lookout for them. After all, if many trout feed opportunistically, why should not fly fishermen fish in the same manner?

Do adult lepidopterans present a viable food source for trout? That's a question worth asking. Gerald Almy makes the statement that "most anglers have seen trout leaping out of the water to catch a cabbage or sulphur butterfly fluttering low over the water." Have you?

I frankly don't have any idea how important adult lepidopterans may be in a trout's diet. I have never observed what Almy describes, and I've been fly fishing for more than forty years. But I am sure that no self-respecting trout will pass up an easy meal, and for that reason alone I'm sure they eat adult lepidopterans. On many mountain streams, there are relatively few good caddis hatches. Be that as it may, I have had great success on dry caddis patterns, particularly the lighter-colored ones. On these streams, I have often shaken the streamside vegetation to see what could be dislodged and have been rewarded by a swarm of smallish moths. Most of these have been light colored. I cannot help but think that sufficient numbers of these find their way into the stream and provide an easy source of food. A cream-colored elk-hair caddis is a superb match!

—H. R. S.

What we have here is a group of insects in which the adult may occasionally flounder into a stream and be eaten. On the other hand, the larvae, because of their habits and their numbers, may frequently (although transiently) represent an important food item and should be treated as such.

MOTHS AND BUTTERFLIES— WHAT'S THE DIFFERENCE?

The lepidopterans were once divided into two suborders, the Heterocera (moths) and the Rhopalocera (butterflies), on the basis of certain anatomical differences, the major factor being characteristics of the antennae: Moths were described as having feathery antennae and butterflies as having slender antennae, usually with a "knobbed" tip. This is not the case today, however. The current system of classification divides the order into five suborders, with various superfamilies included in each. In science, things are seldom as simplistic as they may initially appear to be. What this means to the fly fisherman is simply that you can't just eyeball one of the lepidopterans and immediately call it a moth or a butterfly. Does it really make any difference to most of us? Probably not, and we likely will continue to call those with feathery antennae moths and those with slender, clubbed antennae butterflies.

As far as their development is concerned, both moths and butterflies exhibit what is termed complete metamorphosis: The larvae enter a pupal stage and emerge as fully formed adults. Many species form an elaborate silken cocoon in which the pupal stage is protected during this transformation. Others form a very simple cocoon, and still others build no cocoon at all. As a rule of thumb, many moths construct silken cocoons, while most of the butterflies do not. The developing pupae of butterflies, termed chrysalids (chrysalis in the singular), frequently appear as rather medieval-looking armored cases attached to twigs.

DESIGNING LEPIDOPTERA IMITATIONS

Because of the large size of many of the adult moths and butterflies, there are relatively few patterns on the market. If you really feel a crying need to tie up a few of these, we would recommend nothing more than a hair-

winged and hair-bodied bass bug in the color or colors of choice. The only problem with flies this size is that you are going to have to rethink your terminal gear. A large-size hair-bodied bug on your 6½-foot, 3-weight rod is not going to be very pleasant to cast. Likewise, fragile tippets are going to be useless, and you will have to go to something like 2X or 3X. But if you're convinced that there's a night-feeding brown in your favorite stream that is just aching to chomp down on a size 6 white moth, our advice is to go for it. What have you got to lose?

What about the smaller members of this group? An elk-hair caddis, an Irresistible, or a Wulff pattern can each do a very good job of imitating the smaller butterflies and moths, and we have had excellent luck with all. They seem to be particularly productive on mountain streams where small moths may represent an integral and necessary part of the diet. Besides, many of these smaller streams are located in heavily wooded terrain, where the light along the stream is usually rather dim, and you can actually see these flies! Do the fish really think they are moths or butterflies? Who cares! In the long run what matters is whether the fish takes the fly, not whether it can identify the genus and species.

Lepidopteran larvae, on the other hand, present a different challenge. Take gypsy moths, for example. Here you get into almost a hatch situation. The larvae can be so numerous that unless you have something that is a fairly good approximation, you could go hitless into the ninth inning. Also, gypsy moth larvae must sometimes even be matched to a specific size range. In regions where these are prevalent and trout feed on them, it is reported that the trout have a real preference for the smaller members of the population. We do not know why—perhaps the larger ones become distasteful or uncomfortable to swallow (they do get pretty hairy!).

I have never fished a gypsy moth caterpillar imitation, although the opportunity has presented itself. In June 1990, Cliff Rexrode and I were camped along the West Branch of the Delaware, and there was a large population of gypsy moth larvae in certain areas along the river. You could lie awake at night and listen to the "frass" rain down on the tent. "Frass," by the way, is the foresters' word for excrement. We never listened to it for very long, though. Fishing from dawn to dark (topped off by a late-night sandwich washed down with a few cold beers) usually puts you away in about two minutes. But we sure knew they were there—each morning there would be quite a few of the nasty-looking larvae hanging on to the tent, and the amount of "frass" on the tent roof was phenomenal. I think Cliff tried an imitation a few times, but I'm not sure. It was just that there was so much other insect life about that it seemed to be a waste of time. Who wants to fish a caterpillar when there are blizzard hatches of sulphurs, olives, and caddis coming off? Maybe I missed a great opportunity, but I don't think so.

—H. R. S.

Larvae of other lepidopteran species may also be quite prevalent in specific trees along trout streams but not along the stream in general. It might be well worth the angler's time to tie more or less specific imitations for some of these. Any tree with tent caterpillars is going to supply a few to the stream at some point, if the branches extend over the water. If you find one of these potential delicatessens along the water, it's probably worthwhile to fish an appropriate imitation along the water below it, even if no fish are rising. The caterpillars are not going to be constantly raining down on the water, but every now and then one falls. When it does it could well disappear into a suckhole the size of a washtub. It would be very nice to have some imitations in the fly box when this occurs.

In those cases where an imitation caterpillar seems called for, we have the professional tier's dream. The patterns are the epitome of simplicity. One of the oldest, simplest, and probably most effective patterns is the Woolly Worm fished dry. The body of this pattern does tend to get a little waterlogged, but that problem is easily solved by substituting closed cell foam for chenille. Hackle alone produces a highly effective floating caterpillar that we've used with great success. Other floating patterns have been designed with bodies of cork, feather shafts, balsa wood, and deer hair. We feel, however, that the new closed cell foams (polycelon) produce such realistic and lifelike bodies that there is really no reason to fool around with anything else. If you like fiddling around with wood and cork or even wing quills, fine, but foam is really an unbeatable material. It is available in either flat sheets or round "ropes" and in a variety of colors. Rainy Riding of Logan, Utah, currently markets one of the nicer round forms of this material, which should prove highly useful for forming caterpillar bodies.

A few last words about lepidopteran larvae. Many of them are rather frightening looking and tend to intimidate those few fly fishermen who would like to pick them up and take a closer look. This avoidance was probably initiated by our parents. How many of you were told not to pick that thing up because it would sting you or make you itch? Well, the fact is that very few can actually harm you by stinging you with the body "hairs," but being able to pick out which ones is another story! The saddleback caterpillar (*Sibine stimulea*) can induce severe skin irritation, so watch out for this one. These larvae are about 1 inch long, green in the middle and brown at each end, and have a brown saddle-shaped patch edged with white on the back. It's hard to misidentify this critter! Those hairs that are present are more like bristles and can do a good bit of damage. Even worse are the larvae of the flannel moths. One of these (*Lagoa crispata*) is very common in the eastern United States. If in doubt, collect any of the unknown "hairy" larvae using a pair of tweezers, or induce one of your fishing partners to pick it up for you.

Other larvae will give off an unpleasant odor when handled, and some are poisonous, but only if eaten. We don't think there is too much for fly fishermen to worry about in the latter instance. One species with toxic larvae is the common monarch butterfly. This larva feeds on milkweed and retains the toxins of the plant (cardiac glycosides) in the tissues of the body. Any predator consuming one of these is in for a very unpleasant experience. It probably won't kill them, but it's going to make them feel very ill. If a trout eats one will it make it sick? If so, will it never take another one? Birds learn not to eat them, but birds are a great deal smarter than trout. In the long run, there are probably very few of these that wind up in trout streams, and those that do will probably be snatched up by a fish. So what if it makes them sick? It may happen only once a summer, and the trout isn't going to remember it for very long. If you have a big, old fat black, yellow, and white banded caterpillar imitation in your box, then use it! There's no telling what might happen.

COMMON FAMILIES OF LEPIDOPTERA

Only those families that might be of importance to the fly fisherman are included here.

Family Geometridae: Inchworms or Measuringworms

This is a large and diverse group (more than 1,400 species in the United States and Canada) that contains the familiar inchworms, or measuringworms, which are of prime importance to fly fishermen. They are often seen dangling from the streamside foliage, suspended by a silken cord. The "dapping" technique of fly presentation lends itself well to fishing an imitation of these larvae, provided the angler is able to work himself into an advantageous position. These larvae are of variable size and coloration and usually have no hairs (setae). Imitations should be tied accordingly. Both floating and sinking imitations have proved extremely effective, and every terrestrial fisherman should have a good assortment in his box.

In some instances, infestations of larvae of certain members of this group may cause severe defoliation. Cankerworms, for example, may seriously damage deciduous trees, and the hemlock looper (*Lambdina fiscellaria*) may frequently do the same to hemlocks as well as other conifers.

Family Lasiocampidae: Tent Caterpillars
The social nature and habits of the larvae of these moths may frequently put them in the position of becoming trout fodder. Most of the tent caterpillars appear in the early spring, form large social groups, and spin a silken communal "tent" in which the community lives. The tent is frequently formed in the crotch of branches of the infested tree. At intervals the larvae emerge from these tents to feed, during which time, if the tree overhangs a stream, a few unlucky ones will undoubtedly wind up in the water. The larvae of the common American tent caterpillar moth (*Malacosoma americanum*) is probably the most frequently encountered and can occur in such large numbers that the infested tree is sometimes entirely defoliated. In some instances trees are even killed. The larvae of some species are quite hairy, but others are smooth, and it may be in the angler's interest to take a close look in order to match the imitation to the natural.

Family Lymantridae: Tussock Moths and Others
Certain members of this family are of extreme interest. It is within this group that the gypsy moth (*Lymantria dispar*) is found, and it is difficult to assess the economic importance of this insect. It was apparently accidentally introduced to Massachusetts from Europe sometime between 1866 and 1869. Since then its destructive march south has been slow but inexporable. Anyone who has had the opportunity to observe the impact of this insect on the hardwood forests of the eastern United States is well aware of the damage the larvae do. From southwest Virginia north, large sections of forest have been decimated by these voracious and apparently ineradicable

pests. The best efforts of the Forest Service at times seem futile against these larval hordes. At any rate, where they occur along trout streams, they do provide food for the trout. They may, however, also destroy the fishery. Defoliation of the forest may certainly contribute to raising water temperature, which is a critical factor in mountain brook trout streams. The production of huge quantities of "frass" (excrement) may likewise have a detrimental effect on the ecology of trout streams, although what that effect might be has yet to be determined. Some of the pesticides used to control these insects may also have a harmful effect on streams within the area. So in the long run, the little benefit they may provide trout in the way of nutrition is far outweighed by their adverse effects. We would be better off without them, that is a certainty. But if you do happen into an area where there is an infestation of these pests, do not hesitate to fish a larval imitation. Trout do take them, although you may experience a strangely ambivalent feeling when fishing with an imitation gypsy moth larva. This larva should be tied on the smallish side with a gray body and dark palmered hackle trimmed off on the upper and lower surfaces.

In New England, the browntail moth (*Nygmia phaeorrhoea*) may also be a serious forest pest. Like the gypsy moth, this is also an introduced species. It first appeared around Boston about 1890 and subsequently spread over a large area. Luckily (or unluckily, depending on where you live) its range seems to be restricted to the New England states. The hairs of the larvae will cause skin irritation, so if you try to collect these, be careful.

Another introduced species, the satin moth (*Leucoma salicis*), was once considered a pest of poplars and willows. It has, however, been brought under control through the introduction of natural parasites from Europe. Thank heaven we occasionally manage to do something right!

In the above families we are primarily concerned with the larvae as potential trout food. Though there is no question that adult moths and butterflies do blunder onto the surface of streams, the numbers that do are probably quite small. For that reason we are not including a detailed analysis of the following families but simply list them with some of their more common members.

Family Hesperiidae: Skippers

Very common. Usually a tawny brown, sometimes with orange markings. They have a rapid, bouncing flight, hence the common name.

Family Papilionidae: Swallowtails and Their Allies

Frequently encountered, particularly in clouds around puddles. These are probably some of the most easily recognized of all the butterflies.

Family Pieridae: Sulphurs, Whites, and Orange Tips

This family contains some of the the most familiar of the butterflies (such as the cabbage looper). They are easily identified, being white, yellow, or orange in color and having rounded wings. These frequently gather in clouds around mud puddles or along streambanks.

Family Lycaenidae: Coppers, Blues, Harvesters, and Hairstreaks

Small butterflies with brilliant blue, violet, or copper wings. Hind wings sometimes have small projections resembling tails. Wings held tightly together over the back when resting.

Family Zygaenidae: Smoky Moths

This family is worth mentioning because the larvae of many feed on the foliage of grapevines and Virginia creeper. Since both of these vines are commonly found along trout streams, it is well worth keeping an eye peeled for skeletonized leaves, which would indicate the presence of these caterpillars. The caterpillar of the grape leaf skeletonizer (*Harrisina americana*) is about ½ inch long, yellow with black spots, and spiny.

Family Arctiidae: Tiger Moths

This family includes the common woolly bear caterpillar moth (*Isia isabella*), which has had its name since Colonial times. Every fall we see these cute little guys hurrying across the road on the way to somewhere. These are so neat looking that it just seems natural to tie and fish imitations of them, and they do produce!

Family Noctuidae: Owlet Moths

More than 3,000 species of owlet moths are found in North America, which makes this the largest lepidopteran family on the continent. A few of the more interesting species include the eight-spotted forester (*Alypia octomaculata*), whose larvae feed on grape leaves and the leaves of Virginia creeper; the sweetheart underwing (*Catocala amatrix*), the larvae of which feed on willow and poplar; and its relatives the widow underwing (*C. vidua*), whose larvae eat hickory and walnut leaves, the white underwing (*C. relicta*), whose caterpillars feed on poplar and willow, and the tiny nymph (*C. micronympha*), whose larvae feed on oaks in eastern North America. Another member of this family is the locust underwing (*Euparthenos nubilis*), which can be quite common in those areas of the United States with large stands of black locust. The larvae feed on the locust leaves and are dark mottled brown, twiglike in form, and difficult to see.

Well, if you made it this far, we congratulate you! As you can easily see, the moths and butterflies are a prominent group of insects. How important they are in the diet of trout is, however, a matter of availability, and in many instances that is a matter of chance. In most cases, the larvae are more important than the adult, so keep an eye out for anything that might indicate the presence of large concentrations of these critters. Silken nests in the branches, skeletonized leaves in trees along the stream, the sound of "frass" raining down on your tent (which is difficult to ignore), and other clues can sometimes turn a so-so day into a real experience.

LEPIDOPTERA PATTERNS

As stated earlier, the adult lepidopterans may be well represented by patterns such as the elk-hair caddis, the Wulff series of flies, the Irresistible, and an assortment of clipped-hair bass bugs. These patterns are so well known that there is little point in including them in this volume. Since the caterpillars probably represent a much more important food item for trout than the adults, we will, with one exception, confine our pattern section to the larvae.

THE NEVERSINK SKATER (EDWARD RINGWOOD HEWITT)

Gerald Almy, who mistakenly says that Hewitt developed this as a butterfly pattern, gives excellent directions for tying this pattern, and we refer you to his *Tying and Fishing Terrestrials* for the technique. We include this pattern here for a number of reasons. Hewitt originally developed the pattern as a cranefly imitation and managed to keep the tying procedure a secret for quite a while. Marinaro figured out the procedure and in 1977 let the cat out of the bag in an article for *Outdoor Life*.

From the anatomical point of view, the Neversink Skater doesn't look anything like a butterfly. It lacks the heavy body of most Lepidoptera, and the "wings" look nothing like those of a butterfly. On the water it behaves like a butterfly, skipping and skimming lightly over the surface. But this behavior of the pattern on the water, to our way of thinking, puts the fly into the general category of an attractor pattern along with many others (such as the Royal Wulff). We feel that it is the *action* of the fly rather than the physical characteristics of the design that elicits the agressive response in fish. You can do the same thing by tying a heavily hackled caddis pattern and skittering it across the surface, even when there are no caddis on the water! So what we really have here is a general attractor pattern, the effectiveness of which is dependant on its action, not its anatomy.

THE CLIPPED HAIR CATERPILLAR

Hook: 2X long dry-fly hook, size as desired.
Thread: Since this is a spun deer-hair procedure, we recommend nothing smaller than 3/0 thread. Monocord is actually a better choice for most tiers. Color to match deer hair used for the body.
Body: Deer hair, color at discretion of the tier.

We recommend any fly-tying book that gives directions for spinning deer hair. This is a basically simple procedure, but to spin hair correctly takes some practice. The caterpillars produced float well, are highly durable, and can be tied in any color. To tie one of the fuzzy or hairy caterpillars using this procedure, simply tie in a hackle at the butt of the fly and palmer it through the clipped deer hair.

CORK AND BALSA CATERPILLARS

Gerald Almy makes the statements that "cork caterpillars are extremely simple to construct" and "balsa can be substituted for the cork to make an equally effective inchworm imitation." He gives adequate directions for tying these in his book *Tying and Fishing Terrestrials,* and we refer you to this for directions. But why go to all the trouble of forming cork and balsa bodies unless you are just dying to try this technique? OK, they *were* very effective when they were first produced (George Harvey, back in the thirties), but they were the only game in town at the time. With the advent of the new closed cell foams, you can crank out floating inchworms in a fraction of the time and enjoy the results much more rapidly.

DRY WOOLLY WORM

Hook: 2X long dry-fly hook, size as desired.
Thread: 6/0 or 8/0, color as desired.
Hackle: Good-quality dry-fly hackle, color as desired. Use a
    size somewhat (at least one size) smaller than that required
    for the size hook used. Palmer the hackle through the
    dubbed body.
Body: Polypropylene or fur dubbing, color of choice.
When dressed with a good floatant, the dry woolly worm is an excellent floating caterpillar imitation.

WRAPPED HAIR LARVA

Hook: 2X long dry-fly hook, size as desired.
Thread: 6/0 or 8/0, color to match body.
Body: Good-quality deer body hair, color as desired.
There are many books that give more than adequate directions for constructing this fly. It is extremely easy to tie, but it is rather fragile and will self-destruct after a few fish. We again feel that the modern closed

cell foams are a more desirable material than deer hair, but we include this pattern for historical purposes. Ed Shenk still likes this pattern, though ("'T' Time," *Fly Fisherman,* September 1986), and fishes it when the proper occasion presents itself.

CHENILLE INCHWORM

This pattern was apparently developed by Matthew Vinciguerra and consists of nothing more than a piece of fluorescent green chenille tied to the front portion of a standard dry-fly hook. An oval head is then formed by thread wraps. Vinciguerra indicated that the fly fished well either dry or sunken (although he thought it was a better producer when fished dry).

We again feel that the modern materials have replaced this pattern, but it is of historical interest since it seems to represent the forerunner of the modern sinking vernille inchworms, as well as others tied with different materials.

McMURRAY INCHWORM

This pattern is mentioned by Art Lee ("The McMurray Flies—II," *Fly Fisherman,* July 1983), but none is pictured and we have never seen one. What happened to it? Is it still in production (if so, who carries it) or has it been discontinued?

POLYCELON CATERPILLARS AND INCHWORMS

We feel that these artificials are far ahead of any of the other floating designs. They are extremely easy to tie, are highly visible, float until they are literally torn apart, and can be tied in most of the desirable colors. They can be tied plain to resemble inchworms or hackled to imitate any of the hairy caterpillars (gypsy moth larvae and woolly bears, for example). An excellent article by David Lucca (*American Angler and Fly Tyer,* Summer 1989) gives simple instructions. In essence, a strip of polycelon (closed cell foam) is attached to the hook and segmented with the tying thread. If hairs are required, a hackle is palmered through the segmented body and reinforced with tying thread. We refer you to the article by Lucca for details of tying the following two patterns.

REGULAR-BODY FUZZY CATERPILLAR

Hook: #6 to #16, Mustad Aberdeen #3261. Lucca indicates
  that any other "long shank light-wire hook" may be used.
Thread: 6/0, color to match body foam.
Body: Any closed cell foam.
Hackle: Color to match "hairs" of natural. Palmered.
Eyes: Optional, applied with lacquer.

EXTENDED BODY INCHWORM

Hook: Mustad 94833, 94831, or equivalent.
Thread: 6/0, color to match body.
Body: Closed cell foam cut into a $\frac{1}{16}$-inch-wide strip.
Head: Dark dubbing.

SINKING VERNILLE INCHWORM

This pattern was first written up by Barry Beck ("The Sinking Inch-worm," *Fly Fisherman,* July 1990). It was, however, in popular use for quite a few years prior to that article, so we don't know who gets credit for it. What is important about this fly, however, is not who invented it but the simple fact that it can be deadly at certain times of the year. It is simplicity personified, even simpler than the San Juan Worm! All you do is to tie down the vernille well into the bend of the hook, wrap it forward, tie it off, remove the excess, and form the head.

Hook: #10 to #14, 2X long, fine-wire dry-fly hook.
Thread: 6/0 black or color to match body.
Body: Appropriate color of vernille. There are many from
  which to choose. We recommend you try more than just
  the fluorescent green that Beck employs.
A variation of this pattern can be tied by palmering a hackle of the

appropriate color through the vernille. There have been occasions when this "hairy" inchworm has outproduced its smooth counterpart.

THE KREINIK SINKING INCHWORM

This pattern is tied like the vernille inchworm but with Kreinik round braid for the body. The size of the braid (small, medium, or large) used to tie the fly depends on the size of the hook. Inchworms tied with many different colors of braid have proved productive, but the fluorescent green, yellow, and white seem to be the most attractive. There are so many colors available in these braids that you could spend an entire summer fooling around with inchworm patterns! Green, caddis larva green, bronze, and salmon have all been effective for inchworm patterns. If you desire, a hackle may be palmered through the body to produce a "fuzzy" sinking pattern.

Do the sinking inchworm patterns really work as well as Barry Beck says they do? The answer is an unequivocal yes. When nothing else seems to work, they can be deadly, and for some reason they seem to work long after inchworms have disappeared from sight. Steve Hiner and I were fishing in early December a few years back, and just for the hell of it I tied on a sinking fluorescent green inchworm. I caught fish steadily on it for the remainder of the afternoon. Why it worked so well that day is anybody's guess, and I am at a loss to come up with any sort of explanation. Maybe the fish were just bored and wanted to play.

—H. R. S.

10

Order Homoptera: Cicadas, Leafhoppers, Treehoppers, Froghoppers, and Planthoppers

JASSIDS! THE BREEZE along the Letort seems to whisper the word, and one cannot help but visualize Vince Marinaro crouched low to the surface of the water, collecting seine in hand. Imagine his excitement upon the discovery of "many tiny insect forms." The echoes of his silent "Eureka!" may still be heard today. But read his account carefully (*A Modern Dry Fly Code*), and you will find no immediate reference to the jassids. Marinaro was most excited about the very small ants, tiny beetles, and large, partially submerged ants his seine collected. He makes no mention of "leafhoppers of minute dimensions in astonishing numbers," as Schwiebert states in *Trout Strategies*. It is almost as though the presence of leafhoppers in his collections took a backseat for awhile to the small mayflies and ants. They did not remain there for long, however!

Several seasons of experimentation with numerous leafhopper imitations proved fruitless. Vince, the innovator and perfectionist, was given the task of producing the pattern. He and Charlie discussed hundreds of ideas for imitations, only to come up unsuccessful.

Finally, Vince tied a pattern that he was certain would work. He met Charlie on the Letort behind Charlie's house in the lower meadow. They sat down, and opening a pocket on his vest, Vince produced a box with a half dozen or so new flies. Holding a fly by the bend of the hook between thumb and forefinger, Vince began to expound on the design of the new leafhopper. Certain criteria had to be met, of this they were both certain. The real leafhopper did not ride high on the water's placid surface as did the mayflies, their delicate tails and legs holding their bodies just millimeters above the surface. Rather, the leafhopper's legs broke the surface film, and its oval or football-shaped body floated in the surface film. Silhouette was critical. The oval shape of the body, the tiny legs in the surface film had to be just right if there was any hope of fooling the finicky, selective, surface-feeding browns. Vince was certain he had the answer. He called the first pattern a Jassid. (The leafhoppers used to be of the family Jassidae.)

The pattern looked strange to Charlie, unlike anything he had ever seen or imagined in thinking about how to imitate the leafhoppers—a slim, evenly tapered body of dubbed black fur, a closely palmered hackle with a V clipped top and bottom, and a lacquered jungle cock eye tied flat over the back. It didn't look much like a leafhopper to Charlie as he examined the fly. Vince had several other ties, with brown, olive, and cream bodies, brown and grizzly hackle. There had been color variations in the samples they had collected, with black and green being the predominant colors.

The possibility of failure troubled them. So many previous tries, so many failures. They talked for what seemed like hours about finding several of the early-feeding risers, observing them intently as they fed, making certain of the line of drift of the naturals as they floated helplessly close to the weed-filled banks, and timing the trout's rises. Did they take every natural? Were they taking leafhoppers? Anticipation combined with the fear of failure appeared to inhibit Charlie and Vince from making their first test of the new Jassid.

They finally walked upstream through the meadow. At least a dozen browns called the long, broad runs of the S bend home. The two anglers had encountered them hundreds of times in seasons past. As they approached the tail of the lower bend, they stopped and watched the water. As expected, three browns were rising regularly. The anglers watched and talked, watched and planned.

Finally, Charlie moved back in the meadow away from the river and headed upstream. Vince stealthily began his approach to the first brownie. Charlie's job would be to direct Vince's casts so as not to spook the trout. He stayed low in the weeds directly in line with the brown.

Vince knew exactly how long his cast had to be. Working out line, he made a cast far to the right of the feeding brown. Charlie watched as the Jassid softly landed. "About two feet longer," he told Vince. Stripping line from the Hardy, Vince cast again, this time placing the fly about a foot and a half ahead of the brown. "Right on," Charlie confirmed.

The moment of truth had arrived! Three false casts, and then Vince let the line and 12-foot leader tapered to a 6X tippet go. The loop turned over beautifully as Vince sharply turned his wrist to the left, curving the last 6 feet of leader as the tiny Jassid touched the surface 2 feet ahead of the brown and perfectly in the line of drift, bringing the naturals to his quarry. Charlie watched intently and talked nervously as the tiny imitation approached the trout. "He's coming up, inspecting, drifting back under the fly, and dropping down! He's heading upstream to his feeding station. Everything looked good!"

Vince let the Jassid drift well behind the trout before picking the line off the water and making his second cast. This time the fly landed about a foot to the right of the brown—too far out of his feeding lane to even be seen. Vince's third cast was perfect, a duplicate of the first. "Perfect," Charlie said. Drag-free, the tiny terres-

trial drifted to the brownie. "He's coming up, drifting back, he's got it!" Charlie called. Vince had seen the surface break, instinctively raised the rod, and felt the weight of the trout. "You got him!" Charlie exclaimed.

"Yes! Whoopee, great, fantastic!" Vince yelled as he stripped in the line to control the brown. The take was sure; the tiny fly was embedded firmly in the upper jaw of the trout.

Emotions drained as Vince returned a 14-inch brightly colored, heavy-bodied, stream-bred brown to the river. They slapped each other on the back, shouting, "It worked, it worked! Maybe we have it, please, please! Let it be for real!" All the testing, trying, failing, and frustration had disappeared. They were like two young kids that historic day along the banks of the S bend on the legendary Letort. What followed would become fishing history as future seasons passed.

—E. K.

The jassids that Marinaro collected are members of the order Homoptera, which includes such diverse terrestrials as the tiniest of leafhoppers (only a fraction of an inch in length) and the largest of the cicadas (about 2 inches in length). They are related to the true bugs (Hemiptera). This is the fourth-largest order of insects in North America (north of Mexico), with more than 6,000 species.

They feed exclusively on plants, and many species are responsible for severe damage. In the process of feeding on plants, they may act as vectors for certain plant diseases and therefore may be doubly injurious to the host plants. Some members of this order are, however, economically beneficial. Cochineal, for example, is a vivid red dye produced by collecting females of the scale insect *Dactylopius coccus.* The dried bodies of these females are then pulverized to produce the dye. This was once a highly prized, expensive, and much sought-after material, but introduction of the aniline dyes toward the end of the nineteenth century pretty much did away with the demand for cochineal. The resinous secretion of the females of certain species of the lac insect, primarily *Laccifer laca,* is used in the production of shellac. This is still of great economic importance, since about 4 million pounds of this material are used annually in the production of shellac. But when you consider that many of the common garden and houseplant pests such as aphids, mealybugs, scale insects, and White Flies belong to this order, it is difficult to get excited about the few from which you can make a profit. Unless, of course, you happen to be in the pesticide business!

Those homopterans that have wings usually possess two pairs. The front pair may be slightly thickened, but both pairs are usually clear and membranous. In certain species, the wings may be difficult to see because of the rearward extension of the pronotum of the thorax. In many of the treehoppers, the structure of the pronotum is bizarre, to say the least, and gives the insects a decidedly humpbacked, horned, or otherwise deformed appearance.

Development of the Homoptera is usually through simple metamorphosis. The young that hatch look essentially like the parent and go through a series of instars (nymphal stages) before reaching maturity. In the case of the wingless Homoptera, each instar is nothing more than a miniature adult. In certain winged members of this order (White Flies and scale insects), a type of complete metamorphosis is present in which a pupal stage is interposed between the last nymphal stage and the adult.

The Homoptera represent a large, diverse, and common group of insects that are found on virtually all plant life. As such, they are common residents of the vegetation present along the banks of trout streams, but it was not until Marinaro, seine in hand and brain at work, that it was discovered that the surface of the stream was awash with these tiny critters. It did not take him long to produce a very functional and highly effective imitation for these insects.

The term *jassid* comes from the old name of the family, Jassidae, in which the leafhoppers were originally placed. After some time, and for whatever reasons, entomologists changed the name of the family to Cicadellidae. But when the entomologists decided to change the name of the family, Vince balked. It is best expressed in his own words from *A Modern Dry Fly Code:*

> The last of the most worthy patterns of the minutiae are the jassids, a name that has been dropped and replaced by the term Cicadellidae, recently revived by the entomologists. Though this name has a liquid and lilting sound, it is an effeminate and maudlin thing that I cannot stomach no matter how much the revision is justified. So contrary

to the wishes of the entomologists I shall continue to use
the former name, a compact and more vigorous term befitting the nomenclature of things connected with outdoor
activity—things like rod, reel and trout.

In other words, you can do what you want to and you can go to hell
in the process. You may be professional entomologists, but I am a professional fly fisherman. I like the old name and I will use the old name.
Apparently everyone else agreed, but what do you expect from a host of
kindred spirits? And so the name "jassid" stands today in fly fishing literature as a wonderful monument to a crusty, opinionated, dedicated,
observant, and intuitive man whose contributions to the sport may well
be without peer.

The development of Marinaro's Jassid pattern was the logical outgrowth
of his original pattern for the Japanese beetle. If you look at the two imitations together, it is immediately obvious that the Jassid is nothing more
than a scaled-down version of the Beetle. Marinaro's idea was to imitate
the minuscule leafhoppers he collected, and while he undoubtedly collected many of these, he also undoubtedly collected quite a few treehoppers,
froghoppers, and planthoppers as well. The treehoppers and froghoppers are
in different families from that of the leafhoppers, and the planthoppers
are in a different superfamily, but all are sufficiently similar to one another
to warrant the all-inclusive term of jassid.

For our purpose, the term jassid can probably be used for *any* of the
small Homopterans, although Marinaro used the term only for leafhoppers.
The term would not apply to small beetles, true bugs, or any other tiny
terrestrial, but our imitations for these forms might well serve as very
effective jassids. If a pattern is of the correct size and color, if its presentation is acceptable to the trout, and if the trout takes it with confidence,
the name matters not at all.

What is extremely interesting is the fact that there is only a single
commonly used Jassid pattern! It survives today in virtually the same
form as that originally tied by Marinaro (at least for those of you who still
purchase real jungle cock feathers). Why are there not more patterns for
these common and innumerable streamside residents? After all, they
come in many sizes (but mostly small), range in color from drab brown

to the most spectacular color combinations imaginable, and have body forms that run the gamut from "cute" to bizarre. The plain fact of the matter is that it's impractical to reproduce all these different color, body, and size combinations. In the first place, you have no idea which one might be on the water and might thus be taken by a trout. In the second place, there is the obvious impossibility of carrying around a fly box with every imaginable imitation of the naturals that you might encounter. They are therefore a bit like beetles in that a few good, basic patterns will suffice in most instances.

Marinaro recognized these impossibilities: "The great variety in species and color made standardization an impossibility." After examining the collection at the Bureau of Entomology of the Pennsylvania State Department of Agriculture, he stated, "I determined then and there to quit any more senseless attempts to establish a color standard, at least for the jassid." So, many fly fishermen use only a single Jassid, usually the original Marinaro pattern. If not the original, then it will probably be nothing more than some bastardization of this innovative imitation.

But is this really true? Many of the fraternity of the confirmed terrestrial fishermen use patterns in the size range of 20 to 24, which are routinely defined as beetles. Why beetles? Why couldn't they be leafhoppers or treehoppers? Well, they don't have to be beetles, we just call them that because that's what we set out to tie, and if that's what we tied, then that's what it is. Well, maybe to you, but maybe not to the trout. As we have said many times before, we have no idea what the trout imagines these minuscule things to be. It could be a tiny beetle, a leafhopper, a treehopper, or some other little terrestrial, but there's no way we will ever know for sure. So in fact we might really be fishing jassids and never even know it. The next time you take a nice fish on one of your little beetle imitations, tell your partner you took it on a size 22 green-bodied Jassid and see what he says.

I have a confession to make. It's a damning confession, something like telling your best friend that you're sleeping with his sister, but I've got to get it off my chest. I don't have any of Vince Marinaro's Jassids in my fly boxes.

I live in horror of the day some distinguished-looking gentleman stops me on the streambank and says, "Pardon me, do you happen to have any Marinaro Jassids? I seem to be all out."

My answer will simply have to be, "No, sir, I'm terribly sorry, but I don't."
Wham! A lightning bolt rips off my neoprenes and melts my Wheatley Ritz-
Carlton into a shapeless lump. My Leonard is transformed into a well-chewed lead
pencil, and I'm suddenly the proud possessor of an old Ocean City reel instead of a
Bogdan. More than that, a tremendous wind comes along and whips up the damndest
dust storm you've ever seen, and riding along in its swirling bowels are millions
of demonic terrestrials. They look hungry. Out of the dust storm comes a great,
hollow voice.

"You idiot, how can you write anything about Jassids if you don't fish them?"
booms the Voice of Vince.

"Hold it," say I. "All I said was that I didn't have any Marinaro Jassids in
my fly box. I never said I didn't fish Jassids."

"Look, beetle brain," says the Voice of Vince, "what do you take me for, a
midge? I heard what you said. A Jassid is a Jassid! If you don't have 'em you can't
fish 'em."

"Wait a minute, sir," say I. "To most of the fishermen of today, Jassid means
only one thing—your pattern. I don't have any of those. I can't afford real jungle
cock."

"That I can understand," says the Voice of Vince. "It's never been cheap. But
please, explain to me how you can write about jassids without fishing that pattern."

"Well," I begin, "to me the word jassid means anything that looks like a little
homopteran. I've got a lot of little bitty stuff tied with different materials that could
be anything—leafhoppers, treehoppers, beetles, messed-up ants, true bugs, maybe
little terrestrial dipterans like fruit flies, just about anything. I don't know what the
fish think they are. For lack of a better term I just call 'em all jassids. Frankly, I
like the name. It's a compact and vigorous term befitting the nomenclature of things
connected with outdoor activity—things like rod, reel, and trout."

"Nice," says the Voice of Vince. "I like that idea. I particularly like the way
you put together that last sentence. It's very good. As a matter of fact, it's excellent.
Your argument makes a lot of sense and I guess I'll go along with it. But do me a
favor, will you?"

"Sure," say I, "just name it."

"Go buy some jungle cock nails. It won't break you, and you might find that
my pattern works better than what you've been fishing."

"That's not a bad idea," I admit. "I'll do it. But could you in return do a
great favor for me? There is something I would like to know."

"What's that?" asks the Voice.

"Well, seeing as how you're now in a position where you have access to some pretty highly classified information, would you please tell me, honestly, what the hell trout think these little tiny imitations really are?"

"Ha," says the Voice. "If I told you that it would ruin everything for you. Better that I don't. Besides, someday you'll be in the position to find out for yourself."

"Right," say I, "I know that, but by then it will be too late. I need to know now, while I can still fish for trout."

"Look, sonny, you think you're fishing for trout now? You ain't seen nothing yet," says the Voice of Vince.

—H. R. S.

At the other end of the homopteran size spectrum are the cicadas, the largest of which are a bit over 2 inches long. But if you look at these carefully and compare them with certain of the smaller homopterans, it is obvious that they are closely related. The cicada looks like nothing more than a giant leafhopper!

Of what importance are these to fly fishermen? They appear only every thirteen or seventeen years, depending on which species of *Magicicada* you happen to be dealing with. So then, why bother to ever tie imitations in advance, in the hope that a major hatch of these monsters will occur? Simple! In the United States there are at least thirteen separate broods of those species with a seventeen-year cycle and five broods for those species with a thirteen-year cycle, so your chances of running into them are better than you think! Some broods are much larger than others, however, and when these hatch you have a major occurrence. In the eastern United States, these periodical cicadas with thirteen- to seventeen-year life cycles are identifiable by the reddish venation of the wings, the red eyes, and the blackish coloration of the body. They are also somewhat smaller than other eastern species. Because of their feeding habits, it takes the larvae quite some time to reach full growth. They feed on the xylem sap from the roots of plants, which is notoriously low in nutrients. As a result, it takes them a rather long time to reach maturity, since they grow so slowly.

What is of major interest to fly fishermen, however, is the fact that the different species of *Magicicada* (periodical cicadas) are by no means the only cicadas around. The other common types of cicadas (and there are various species of these) are known as the dog-day cicadas and appear *each year*. Though the entire life cycle of these species is unknown, the shortest life cycle reported is only four years. But even in those species with relatively long life cycles, there is brood overlap, so that a certain number of adults will appear each year. In certain regions of the country, this makes it nice for fishermen. The area around Utah's Green River is a prime example of a spot where the annual "cicada hatch" is looked forward to as a time for many and large fish. Granted, it's better in some years than in others, but that's the chance you take. This annual hatch was the subject of a recent article, "Cicada Madness" by Rex Gerlach in the May 1993 issue of *Fly Fisherman*. The hatch, as stated, begins sometime in April and lasts through about the first week in June. For those of you who have never experienced something like this, it is a memorable event.

I've seen Cliff Rexrode take off down the side of one mountain, head through a laurel thicket, and go halfway up the side of the next mountain without breaking a sweat. Pete Bromley can verify this statement because he was with us. We were chasing a spring gobbler, and those of you who hunt during the spring gobbler season can understand this sort of madness. When Cliff finally stopped, it was all Pete and I could do to keep from throwing up a lung. But Cliff is a professional forester, so he has an advantage. By the way, we got that turkey, and that afternoon we hiked about 10 miles while fishing a pretty rough native trout stream in the area. Cliff did admit that he was kind of tired that evening, but Pete and I were a lot more than "kind of tired."

What's the point to this story and what does it have to do with cicadas? The point is simply that Cliff is a full-bore sort of outdoor guy. With Cliff, fishing (or hunting) is dawn to dark, don't stop, drink plenty of fluids, don't worry about where you are or when you're going to get back—serious business. Funny, now that I think about it, most of the people I fish with are like that, but Cliff is at the top for pure raw endurance. What it has to do with cicadas is simply that the only, and I mean ONLY, time I have ever seen Cliff stop, sit down, slip the fly into the hook keeper, and invite someone else to take over was during the cicada hatch on Utah's Green River.

To this day, I will never forget that moment when Cliff turned to me and said,

"My wrist hurts. Why don't you come up here and fish from the front of the boat for a while." Being an accommodating sort of guy and always willing to help others out, I did just that!

I might add two other comments. It's the only time either of us had ever purposely yanked the fly away from 16- to 17-inch fish in hopes that a bigger one would come up for it. It was also the only time either of us had ever become bored with catching big trout. Why? It was too easy and the tackle was too heavy. You can't throw huge cicadas on small rods from a drift boat (at least not easily), and you have to fish them on a fairly heavy tippet (6X just won't do it). It turned out that the fun part of the trip was not the cicadas but the large trout cruising the scum lines and sipping small stuff. Now these on little rods, light tippets, and tiny flies were fun!

And by the way, any big, black fly will work fine during the cicada hatch! We had no trouble proving that. As a matter of fact, it didn't even have to be black.

—H. R. S.

Cicadas are noisy insects, to say the least, but it is only the males that produce the characteristic "song" for each species. This is accomplished through a series of complicated muscular movements that cause riblike portions of the abdomen to bend rapidly. The resultant sound is amplified by a large internal air sac that acts as a resonance chamber. During a major hatch of these insects, the sound produced can be almost unbearable!

DESIGNING HOMOPTERAN PATTERNS

In designing patterns for homopterans, there are a few general rules to follow. First of all, the pattern is going to be either very large (to mimic a cicada) or very small (to mimic everything else). There really is no in between. Second, color can be pretty much anything you like, except for cicadas, for which black is usually going to be the color of choice for the body. Third, use any material that strikes your fancy and suits your purposes. The following represents those materials that we have found particularly useful.

Cicadas

Body. Spun and trimmed deer hair, macramé cord, closed cell foam,

Ice chenille, Micro-Ice chenille. Bill McIntyre has also employed shaped cork very successfully in the production of the Corker Cicadas.

Wings. Krystal Flash, white calf tail, or a combination of the two; bleached elk hair; fibers of nylon organza; Kreinik ⅛-inch flat ribbon or Kreinik Flash in a Tube.

Head and Thorax. Closed cell foam (extension of the body, which is folded backward) or deer hair tied bullet-style.

Legs. Rubber filaments of different colors are added on certain patterns.

Other Homopterans

Why do we include all the other homopterans in a single category? The answer is simply that there is no reason not to! The important ones to trout are leafhoppers, treehoppers, or froghoppers, and their basic characteristics are so similar that there is no point in tying specific members of each group.

Body. If it floats, use it. Wrapped and trimmed hackle was called for in Marinaro's original Jassid pattern, but anything that floats will do. Bodies may be formed using nothing more than a bit of deer or elk hair, and the "jassid" may be tied as nothing more than a minute Crowe beetle. On the other hand, closed cell foam is a more desirable material, and very small bodies may be formed using this material.

But all foams are not created equal, and some are better than others for tying jassids. The three types we have experimented with range in thickness from ⅛ inch to about 3⁄16 inch, and the physical character of each is vastly different. The thicker foams are more difficult to work with for the smallest of jassids. When dealing with a 3⁄16-inch-thick block of foam, you must first cut 1⁄16-inch-wide strips from the block and then split these to obtain a workable size. The thicker foams also must be stretched in the tying process to obtain the slender body necessary for a jassid imitation. On the other hand, the 1⁄16-inch-thick foam obtainable from Dale Clemens, 444 Schantz Spring Rd., Allentown, PA 18104, is ideal for Jassids in the size 20 to 24 range. Very thin strips are easily obtained using a straight-edge and single-edged razor blade. The foam from Clemens is also very dense, tough, and durable, and comes in a wide variety of colors, including a lovely tan that is unavailable in the other foams.

We must also include the jungle cock nail in this section as well (see explanation below). As a matter of fact, any small feather, particularly if treated with Flexament and trimmed to shape, will produce an elegant body for a jassid.

Wings. Marinaro indicates in his original directions that the wings are tied using "one small to medium jungle cock nail, any color." This is rather misleading, for the jungle cock nail (along with the wrapped hackle) was really employed to form the outline of the body. We cannot therefore really look upon it as representing a wing, particularly since the wings of homopterans are not opaque but clear and membranous.

An excellent material for forming wings is the 1⁄16-inch flat metallic braid manufactured by the Kreinik company, particularly the mallard and star green colors. These are very translucent and produce the desired effect. Fibers of nylon organza produce lovely wings on the smallest jassids. This material is usually available through fabric shops, and a half yard will last you for years. Other winging materials include Z-lon, poly-yarn, and fibers taken from macramé cord or plastic canvas yarn.

Legs. Wrapped hackle as an underbody seems to be all that is necessary, particularly if it is trimmed flat along the top and bottom.

Color. Color to Marinaro was a very real stumbling block, and he gave up on trying to come up with any standardization. This does not mean, however, that you should tie only "jungle cock jassids." The important small homopterans come in every conceivable color, so try some with bodies of green, red, black, yellow, tan, brown, or other colors. Combinations of these colors are also common, so don't be afraid to experiment using different colors of tying thread to form an underbody on foam-bodied jassids. You do not have to have hundreds of these things, but that 20-inch brown just might take a small foam jassid with a green body when it has consistently refused everything else. If it doesn't, then the most you have wasted is a tiny bit of material and about two minutes at the bench—the hook can always be recycled!

HOMOPTERAN CLASSIFICATION

There are only a few groups of homopterans of interest to fly fishermen. They are as follows.

Superfamily Cicadoidea

Family Cicadidae: Cicadas. No one should have any problem recognizing these! Compared with everything else in this order, they are huge. We assume that all of you have seen one and that no description is necessary.

Family Membracidae: Treehoppers. Very common, found in all types of vegetation, not just trees. Many of these have a highly modified pronotum, which gives them a bizarre and deformed appearance, so they are (for the most part) easy to recognize. If it looks like a thorn, the hunchback of Notre Dame, or something out of Star Wars, it's probably a treehopper.

Family Cercopidae: Froghoppers and Spittlebugs. Froghoppers look so much like leafhoppers and planthoppers that you should not waste your time trying to tell the difference. The only ones of this group that are easy to identify are the nymphs of spittlebugs, which secrete the characteristic foamy or spitlike mass of material within which they mature.

Family Cicadellidae: Leafhoppers. Here we have Vince Marinaro's jassids. This is a very large and abundant group, most being well under ½ inch long. If you can catch one of these and look at it with a magnifying lens, its similarity to a cicada will be quite surprising.

Superfamily Fulgoroidea

Within this superfamily are found all the families of the planthoppers. These are too numerous to mention, and besides, they look so much like the leafhoppers and froghoppers that only an expert is going to be able to tell the difference.

HOMOPTERA PATTERNS

Jassids

MARINARO'S JASSID

These are the original instructions given by Marinaro. With the modern materials and hooks available today, you are certainly free to make substitutions!

Hook: 20 short or 22 regular, Model Perfect.

Body: Tying silk, any color.

Wings: One medium to small jungle cock nail, any color.

Hackle: Two or three very small ones turned as for a ribbing
hackle, any color and as short fibered as possible.

As we mentioned earlier, any small feather may be used for the wing, but we recommend that it be pretreated with Flexament and trimmed to shape.

FOAM-BODIED JASSIDS

Hook: #20 to #26 standard dry-fly hook.

Thread: 6/0 or 8/0, depending on the size of the hook or the
desired color of the thread. (We tie many of our foam-
bodied patterns with fluorescent thread, which is
unavailable in 8/0.)

Underbody: If desired, peacock herl makes a good underbody,
but on the smallest of these patterns, use the very fine herl
from the eye of the peacock feather. In most cases, the
underbody is not necessary, as the color of the thread is

used to produce a strong contrast with the color of the body foam.

Wing: On the larger-size imitations, we recommend the ⅟₁₆-inch Kreinik ribbon (mallard #850 or standard minnow #095). On the smaller sizes, we use fibers of nylon organza. (There are, of course, alternatives to these.)

Head: Formed by folding the body foam backward and tying it down to form a semi-bullet head.

Tying Instructions

1. Wrap shank of hook with thread of appropriate size and color.

2. Tie in the piece of foam at the bend of the hook, and wrap the thread forward to a point about ⅟₁₆ inch back from the eye of the hook.

3. Fold foam forward and tie down. *Do not trim the forward-projecting portion of the foam.*

4. Tie in the winging material projecting backward, and wrap the thread all the way to the eye of the hook. Wrap thread backward to the front of the formed body. Fold foam backward and tie down to form the head. Trim excess foam and whip-finish.

5. Trim wing material slightly longer than the body.

These are so simple to tie that a few hours at the vise should produce two or three dozen assorted Foam-bodied Jassids.

Cicadas

There are more patterns for cicadas than for jassids. This is perhaps because of the greater visibility of the cicadas, and maybe also the hesitancy of many individuals to fish the very small patterns necessary for jassids (although most have no problem fishing comparably sized midges!). Whatever the reasons might be, cicada patterns have bloomed over the past few years. Perhaps the preponderance of these insects on Utah's Green River has had something to do with this.

SEVENTEEN-YEAR LOCUST (ED SHENK)

Hook: #8 to #10, Mustad 9671.

Body: Burnt-orange dubbing fur tied very full or, preferably, burnt-orange deer hair trimmed very full, and flat on bottom.

Wings: Blue dun hackle tips tied in a narrow V, or a broad body feather tied flat, coated with vinyl cement, and trimmed to a delta-wing shape with rounded wing tips.

Hackle: Orange, clipped on the bottom.

Head: Large, rounded, clipped orange deer hair.

STALCUP'S CICADA (SHANE STALCUP)

Hook: #8 dry-fly hook, 2X long.

Thread: 6/0 black.

Body: Black poly yarn or similar material.

Wing: Pearl Krystal Flash over which is tied white calf tail hair, over which is tied orange-dyed squirrel tail.

Bullet head and collar: Black deer body hair tied reversed.

Legs: Black rubber hackle.

GREEN RIVER CICADA

I have no idea who developed this pattern, but it's deadly. I fished it years ago on the Green River with Rick Lee, Stuart Asahina, and Marty Howard. It is similar to the MacSalmon Stonefly in that the body is formed from macramé cord.

—H. R. S.

Hook: #8 or #10 dry-fly hook, 2X long.

Thread: 6/0 black.

Body: Black 3-mm macramé cord, threaded on the hook to a point halfway down the shank and trimmed to extend beyond the bend of the hook. The extended end is then

flamed to prevent unraveling. The forward portion is tied down, trimmed at an angle, and wrapped firmly in place with the tying thread. *The body must be threaded over the hook shank before any tying thread is employed.*
Wing: Peacock or pearlescent Krystal Flash. A little orange Krystal Flash may be mixed in if desired.
Head and collar: Dyed blue dun or gray elk hair tied in bullet-head style.

The following three patterns for cicadas were taken from an article, "Cicada Madness," by Rex Gerlach (*Fly Fisherman,* May 1993).

BULLETHEAD CICADA

Hook: #8 to # 10, Mustad 94831.
Thread: 6/0 black.
Body: Black polypropylene rope (macramé cord) tied to form a slightly extended body.
Underwing: A few strands of Krystal Flash.
Wing: White calf tail, dressed sparsely, extending slightly beyond the hook bend.
Hackle: Gray deer hair, dressed bullet-head style.
Legs: Two brown, rubber microfilaments. Tie one on each side of the body where the bullet-head tie-down is made, to form two long rear legs and two short front legs.

TRUDE CICADA

Hook: #8 to #10, Mustad 94831.
Thread: 6/0 black.
Tail: A dozen fine black moose mane hairs.
Underbody: Black foam.
Body: Peacock-colored or black Krystal Flash chenille (Ice chenille or Kreinik Micro-Ice chenille may also be used).
Wing: Medium-size bunch of white calf tail, tied to extend slightly beyond the hook bend in Trude style.
Hackle: Grizzly.

FOAM CICADA

Hook: #8 to #10, Mustad 94831.

Body: Black foam, tied down at evenly spaced rear, middle, and forward locations to form a slight rear-body extension and two forward segments.

Legs: Two black and one yellow rubber microfilaments laid crisscross on the shank and wrapped into place.

Underwing (optional): A few strands of Krystal Flash extending slightly beyond the hook bend.

Wing: A sparse bunch of light gray elk hairs, same length as the underwing.

Hackle: Furnace, dressed sparsely.

RAINY'S CICADA (RAINY RIDING)

Hook: #8 to #10, Mustad 9672.

Thread: Yellow monocord.

Body: Rainy's Float Foam, black, large size.

Underwing: A few strands of pearlescent Krystal Flash.

Wing: Natural or bleached elk hair.

Head: Formed from a folded-back portion of the foam used to tie the body.

Legs: Black rubber microfilaments, one tied in on each side at the point where the foam used to form the head is tied down.

CORKER CICADA (BILL McINTYRE)

This pattern will last so long you may want to throw it away before it wears out, and it's an excellent producer. There are at least four variations of this pattern available, and they may be purchased from Bill at the following address: Bill McIntyre, W. S. M. Ind., 106 White Gate Rd., Pittsburgh, PA 15238, telephone (412) 828-8668.

We do suggest that you buy these rather than tie them. Bill has the procedure down pat, and most of you won't want to spend the time it takes to produce them. They aren't cheap, but quality never is!

Just as with other terrestrials, there are undoubtedly patterns of which we are unaware or for which we cannot give a materials list or tying directions. An example of the latter is the cicada pattern presented by Larry Tullis in his article "How to Tie Foam Flies" (*Fly Fisherman,* March 1993), in which no directions were given.

11

Lesser Terrestrials

IN HIS CLASSIC book *A Modern Dry Fly Code,* Vince Marinaro describes an autopsy done on a 2½-pound Letort brown. In its stomach were the following identifiable insects: fifteen or sixteen ants, five or six house flies, three or four lightning bugs, and two cress bugs. If we use the high figure for all food items, we get twenty-eight items present in this trout's stomach. The house flies account for 21 percent of all food items ingested, and because of their size probably represent a large percentage of the total caloric value. *This is the only conclusion we can draw regarding Marinaro's autopsy observation.* Any statements regarding the fish's preference for ants, its selection of ants over flies, its dislike of cress bugs, or anything else is pure speculation. Marinaro had no idea what the ratio of insects available to the fish might have been or where or how the fish picked up the cress bugs or beetles. In short, all we have is a simple observation. Interesting, but not conclusive. If house flies were as prevalent on the surface of the stream as ants, would there have been an equal number of both or would house flies have made up the majority of the stomach contents of this trout? An interesting question, and one that cannot be answered. On the basis of what we do know, however, it is obvious that trout, even on the hallowed spring creek water of the Letort, become opportunistic feeders during terrestrial time. Herein lies the importance of the lesser terrestrials.

Our terrestrial boxes are crammed full of beetles, ants, hoppers, and crickets. There may be a few inchworms and a couple of other items, but in general the terrestrial fisherman relies mostly on the major groups of terrestrials. At least that's what he believes. But how many fish take that small beetle or leafhopper imitation for something other than a beetle or a leafhopper? A little black beetle could very well be a good imitation of one of the land flies, and a small brown or green beetle does a pretty good job of representing any number of small, green bugs. We don't know what the trout take these imitations for, and there is certainly no way they will ever tell us. We are thus happy in our ignorance and continue to make statements to the effect that the trout "took a size 18 brown Crowe beetle." The trout may have taken it for something quite different, however, and only if we are quite aware that the water is covered with little, brown size 18 beetles and have adjusted our technique accordingly can we make such an assumption.

Well, then, if the trout are inclined to take many of our terrestrial imitations for something other than what they are meant to be, why bother fooling around with any of the lesser groups of terrestrials at all? We could probably get by very well with what we already have in our fly boxes.

There are a number of reasons why we tie imitations for some of the lesser terrestrials. First of all, some of them do occur in considerable numbers. When they do, and when they are on the water, the prepared fisherman is often overcome with a terminal case of smugness. Both his reel and his heart sing as he casts sideways glances over his bowed rod at the unlucky mortals above or below him. It might be the first time he's ever used that fly, but it won't be the last. Once a particular "off the wall" terrestrial pattern has been used with success, the fisherman tends to use it more often. As he does, he learns that it indeed produces with startling regularity, and it winds up a standby in his fly box. This probably accounts for the regional preferences of terrestrial fishermen across the country. But the wonderful thing is that many of these little-used or unknown patterns produce well no matter where we are—another testimonial to the marvelously plebeian palate of the trout, and thanks to Mother Nature for the hordes of terrestrials that blanket the country.

A second reason to tie and fish patterns that represent the lesser terrestrials is simply that it is our nature to be curious. It is fun to experiment! Just think, none of the present-day patterns ever would have been conceived if we did not have this insatiable curiosity. Unlike many older patterns, however, today's fly designs are not simply pulled out of thin air because they look pretty. Far from it. Modern patterns have been developed with a great deal of attention paid to either realistic or impressionistic design. They represent very careful thought on the part of the designers, most of whom possess more than their fair share of both knowledge and curiosity about the world of the trout and the insect. Suffice it to say, then, that we are possessed with an abundance of natural curiosity and will always attempt to tie new patterns that we hope will work at least as well as the old ones.

Finally, when we consider the incredible numbers of what we have termed the "lesser terrestrials," it becomes obvious that they are not really "lesser" after all. There are more than 3,500 species of Hemiptera (true

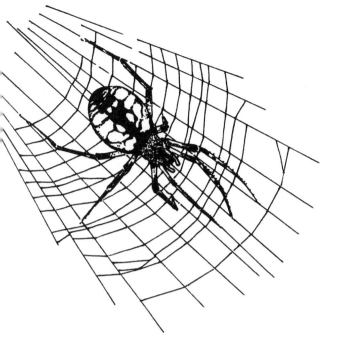

bugs) and 2,500 species of spiders found within the United States. When you take into consideration that there are therefore roughly three times as many species of "bugs" and well over twice as many species of spiders as there are grasshoppers and crickets, the "lesser terrestrials" begin to assume their rightful importance. Also, there are probably in the neighborhood of 9,000 species of terrestrial dipterans (flies).

Nevertheless, species numbers notwithstanding, we still think of all of these groups of insects as being "lesser." This is very strange, but it is probably because of the relatively reclusive ways of most of these groups of terrestrials. You do not, for example, kick up hordes of "bugs" by walking through a meadow along a stream. Or do you? The plain fact is that you disturb untold quantities of these lesser terrestrials. But unlike the grasshopper, that court jester of the insect world, these insects do not flee helter-skelter, buzzing and hopping about in mass confusion. Rest assured, however, that they are there, hiding under leaves, creeping along the ground, blending in with the bark, and doing everything they can to remain as inconspicuous as possible. If every fly fisherman, just once, took the time to thoroughly examine a few plants or bushes along the stream-bank, they would be overwhelmed by the numbers of "lesser" insects they found.

SUBPHYLUM ATELOCERATA

Class Hexapoda

Order Diptera: Flies. As previously indicated, there are about 9,000 species of truly terrestrial dipterans. These flies are readily distinguished from other insects known as flies by the fact that they have only a single pair of wings. The hind wings are reduced to a pair of knobby, stunted outgrowths (the halteres), which are completely without function as far as flying goes. They are, however, important in maintaining balance and equilibrium. It is interesting to note that with the other flies the fisherman must deal with, in entomological texts the term "fly" is included in the common name as a suffix—for example, caddisfly, dragonfly, and stonefly. With dipterans, the term "fly" is separated from the descriptive or common name: house fly, face fly, fruit fly, and so forth. A small point of difference, but interesting.

The size of terrestrial flies ranges from extremely small to several inches long. Needless to say, one of the latter, if suddenly forced down upon the surface of a trout stream, is going to attract an unwanted amount of attention to itself.

Terrestrial flies inhabit so many different ecological niches that it is impossible to catalog them all. Many of them assume extreme importance as disease vectors, destroyers of crops, bloodsucking pests, and general nuisances. Others, on the other hand, are of economic benefit. Some act as scavengers to clean up rotting plant or animal matter, others are predators of economically harmful insects, and still others are important as plant pollinators.

All dipterans undergo a complete metamorphosis in their life cycle, going through the stages of egg, larva, pupa, and adult. The wormlike larva is known as a maggot. Other than the adult, none of the developmental stages would ordinarily be available as a food item for trout.

Only twice in more than forty years of fly fishing have I ever been tempted to fish a maggot imitation. The first occasion was on Little Stony Creek in Virginia, a wonderful freestone mountain stream filled with native brook trout and naturalized rainbows (planted over fifty years ago). During the high water that occurred in the spring of that year, an unlucky deer had apparently been swept off its feet while trying to cross the stream. Its head had by chance been securely caught in the crotch of a tree that had fallen across the stream. I could not tell whether the deer had died of suffocation, drowning, or trauma (though I like to think it died quickly). Nor would I have wanted to autopsy the deer to determine the cause of death, as it was in a fair state of decomposition when I found it. The fly-blown carcass was about half out of the water, suspended by its neck, and from a distance (aided by a small pair of binoculars) I could see that the carcass was infested with maggots. It was natural to assume that quite a few of these maggots would drop into the stream. I was tempted. In my fly box were some cream caddis larvae that probably would have passed inspection, but I let the opportunity go. Somehow it just didn't seem proper.

The second occasion was on the West Branch of the Delaware. Cliff Rexrode, Norm Shires, Ed Koch, and I had gathered for a weekend, hoping to catch the early July hatches. (We were not disappointed.) In the area where we were fishing, there was a strange object, unidentifiable from a distance, but definitely something that did not belong in the stream. I ignored it for a few days, but finally my curiosity got the better of me, and closer inspection revealed a deer carcass stranded in the shallow water of a gravel bar. The location was terrible. There was no decent holding water below the carcass, and as a result none of the larvae were being swept down-stream to holding fish. Another opportunity gone.

—H. R. S.

There are probably only a few families of flies the fisherman has to deal with. Those that would be most important are as follows.

Family Tabanidae: Horse Flies and Deer Flies. These are quite common, with well over 300 species being represented in the United States. Most of us have had at least one encounter with these critters, so there is no need to recount what it's like when a female of one of these species drives a ten-penny nail into some portion of your anatomy. Yes, it's only the female of the species that is the bloodsucker. The male is a meek and harmless organism, feeding on pollen or nectar, and is therefore often encountered on flowers along the streambank. One interesting fact about this group is that though we consider them to be terrestrial, the larvae are actually aquatic and predaceous. No wonder they are often encountered in marshy or wet areas along trout streams. All of the Tabanidae are power-ful fliers, with a considerable range in body size. It is also of interest to note that in the United States certain of the tabanids act as vectors of diseases such as anthrax and tularemia.

Family Asilidae: Robber Flies and Grass Flies. These are quite common in the United States, with more than a thousand species described. Most fishermen have seen them along streams but may not have recognized what they were. The adults of this group are all predaceous, feeding on other insects. It is not uncommon to come across one of the robber flies dining on another insect as large as or larger than itself. Wasps, bees, grasshoppers, and even dragonflies are all fair game to this predator. Don't try to grab one of these if you come across it in your streamside perambulations—the bite is quite painful, and it won't hesitate to lay one on you.

Family Muscidae: House Flies, Face Flies, Stable Flies, and Others. Most people probably are familiar with this group of flies. Its members can be found everywhere and probably cause more general annoyance than any of the other flies. The common house fly, while certainly annoying, can also act as a disease vector for such things as typhoid fever, anthrax, and dysentery, but at least it doesn't bite. Others do. Both sexes of stable flies and horn flies are perfectly capable of biting and often do. On trout streams adjacent to fields in which cattle are pastured or adjacent to dairy farms, the opportunistic angler should certainly not overlook the importance of this group of flies in the diet of the trout. On Falling Springs Branch outside Chambersburg, Pennsylvania, the proximity of a dairy farm undoubtedly contributes a great many flies to the overall food web of the trout in this stream.

Family Anthomyiidae: Dung Flies and Others. These flies are indistinguishable from the preceding family, Muscidae, by the layman. Adults of this group (about 500 species in North America) are black and about the size of a common house fly. Larval stages feed on plants, and some of these can cause considerable damage to gardens and field crops.

Family Calliphoridae: Blow Flies. Everyone is probably familiar with these metallic blue or green flies. A bit larger than the average house fly, the adults are scavengers, while the larval stages live and feed in decaying flesh, excrement, or some other delightful media. Regardless of how we feel about the habits of this group of flies, we should be glad they are around, for they do provide a valuable service. In effect they act as sanitary engineers, cleaning up the mess that nobody else wants to deal with. Even so, some of these flies act as vectors for diseases such as dysentery. Others have a particularly nasty habit of laying eggs on wounds of people or animals. In some cases, the larvae of these flies feed only on decaying flesh associated with the wound, but others feed on healthy tissue as well. Screwworm flies fall into the latter category, and the larvae of this fly may cause considerable damage to cattle.

Family Sarcophagidae: Flesh Flies. This group is quite similar to the blow flies, but the adults are generally black with gray stripes on the thorax. Adults are quite common and may be seen feeding on any material that has a high sugar content (tree sap, flowers, and melons and other fruits). The larvae are more cosmopolitan in diet; most are scavengers or parasites and depend on some sort of animal material for their sustenance.

Note: Some authors include both the blow flies and the flesh flies in the same family, the Metopiidae.

Family Tachinidae: Tachinid Flies. The larval stages of these flies are parasitic on other insects, and for this reason the family is of considerable economic importance. Many of these flies are quite similar to the common house fly, others resemble flesh flies, and still others look like bees or wasps. This group is quite large, being the second-largest family of Diptera, and its members are widely distributed.

While this list may cover the more important terrestrial dipterans, it certainly does not preclude those that might be of local significance. An example of this would be the march fly (family Bibionidae). As indicated in *Tying and Fishing Terrestrials* by Gerald Almy, Charlie Fox considered this to be an important terrestrial along certain trout streams. He also noted, however, that it was "highly cyclic," which simply means, *don't count on its being there at the same time next year.* Fox also indicated that at such times "a floating imitation, like the right size John Crowe beetle, is just about necessary."

This last statement by Fox is of particular interest. After all, is there that much difference between a fly and a beetle as far as general body shape and outline are concerned? Probably not. The shape of most flies falls into our general body classification for certain of the beetles, namely, elongate-robust. Flies may initially float a bit higher in the surface film than do beetles, but we doubt if the trout are that cognizant of this fact. The color of flies is also fairly close to that of many beetles, black being the predominant color, but brown, yellow, iridescent blue, and iridescent green are also well represented.

In short, then, is there anything about a fly that might set it apart from a beetle, and if so, should this difference be taken into account when designing a pattern? The answer to this question is an emphatic *yes.* Remember in beetles that the first pair of wings is modified to form the wing case? This condition does not exist in flies. The single pair of wings lie open and exposed in all their iridescent glory. So while the chunky body of the fly may act as a major stimulus for a hungry trout, the wings should also be taken into consideration. For this reason, fly imitations should be tied with prominent, flashy wings. Any pattern tied without them is lacking in one of the major stimuli that elicits the feeding response in trout. As far as the legs of flies are concerned, they probably make little if any difference in the efficacy of the pattern. There is no indication that they play a major role in beetle design, and many beetles have legs that are, if anything, more prominent than those of flies.

In designing patterns for flies, the shape of the body and the prominent and translucent wings are of primary importance. Color may also play a key role, particularly if you are dealing with the iridescent bluebottle or greenbottle flies or some of the more brightly colored bee and wasp mimics. While certain patterns have been developed in the past and undoubtedly have worked on occasion, little attention seems to have been paid to the key sign stimulus of the wings. Almy, in *Tying and Fishing Terrestrials,* describes his Polywing Housefly, in which the wings are formed from either gray or white polypropylene. This is a poor substitute for the wings of most flies! Almy states, "Select a small parcel of polypropylene for wings, ranging from grey to white, depending on the opacity of the naturals' wings." Now, a house fly's wings are anything but opaque. Opaque means impenetrable to light, and the wings of practically all flies (terrestrial or aquatic) certainly are not impenetrable to light. The body is opaque, the legs are opaque, the head is opaque, but the wings are not opaque!

A second pattern listed by Almy, Lively's Horse Fly, likewise pays no attention to the translucent quality of the wings. This pattern, first described by Lively in the February 1977 *Pennsylvania Angler,* is tied totally with black deer hair, with the wings formed from the black hair as it is folded back over the body. Again we have a pattern in which the wings are opaque rather than translucent. Now there is nothing *wrong* with either one of these patterns. They do catch fish. They could be improved, however, by paying more attention to the wing qualities exhibited by flies.

Order Hemiptera: True Bugs. Here at last we have the group of insects to which the common name "bug" truly applies. These are indeed often termed the *true bugs* by entomologists in a vain attempt to differentiate them from other insects often called bugs by the uneducated masses. The term Hemiptera means "half wing," and this is the chief identifying characteristic of these insects. If you examine the front wing of these insects carefully, it is immediately obvious why the term is used to describe this group. The basal portion of the wing is modified to form a leathery, thickened region, and the apical portion is the only part of the wing that is translucent. Although two pairs of wings are present in these insects, the second pair is totally membranous.

This is a large order of insects, with well over 3,000 species represented on the North American continent north of Mexico. It is not only a large order, it is a very diverse order. While most of these insects are terrestrial, some are aquatic. The great majority are herbivorous, feeding on the sap of plants. As a result, some are quite damaging to crops and ornamental plants. Others are carnivorous predators, and others are bloodsuckers (certain of the latter act as vectors for disease-causing organisms).

One of the most interesting things about this group is that virtually all have scent-producing glandular structures that open laterally on the sides of the thorax. If one of these bugs is disturbed, the insect gives off a very characteristic odor that is often most unpleasant to humans (hence the name of one type, stink bug). This raises an interesting question. If one of these bugs happens to land in the water, it must become somewhat agitated or disturbed by the experience, and if so, then the odor is produced. Since we know trout have the sense of smell, is this odor as obnoxious to the fish as it is to humans? There are unfortunately no controlled experiments to help us gain insight into this question. Given the proper equipment, the money, and the time, it would be relatively easy to come to some conclusions concerning this question. Standing on the side of a stream and throwing stink bugs to a rising fish would give you some idea as to the palatability, but it wouldn't give you the complete story. Why not? Simply because handling the bug will cause it to secrete these obnoxious chemicals, and you really want to know if just falling in the water is enough of a stimulus to cause this. But enough of scientific procedure. We have examined the stomach contents of enough trout to know that the fish do eat these bugs on occasion, or when they are available, so they must be considered part of the normal diet.

Of all the different true bugs, which ones might be of primary importance to the trout fisherman? This is not an easy question to answer. A lot is going to depend on the type of foliage present along the streambank. In general, however, members of the following families might be expected as normal streamside residents.

Family Miridae: Plant Bugs. Members of this group, the largest family of true bugs (about 1,700 species in North America), can be found just about everywhere. They range up to about ⅜ inch in length and come in various colors (white, red, orange, and green). One of the largest, the meadow plant bug (*Leptopterna dolobrata*), is a common inhabitant of meadows and pastures, where it may be quite damaging to grass during the early summer months. The tarnished plant bug (*Lygus lineolaris*) is also very common. Keep an eye out for this one, as it is frequently found feeding on flowers and legumes (often abundant around trout streams). It is about ¼ inch long, is brown, and is common throughout the eastern states. Western fishermen should also be aware of this bug, as other species are damaging to western crops.

Other members of this family also are frequently encountered along trout streams. The rapid plant bug, *Adelphocoris rapidus,* feeds primarily on dock (burdock), which is quite common along meadow streams. This bug reaches a length of about ⁵⁄₁₆ inch and is easily recognized, with a brownish body and yellowish margins on the front wings. Fleahoppers, *Halticus bractatus,* are also frequently encountered. They are quite small, reaching only about ³⁄₃₂ inch in length. This shiny, black bug is often found feeding on legumes and other cultivated plants and can cause considerable damage. It is named for its flealike ability to avoid danger by making rather spectacular jumps.

Family Nabidae: Damsel Bugs. Anywhere you encounter concentrations of aphids or caterpillars, be on the lookout for damsel bugs. They are predators of these other insects, and concentrations of the prey species will almost certainly mean concentrations of the predators. The most common of the nabids are usually brown to yellowish in color and can reach a length of about 7/16 inch. One of the nabids, *Nabicula subcoleoptrata,* is a predator of the meadow plant bug described above.

Family Reduviidae: Assassin and Ambush Bugs. Members of this family are all predaceous, can reach a considerable size (up to 1½ inches), and can inflict a severe bite. If you are in doubt as to what you are looking at, see if you can locate a beaklike structure folded flat under the head and thorax. If you can, then leave the bug alone. While most of these will be black or brown, some are very brightly colored and are easy to locate. We have seen many of these along trout streams, but their place in the trout's diet is open to question.

Family Lygaeidae: Seed Bugs. There are more than 250 species in this family, which makes it the second largest of the true bugs. Many of its members are common inhabitants of plants adjacent to trout waters. To this group belong the chinch bug, *Blissus leucopterus,* and the small and large milkweed bugs, *Lygaeus kalmii* and *Oncopeltus fasciatus.* The chinch bug is a common pest of cereal crops and is frequently encountered on corn and wheat. It is about ⅛ inch long, with a black body and white front legs (which make it relatively easy to identify). The milkweed bugs are common along many trout streams, since, as their name implies, they feed on milkweed plants. They are quite easy to identify, with brightly marked red and black bodies. Anything (including monarch butterfly larvae) that feeds on milkweed is a pretty tough critter. The sap of the milkweed plant is loaded with toxic substances, which, as the larvae or juveniles feed, are concentrated in the tissues; the toxins are carried over to the adult following the final molt. Anything, presumably including trout, that eats one of these poison packages may very well regret its action. For example, blue jays that are fed monarch butterflies (under laboratory conditions) will eat one or two and become violently ill. After a few of these experiences, they refuse to touch them again. What about trout? Well, milkweed bugs (and also monarch butterflies) probably don't come along very often. Both are brightly marked and conspicuous, both are large, and both represent a potential food item. A nice, big red and black milkweed bug imitation may prove to be just the item that selective brown has been waiting for, so why not try it? You can rest assured that there is little chance anyone else has tried one on him, and you only have to fool him once!

I know that trout will take milkweed beetles, so why not milkweed bugs as well? In late July 1992, I collected a handful of these beetles from the milkweed growing along the banks of a section of the Letort. When flipped into the current well above a group of rising fish, every single one of them was taken. The only question I couldn't answer was whether it was a single fish that took every one of them or whether each individual beetle was taken by a different fish. Now that would have been something worth discovering!

—H. R. S.

Family Pentatomidae: Stink Bugs. You won't have any trouble identifying one of these. Most of them exude a most disagreeable odor when handled, so if in doubt, just smell your fingers! The only other true bugs that have this habit are the broad-headed bugs (family Alydidae), which actually stink much worse than the common stink bugs. Many of the stink bugs are shield shaped and brightly colored (such as the harlequin bug) and are easily recognized. More than 200 species are found in North America, so this group of bugs is quite large and widely distributed. The great majority of these bugs are herbivorous, but they usually feed on plants that are of little economic importance.

Family Rhopalidae: Scentless Plant Bugs. The only member of this family worth mentioning is the box elder bug, *Boisea trivitattus.* This bug is black with bright red markings, reaches ½ inch in length, and feeds primarily on box elder trees. If box elders are prevalent along a stream, you should certainly keep an eye out for these.

Class Diplopoda: Millipedes

Everyone is probably familiar with the millipedes, since they are common inhabitants of damp places such as the borders of trout streams and forest floors. Whether they make up an important or even an unimportant portion of a trout's diet is debatable. There is no question that they occasionally wander, fall, or are swept into trout streams. If they do, then there is also probably no question that they will be eaten by trout. We feel, however, that this group represents nothing more than a very occasional morsel in the diet of the trout and therefore warrants little attention. Another factor that might contribute to the unimportance of this group in the trout's diet is the fact that many millipedes, like stink bugs, secrete an evil-smelling fluid. This is accomplished in much the same manner as that employed by stink bugs—that is, through openings along the lateral margins of the body. Some of these secretions also are extremely toxic. If insects are placed in the same jar with certain species of millipedes, they will soon die because of these toxic secretions. Some millipedes can even give off hydrogen cyanide in these secretions, which would certainly act as an efficient deterrent to any predator.

Class Chilopoda: Centipedes

Again, most people are familiar enough with centipedes to be able to recognize one. These are characterized by having fifteen pairs of legs and can move quite rapidly (as anyone who has tried to step on one can attest to). In addition, they are all predaceous, actively feeding on insects, spiders, and other small animals. As a result, all have powerful jaws (actually a modified pair of legs) and can inflict a painful bite, during which poison is secreted into the body of the prey. Don't try to pick one up and examine it! It will not hesitate to treat you as it does its prey.

Whether or not the centipedes constitute a viable food form for trout is again debatable. They undoubtedly fall into trout streams, but the frequency of this occurrence is probably so slight that attempting to tie and fish artificial centipedes might well be a waste of time and energy. On the other hand, you never know. If you are so inclined, then as Gerald Almy has pointed out, a Woolly Worm fished dry is probably as good as anything.

SUBPHYLUM CHELICERATA

Here we must make a distinction between one type of arthropod and another. Our discussions up until now have been devoted to members of the arthropod subphylum Atelocerata. In that subphylum, class hexapoda (the insects) is distinguished, among other things, by having three pairs of legs. Also, the structure of the mouth parts is quite different from that of members of the subphylum Chelicerata. The other two classes of the subphylum Atelocerata, the Diplopoda and the Chilopoda, are likewise easily differentiated from members of the subphylum Chelicerata.

The major distinguishing features of the Chelicerata are the presence of four pairs of appendages and the division of the body into only two recognizable portions, the cephalothorax (prosoma) and the abdomen (opisthosoma). (In the Hexapoda, on the other hand, the body is divisible into three separate and distinct parts, the head, thorax, and abdomen.)

Within the subphylum Chelicerata there is only a single group that should be considered an important component of the trout's diet. This is the group to which the spiders belong.

Class Arachnida

Order Araneae: Spiders. Like other members of the subphylum Chelicerata, the spiders are characterized by having four pairs of legs and a body divisible into only two portions. Almost all spiders possess venom glands associated with their mouth parts, but most rarely bite humans. A few, including the notorious black widow and brown recluse, are dangerous to man, but most are not. All are predatory, feeding on other insects for the most part.

This is a large and diverse group of organisms, with more than 2,500 species present in North America. Under certain conditions and during certain times of the year, they can be quite abundant, and they frequently are blown into trout streams. It is therefore not uncommon to find spiders in the stomachs of autopsied trout. The fact that the group is so large and diverse prohibits a detailed examination of the individual families of this class. Luckily this is not necessary, for the general body structure is much the same for all, and the body colors for most are dull brown to black (although quite a few are brilliantly colored).

Spiders have held a certain fascination for the trout fisherman, and most of us who fish terrestrials have a few spider patterns in our boxes. But most of these patterns look nothing at all like spiders! A true spider imitation should be tied with a chunky body divisible into two pronounced segments and with inordinately long legs.

LESSER TERRESTRIAL PATTERNS

Flies

In actuality, many of the patterns developed for beetles, particularly those foam types tied with iridescent blue or green underbodies, may well be taken by trout for flies. As a result, developing specific fly patterns to imitate these insects is probably unnecessary. Unless you are in a situation where there happens to be a real preponderance of a certain type of fly present, your energies are probably better directed to other endeavors.

MARINARO'S "HOUSEFLY"

Hook: Unspecified.
Thread: Unspecified.
Body: Unstripped peacock quill.
Wing: Pale bluish hackle fibers flat over the body and clipped at the rear to make a flat, glassy wing like the house fly at rest.
Forefeet: It is not clear what Marinaro wanted to term these. At one point he refers to them as forefeet, but later he makes the statement that "from that day forward, all my houseflies wore antennae." No matter, he always tied his house fly pattern with "never fewer than two, never more than three" of the hackle fibers protruding over the eye of the hook.

POLYWING "HOUSEFLY" (GERALD ALMY)

Hook: Mustad 94833 or equivalent.
Thread: 6/0, black.

Body: Plump fur body of the appropriate color, palmered with
blue dun hackle. Trim hackle from top of the body. Trim
V-shaped wedge from the hackle under the bottom of the
body.

Wing: Gray to white, sparsely tied polypropylene.

LIVELY'S "HORSEFLY"

Hook: Mustad 94833, 94840, or equivalent.

Thread: 6/0, black.

Body, wings, head, and legs: Black deer hair.

For complete tying directions, see Almy's *Tying and Fishing Terrestrials.*

True Bugs

Very few patterns have been developed for the true bugs. One of the few is
Almy's pattern for the turkey quill stink bug, but we again feel that beetle
patterns probably serve quite well as imitations for this group. If you
encounter a situation in which a certain type of bug is present in abundance, a slight modification of a foam beetle would probably work quite
nicely. With all of the new materials and colors available, imitations
should not be too difficult to produce.

We are including a general "bug" pattern with which we have had good
success. While we call it a bug, it could just as well have been included in
the patterns for the land flies, or even for the beetles, since it does a good
job of imitating all of these different groups of terrestrials. In other words,
it's a good general pattern for a whole bunch of different terrestrials, but it
was originally tied to imitate a bug, so that's where we are going to put it!

STEEVES' HONEY BUG

Hook: #12 to #16 Mustad 94833, Orvis 1509, Tiemco 100.

Thread: 6/0, black or color to match that of the underbody.

Underbody: Ultra or micro chenille (vernille), New Dub, or
Easy Dubbing. Color of choice.

Body: $\frac{3}{16}$-inch-thick closed cell foam cut into $\frac{1}{16}$-inch-wide
strips, color of choice.

Wing: Peacock Krystal Flash.

Legs: Six moose body hairs.

Thorax: Same material as used on the underbody. The color may be matched to that of the underbody, or a contrasting color may be used.

Tying Instructions

1. Wrap hook shank with thread two-thirds of the way to the bend. Tie in the piece of body foam and continue tying it down to the bend of the hook. Wrap the thread forward a short distance and tie in a six-inch piece of underbody material.

2. Wrap the thread forward about two-thirds the length of the hook shank. Wrap the underbody material forward, tie it down, and trim away the excess, which is saved for more flies.

3. Fold the body foam forward and tie it down at the same point that the underbody material was tied off.

4. Tie in eight to twelve strands of Krystal Flash for the wings and trim the portions of the strands that extend rearward so they are even with the butt of the fly. If desired, the wings can be made somewhat longer than this.

5. Invert the fly in the vise and tie in the six moose body hairs. Trim them even with the point of the hook.

6. Turn the fly upright in the vise and tie in a piece of thorax material. Wrap the thread forward to a point slightly behind the eye of the hook, leaving enough room to form the head. Wrap the thorax material foward three or more times to form the thorax. Tie it off and trim away the excess. Form the head and whip finish.

Centipedes and Millipedes

There are probably very few situations in which any pattern for these is called for. If you just have to fish something like this, then a dressed Woolly Worm or a foam-bodied caterpillar palmered with hackle would probably do the trick for a centipede. Millipedes, however, would probably best be represented by a sinking pattern that is not very hairy.

1

2

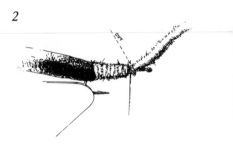

5

6

STEEVES' HONEY BUG

3

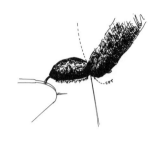

4

7

STEEVES' HONEY BUG

Spiders

There is probably no other group for which more nonrepresentational patterns have been tied. Patterns such as the Neversink Skater, W. C. Stewart's Wet Spider, and the Troth Spider are anything but spiderlike. They were probably dubbed "spiders" for the sake of convenience rather than for their likeness to these insects. There is no question that they can be deadly under certain conditions. Most are better designated as attractor patterns and are fished in a manner designed to provoke strikes by triggering the aggressive actions of trout. At this they have done rather well. The following pattern, on the other hand, was developed in an attempt to actually produce an accurate representation of a spider.

STEEVES' BARKING SPIDER

Hook: #12 to #18 Mustad 94833, Orvis 1509, Tiemco 100.
Thread: 6/0 or 8/0 depending on size of pattern, color to match body.
Body: ⅛-inch-thick foam cut into ⅛- to ¹⁄₁₆-inch-wide strips, depending on hook size. Color at tier's discretion (black, green, yellow, etc.).
Legs: Four ringneck pheasant tail barbs.

Tying Instructions

1. Wrap hook shank with thread from eye to about two-thirds the length of the shank. Form a ball of thread at the end of this wrap, which will serve to separate the legs. Wrap the thread forward to about ⅛ inch or more from the eye of the hook. Tie in the four pheasant tail barbs at this point, with the tips extending backward well past the bend and the butts extending forward well past the eye of the hook.

2. Wrap thread backward to tie the pheasant tail barbs down. When you get to the thread ball, separate the barbs so that two lie on one side of the shank and two lie on the other. Tie them tight into the ball so that they splay out to form the hind legs. Wrap thread forward, and separate the forward-projecting barbs so that two lie on one side of the hook

shank and two lie on the other. Figure-eight wrap to splay them out and form the front legs. Trim both front and rear legs to desired length.

3. Wrap thread back to a point halfway between the front and rear legs, and tie in the foam body piece pointing backward. Tie it in by wrapping backward almost to the rear legs. Wrap thread forward.

4. Fold foam forward; do not stretch or pull it, but fold it a bit backward and then forward to form the abdomen. Hold it in this position with the left thumb, and tie it down. Trim forward-projecting portion of foam to form the head of the spider. Whip-finish. If you tie this pattern with legs that are too long, the fly has a tendency to twist the leader. If this should occur, simply shorten the legs or go to a heavier tippet.

FOAM SPIDER (GARY LaFONTAINE)

Hook: #14 to #16, standard dry-fly hook.

Legs: Four pieces of natural brown deer hair. Place deer hair about three-quarters of the way up the shank. Spin it, and trim the ends.

Body: Foam. Tie down a shaped piece of foam (with a smaller front section and larger rear section) where the deer hair is wrapped. Color brown with a waterproof marker.

LaFontaine (*The Dry Fly*) indicates that the foam used is the large-cell, closed foam that is used as a packing material. He indicates that spiders tied with this type of foam instead of the small closed cell foam sold in fly shops will "pull trout from much further away" and that "there is no comparison between the two types." We don't necessarily find this to be true.

There are other patterns, such as the one developed by Richard Walker (*Fly Dressing Innovations*), that have also been designated as spiders. Walker's pattern, the Daddy Longlegs, is really not representative of a daddy longlegs but, as LaFontaine points out, a "downed" cranefly.

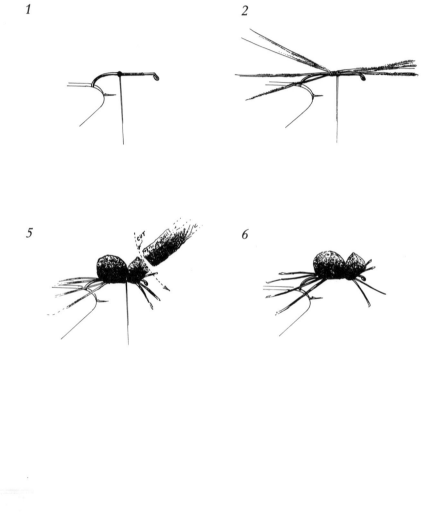

STEEVES' BARKING SPIDER

3

4

STEEVES' BARKING SPIDER

12

Finis

. . . with a disdain akin to that I have for the de-romanticizing of fly fishing with too much science and its wicked step-sister, verification.

—*Art Lee,* Fly Fisherman, *September 1983*

THERE IS A fair amount of science in the preceding pages; there is no getting around that fact. But in this case, how much science is too much, and have we really deromanticized the sport at all by going into some depth on certain topics?

In this book, we have made an attempt to enlighten fly fishermen on the art of fishing terrestrials, and in so doing we have had to delve into certain scientific principles. But these are scientific principles that should be of general interest to all fly fishermen and in most cases do not apply only to terrestrials. We sincerely believe that even with all the science, fly fishing will always remain an art. Indeed, if the "scientification" of this sport goes too far, then God help us all.

The idea of someone standing in a stream feeding data into a pocket computer, coming up with the correct pattern for the specific conditions, and then proceeding to catch fish is abhorrent. Although some science is necessary, to infuse such a gentle sport with too many facts and figures is to do away with its inherent beauty. It would be similar to a parent destroying a child's magic rainbow by explaining its being in terms of Newtonian and quantum physics.

The reason a trout accepts one fly over another, exhibits that ephemeral characteristic of selectivity, or charges a terrestrial pattern will probably always be open for debate. These are problems that we hope will never be solved. Without these topics for discussion, the stew of fly fishing would lack the proper seasoning and be nothing more than pablum for the gourmet's palate. As a matter of fact, it is these very problems that have attracted many of us to this sport. At times we seem to solve them, but then at other times we are left standing in midstream with our neural circuitry in total disarray.

This is as it should be. To solve all of the problems all of the time would be tantamount to relegation to hell, for there would be nothing left to look forward to. How terrible it would be to go astream knowing that no matter what problem presented itself, you would be able to find an answer. There would be no mystery left. And after all, fly fishing is first and foremost, and always should be, full of mystery and supposition.

The intrusion of science is to a certain degree a good thing. We *should* be able to call things by their proper names. In doing so we put to rout the devils of confusion. A sulphur means one thing to one person, and something else to another. On the other hand, *Ephemerella dorothea* should mean the same thing to everyone. It is of extreme interest to know how a trout sees or smells, or senses vibrations in the water. It is nice to know why terrestrials float, or why the exoskeleton of insects has virtually no nutritive value. It's fun to speculate on why fish behave the way they do; why they show certain types of feeding patterns; or why they might refuse certain flies at certain times or accept one pattern over another.

We do not believe that we have dimmed the magic of the rainbow by injecting a modicum of science. If anything, we have intensified the colors of the spectrum. There seems little danger of reducing this sport to nothing more than quantification and statistical analysis. There are too many variables present. Indeed, things change onstream from one hour to the next, and often within minutes rather than hours. Each fisherman will react differently to any given situation. Each cast is distinct; each drift is unique; each day is a new beginning and has a different ending. How wonderful that this is so, and ever will remain thus.

REFLECTIONS IN BARNEY'S POOL

With miles of thread
A web of well-conceived deceit is spun.
A witch's brew of body parts,
Chimeric blend of bird and beast.
A teaser wrapped in tinsel,
Designed to stimulate the appetite
Or trigger uncontrolled aggression.

Years of travel—
Time in cubic feet per second,
Slipping past the loins
As carefully the silken trap is laid.
The sigh of silver thread,
As it passes through our eyes
And parachutes to rest.

Feathered temptress, Babylonic whore
Dancing in the interface,
Calling softly,
"Take me—I am yours,"
It beckons to the waiting beast.

Engulfment, gentle and precise.
The ruse successful, as so many times before.
The moment always magic and unique
And always unexpected,
No matter what our confidence.

And now the pulse of life.
Electric play of prey and predator,
United by a polymeric spider's thread.
The ritual of dance,
The sparring choreography,
As in a cocktail conversation
Between potential lovers.

A bargain finally struck!
Take me for the moment, for the instant.
Admire me while you can.
The contract for today
Portends no promise for tomorrow,
No future certainties,
No conclusions.
But today—today is present,
And for today I'll play your game.

—H. R. S.

Where to Find Materials

Most of the supplies for patterns presented in this book are available from a well-stocked fly fishing shop. If there is not one in your area, you might try one of the following. We have dealt with these shops in the past and have found that they offer good service.

Hook and Hackle Company
7 Kaycee Loop Road
Plattsburg, NY 12901
518-561-5893

American Angling Supplies
23 Main Street
Salem, NH 03079

Pennsylvania Outdoor Warehouse
1508 Memorial Avenue
Williamsport, PA 17701
1-800-441-7685

Flyfishers Paradise
2603 E. College Avenue
State College, PA 16801
814-234-4189

Kaufmann's Streamborn, Inc.
P.O. Box 23032
Portland, OR 97281
503-639-6400

Murray's Fly Shop
P.O. Box 156
Edinburg, VA 22824

Clemens
444 Schantz Spring Road
Allentown, PA 18104

The Fly Shop
4140 Churn Creek Road
Redding, CA 96002

Madison River Fishing Company
P.O. Box 627/109 Main Street
Ennis, MT
406-682-4293
1-800-227-7127 orders only

Cold Spring Anglers
419 E. High Street, Suite A
Carlisle, PA 17013
1-800-248-8937 orders only

Orvis Manchester
Historic Route 7A
Manchester, VT 05254
802-362-3750
(or try any other Orvis store
near you or an Orvis dealer)

Bill Skilton's USA Flies
P.O. Box 64
Boiling Springs, PA 17007-0064
717-486-5656

Fishing Creek Outfitters
Fairmount Springs Road
R.D. 1, Box 310-1
Benton, PA 17814
1-800-548-0093 orders only
717-925-2225

Dan Bailey's
P.O. Box 1019-N
Livingston, MT 59047
1-800-356-4052

Wolf's Sporting Adventure
9191 Baltimore National Pike
Elicott City, MD 21042
1-800-378-1152

Kettle Creek Tackle Shop
HCR 62 Box 140
Renovo, PA 17764
717-923-1416

Hunter's Angling Supplies
Central Square, Box 300
New Boston, NH 03070
603-487-3388

Bob Marriott's Fly Fishing Store
2700 W. Orangethorpe Avenue
Fullerton, CA 92633

Certain tying materials presented in the text are not yet widely available. The following list will help you locate these materials.

1. Kreinik Materials (braids, ribbons, Micro-Ice Chenille): Kreinik Manufacturing Co., 9199 Reisterstown Road, Suite 209 B, Owings Mills, MD 21117, 1-800-354-4255, FAX 301-581-5092.

2. Rainy's Float Foam: Shops have begun to carry this, but if it is not available in your area contact: Rainy Riding, 600 North 100 East, Logan, UT 84321, 1-801-753-6766.

3. Plastic Canvas Yarn: This can be found in most craft shops, Roses, Wal-Mart, Kmart, and similar stores. We use this material for many purposes!

4. Nylon Organza: Your best bet for this is a good fabric shop, or contact a tailor or dressmaker if there is a good one in your area. We expect that fly shops will begin to carry this in the future, but it will be under some other name and cost you a fortune.

5. Macramé Cord: Try your local craft shop; if they do not have it, they can probably order it.

Suggested Reading

Almy, Gerald. *Tying and Fishing Terrestrials.* Mechanicsburg, PA: Stackpole Books, 1978.

Borrer, Donald J., Charles A. Tripplehorn, and Norman F. Johnson. *An Introduction to the Study of Insects.* Philadelphia: Saunders College Publ., 1989.

Borrer, Donald J., and Richard E. White. *Peterson Field Guides, Insects.* Boston: Houghton Mifflin, 1970.

Dennis, Jack. *Western Trout Fly Tying Manual.* 2 vols. Jackson, WY: Snake River Books, 1974.

Koch, Ed. *Terrestrial Fishing.* Mechanicsburg, PA: Stackpole Books, 1990.

LaFontaine, Gary. *The Dry Fly.* Helena, MT: Greycliff Publ. Co., 1990.

Marinaro, Vincent. *A Modern Dry Fly Code.* New York: Nick Lyons Books, 1983.

Marinaro, Vincent. *In the Ring of the Rise.* New York: Nick Lyons Books, 1976.

Schwiebert, Ernest. *Trout Strategies.* New York: E. P. Dutton, 1983.

Stewart, Dick, and Farrow Allen. *Flies for Trout.* Mountain Pond Publ., 1993.

Stoltz, Judith, and Judith Schnell, eds. *Trout.* Mechanicsburg, PA: Stackpole Books, 1991.

Index